READING REFLEX

The Foolproof Phono-Graphix™ Method for Teaching Your Child to Read

CARMEN McGUINNESS
GEOFFREY McGUINNESS

A FIRESIDE BOOK
Published by Simon & Schuster

FIRESIDE
Rockefeller Center
1230 Avenue of the Americas
New York, NY 10020

First Fireside Edition 1999
FIRESIDE and colophon are registered trademarks
of Simon & Schuster Inc.

Manufactured in the United States of America

10 9 8 7 6 5 4 3 2

Library of Congress Cataloging-in-Publication Data

McGuinness, Carmen
Reading reflex : the foolproof Phono-Graphix™ method for teaching your child to read / Carmen McGuinness and Geoffrey McGuinness.
p. cm.
1. Reading—Code emphasis approaches. 2. Reading—Remedial teaching. 3. Reading—Parent participation. 4. English language—Study and teaching (Elementary) I. McGuinness, Geoffrey.
II. Title.
LB1050.22.M34 1998
372.43—dc21 97-33967
CIP

ISBN 0-684-83966-0
0-684-85367-1 (pbk)

With this book goes our sincerest appreciation to all the children and parents of the Read America clinic, without whose trust we could not have tested and proven our work, and to our adult clients, who provided us with so much insight.

In addition, we send our love and appreciation for their support to—

Our daughter Amanda, who put up with our late nights and early mornings, and nursed us through carpal tunnel, sciatica, and writers' cramps and a broken ankle.

Rob Janzer, who taught himself to read at five, while his mommy was busy at college.

Brian McGuinness, whose constant support and unwavering faith in us made our work possible.

Diane McGuinness, who demands so much from her students—especially when they are her children.

Ruth and Joseph Reitano, who made their daughter read every day.

Susan Whitworth, who worked every Monday for no pay.

Each other, because together it was fun.

Our editor, Susan Arellano, whose vision and concern for literacy made *Reading Reflex* a reality.

And our special affection and appreciation goes to Kate Rappoport for her hard work and perseverance in making this book just perfect.

CONTENTS

PREFACE

Every innovation, every major breakthrough has a first cause—an event perhaps unnoticed that lies dormant, tickling the subconscious, making its way to the surface like spring's first blossom. Phono-Graphix had a very inauspicious start. It was the summer of 1982 and my then five-year-old son had spent most of the summer teaching himself to read. I didn't think much of this at the time. I wasn't particularly impressed with this feat, not yet aware of the struggle that some children have reaching even basic literacy. On this particular August day he sat with crayon and chubby pencil, meticulously recreating *Aesop's Fables* onto construction paper. When asked about the need for this task Rob explained he was making a copy of the book before we had to return it to the library. The day went on, words were carefully copied down in a semblance of their original order. Pictures were drawn looking little like the originals. Rob continued working until he was disturbed by a bath and dinner. The next day the task went on—and the next. On the fourth day I noticed Rob had given up his crayons, chubby, and construction paper for a lined notepad and a slimmer, sharper pencil. Intrigued, I approached. As I did I was met by gleaming brown eyes and a beaming smile. He tapped his notepad and said proudly, "Look at all my work, Mommy." Indeed the notepad was filled with words. I was amazed.

"What are you up to here?" I asked.

"I'm writing down all the 'ae' words in my book." He indicated the notepad again. "There's a lot."

Looking more carefully and working hard to decipher Rob's crude handwriting, I saw before me the beginnings of the Phono-Graphix method. There they were on the page of Rob's notepad, word after word containing the sound "ae"—not the letter **a.** I'm not sure if I thought of it then—in my later memories I did, I saw all the crudely written words reorganized systematically to show the sound "ae." I don't think I thought of it as a method then, not really. But the seed was planted and already beginning to grow. A return trip to the library made the book ours for another three weeks, long enough for Rob to make it through the "ee" words. School started, Rob's first year, and soon, with the advent of Cub Scouts and the start of the soccer season, he forgot his task. Unfortunately, I too forgot it, for the time being. We were both busy at school, you see, as I had returned to the university and was working toward a psychology degree and expecting another child.

The next summer was a hectic year for us. With a new baby, I had set school aside for a while and opened a preschool and kindergarten. The years went on, and I taught many children to read. But I soon learned that most didn't take to it as easily as Rob had. In my naïveté I assumed they all learned in time. In 1986 we were busy building an addition on the school—space for grades one through three. The mailbox had been temporarily taken down to allow for the comings and goings of construction vehicles. The postman was kind enough to bring the mail to my classroom, so for a period of about two months I was the person who saw the mail first each day—a job usually managed by Donna, our school secretary. On one particular morning in May 1986, a letter arrived inviting me to join the Orton Dyslexia Society. The letter put forward statistics that stunned me. Reflecting back on how easily Rob had learned to read and how most of my kindergartners left my school reading at least basic words, I couldn't understand how these statistics could be so. I joined, and began to get interested in literacy beyond the gates of my little school.

By the spring of 1988, after two years of teaching grades one to three, I knew of more than one child who had not learned to read in our classrooms. That fall I returned to pursue my psychology degree to find out why. In the spring of 1989 I initiated a reading research project for an independent studies course that would earn the last six credits to complete my psychology degree. It was through that study that I learned of the historical swings back and forth between phonics and whole-language reading instruction. My husband, Geoff, and I also learned that year that our seven-year-old daughter, Mandy, couldn't read. As she sat crying at the dining room table, pointing to the word on the paper before her and sobbing that she didn't see how it could be "eight" without an **a** in it, what Rob had taught me precisely eight years earlier made its way finally to the surface. I picked up the pencil and explained, "Look here, Mandy, there are lots of ways to show the sound 'ae.'" I covered up the **t** and pointed to the remaining **eigh** and said, "This is one way to show 'ae.' So if this is 'ae' and this is 't,' this is 'eight.'" Geoff said that two lightbulbs shone over the table that night, one over Mandy's head, and one over mine. The next four years of our lives were filled with hard work. Teaching Mandy to read was the easy part. Developing Phono-Graphix, researching it, publishing the research, and launching the program internationally were a bit more difficult.

Today is New Year's Day 1999, and the second release of *Reading Reflex* is on the horizon. We've been asked to update it with this preface. Much has happened since that tiny seed was planted and finally bloomed at our dining-room table. Rob, who turns twenty-two on Thursday, will graduate from college this year. Mandy, who is now fifteen, has taught many children to read as a teen literacy volunteer. Well over three thousand teachers have been trained and certified in Phono-Graphix. Another thirty thousand are working with this book and our classroom curriculum without training. These teachers are in the U.S., the U.K., Canada, Australia, and New Zealand. A 1996 clinical study of Phono-Graphix revealed a 98 percent success rate at getting children to grade-level reading in just twelve sessions. This study was published in the journal of the organization that helped awaken me to the issue of illiteracy, *The Orton Annals of Dyslexia*. We've conducted four classroom studies and a volunteer study. In the fall of 1996 KinderCare and Read America initiated a clinical study of the efficacy of the Phono-Graphix Reading Fundamentals programs in several KinderCare classrooms in Central Florida. Four- and five-year-olds received twenty minutes per day in small groups of three to five for eleven weeks. At the close of the study the average reading age of the children was six years, one month, and the average number of correctly spelled words on a trial test was four out of five. At the Milhopper School in Gainesville, Florida, twenty-four grade one through grade three children received Phono-Graphix exclusively for one school year. The average gain across the eight-month period of the study was one year, five months, with poor intake readers gaining one year, eight months and average and good intake readers gaining one year, four months. At Rock Lake Middle School in Seminole County, Florida, twelve- and thirteen-year-olds who were significantly below grade level received Phono-Graphix instruction in their language arts class to determine whether it would improve their reading comprehension. They were pre- and post-tested on the Gates-McInitty Comprehension subtest. Average gains were one year, eight months after eight months of instruction. Seminole County schools have gone on to offer Phono-Graphix training to their teachers at regular training events. In another study conducted in Phillipsburg, N.J., fifty-three middle school students were isolated as needing special reading help. They participated in special nine-week classes in which they received Phono-Graphix reading instruction in groups of six, for forty minutes, five days per week. The average gain on the Woodcock Reading Mastery Word Identification subtest was twelve standard score points. Since completion of this study the county has gone on to implement Phono-Graphix at the elementary level. In September 1998 the district and Read America hosted visiting officials from the Ministry of Education in Great Britain on a tour of Phono-Graphix classrooms in Phillipsburg. And finally the most exciting project of all was initiated by a corporation wishing to involve its employees in a worthwhile volunteer literacy project. Under the direction of community relations director Swen Nater, Costco implemented the Costco/Spring Lake Volunteer study. Forty-three students, age six through nine, were isolated as needing special help with reading. Sixty-four percent were described as nonreaders. All forty-three children received forty-five minutes of help once a week for eleven weeks—a total of eight hours of instruction. Help was offered one-on-one by Costco employees who had received four hours of Phono-Graphix training and used materials from *Reading Reflex*. The Qualitative Reading Inventory was administered before and after. Average gains were eleven months. Costco has not stopped here. Since the completion of this study it has been responsible for the training of over five hundred Costco employees who are now working in schools all over the U.S.—teaching children to read.

Release of *Reading Reflex* (Penguin) in Great Britain in the summer of 1998 brought on a surge of excitement from the British media, with articles appearing in every major publication and a BBC production chronicling the remediation of twin nine-year-olds. The British government became interested in Phono-Graphix and is about to launch a national study of the effect of the method as integrated into the National Literacy Strategy.

As 1999 dawns today, the millennium on the horizon, Phono-Graphix has taken its place as the new paradigm in reading instruction, as evidenced by the thousands of whole language and phonics teachers who have taken it up with renewed spirit for their work. These teachers fill us with hope that the paradigm swings have stopped and that the next millennium will offer literacy to every English-speaking child.

—Carmen McGuinness

CHAPTER ONE

READING EXPLAINED

Learning to read is the most important thing your child will undertake during his school years. I could say that, "it's the foundation of future learning" or "it's the building blocks to his future." But those words are too general, too cool, and lack the small pictures associated with being able, or unable, to read. What learning to read will really do is allow your child to share the information that others have written down. It will allow him to share his own experiences with others, to put his questions, his beliefs, his thoughts and dreams on paper. It will offer him hours of enjoyment, decrease his likelihood of depression, unemployment, and low self-esteem. And certainly of equal importance to him, learning to read is just one of those things he will do that everyone else can do too, that identify him with the rest of us, that prove he is capable and worthy of entrance into the realm of the educated world.

In 1993 I had been teaching reading for eleven years. I thought I understood the importance of learning to read. I thought I, better than most, understood the possible anxiety and trauma that would surely fill the life of the nonreader. I thought I knew it all, until Jack. Jack was my first adult client. At fifty-four he was the oldest nonreader I had worked with by nearly forty years. Jack changed, forever, my understanding of the importance of learning to read. He moved my thinking from big pictures like, "it's the foundation of future learning," to the small pictures like depression, unemployment, low self-esteem, and rejection. I was first contacted by Jack's son Tim, a computer systems engineer with a large multinational communications network. Tim was straightforward and unashamed when he said, "My father can't read. My mother has left him. I'm afraid he might do something awful."

Tim had grown up never knowing that his dad couldn't read, though at our first meeting he confessed that he should have known. "Dad never read to me. He had lots of books. He would keep them by his recliner, stacked on the floor. Every so often one or two of them would get moved to the bookshelf and a new one would appear at the top of the stack. But he never read to me. You know, like dads do. My Mom always put us to bed and read us a story. Dad never did."

After tests which revealed a reading level of late first grade, Jack entered into reading therapy. His avoidance of doing anything like a lesson was pronounced. For the first three sessions we did little more than talk, and his tale began to unfold. Jack had grown up, the son of the local butcher, in a small town near Chicago. He had attended a public school and seemed to be doing well until the end of second grade when Jack's teacher told his parents that he was progressing slowly at his reading and she would be retaining him in second grade.

"I'll never forget how I felt when my mother told me that I couldn't go to third grade. I was really hurt, you know? It really hurt me bad. I think that messed me up, you know. I think it hurt me more than it helped." By the end of Jack's second try at second grade things had gone from bad to worse. Jack had become a behavior problem. His parents were frequently at the school for conferences. "I spent my days at school hating that, and my nights at home in all kinds of trouble over school. It was really bad." Jack recalled, with great detail, one incident when he got caught cheating on a spelling test. "I wrote the words from my spelling list on my arm. I don't know why I bothered, she (the teacher) would have known I'd cheated soon as all the words were right. My parents were real mad. They didn't hit me or anything though. They never did that. They were good parents and all. It wasn't their fault. It was me. I guess I just couldn't remember all the words. I tried. I really wanted to read like the other kids. I guess I just couldn't remember all the words."

Jack dropped out of school when he was sixteen. "I was in the seventh grade," he confessed ashamedly. "The other kids were thirteen. It seemed stupid to stay in." Jack went into the army at sixteen. "They found out right away that I couldn't read. There were a bunch of us that couldn't. So it wasn't so bad." By the time Jack got out of the service his older brother had finished an engineering degree at Northwestern University. He had graduated in the top one hundred in his class and had been hired by a company who had just received a government contract to build a highway. He got Jack a job doing roadwork. "I dug the foundations. It was just like my fifth grade teacher said, 'Jack, you're gonna end up diggin' ditches.' I did okay for us though, you know. I did good. Pretty soon I was a subsupervisor. That's the guy who makes sure everybody is doin' the job. I never got to be a supervisor because he had to read the blueprints and all." Jack's brother was making quite a lot of money by the time Jack had been promoted to subsupervisor. He started investing in real estate around the Chicago area. He brought Jack in on many of the deals and by the time Jack retired at fifty he had a hefty investment income and a thirty-year pension. "We were sittin' pretty. The kids were both out of college and we had nothin' to do but play tennis and bridge and go shoppin'. It was good, I mean for me it was. But then my wife, well you know. She left me."

Jack's son Tim had explained the separation at our first meeting. Jack had a bad temper. He didn't direct it at anyone. He wasn't abusive. He was just, as Tim put it, "very grumpy." "I think she just got sick of me complainin' all the time. You know, about, well, most everything. And I'm real competitive you know. She hates that, like when we're playing doubles with other couples, or bridge or somethin'." Jack recalled one of the last incidents that occurred just before his wife left him. "Timmy was tellin' me I needed to get me a computer. I got it in my head that I could use that thing to learn about stuff. You know, the stuff I hadn't learned from the school books, history, and all. Sal (Jack's wife) told me I was nuts, that I couldn't use a computer if I couldn't read. But Tim had said about all the pictures and how they (computers) talk and all, so I got me one. Timmy helped me pick it out. I told him I wanted the best one, the one that could make lots of pictures, and talk a lot. When we got it home Tim set it all up. He's real good with those things. I was real impressed. He showed me how to turn it off and on and to put in the programs. I memorized all the steps. I've got a lot better at remembering since my school days. Then he had to go. He had a softball game or somethin'. He left me with that thing and I was lost. Makin' it talk was easy. It was the words that were hard. That thing didn't ever help me one bit. I just sat there lookin' at it, gettin' madder and madder. Sal and me had a bridge match that night. I was a real jerk and said Joe (one of the other players) was cheatin'. Sal was real mad at me. I think that was the end really. I don't blame her. She tried to tell me that thing (the computer) wasn't for me." When Jack's wife left him later that week he was forced to share the burden of his illiteracy with his son Tim. He knew that he would need the help of another adult in dealing with daily life in a literate society.

Before I allow my readers to become too saddened by Jack's tale, let me share his happy ending. Jack did learn to read. His wife was so happy for him that she promised to come home if he would engage in counseling, which he did. When I last spoke to Jack he had just completed his GED and was about to start a real estate license course. He hadn't had much time lately for tennis, but he was very happy to report that his favorite activity was reading to his three-year-old granddaughter.

Since Jack I've worked with many adult nonreaders. With each new case I am reminded anew of the small pictures associated with reading failure. I've seen over and over again how these people's lives have been affected, how they have learned to cope and how the coping has taken up all of their energy and filled the spaces that might have been their lives—other lives. Jack's way of coping was to compete. He once said to me, "At tennis I'm a winner." I've come to think of him in that way, as Jack, the "winner." Other adult clients coped in different ways. Soon after Jack was Tina, the dependent. In all situations Tina would immediately notify those involved that she couldn't read. This limited their expectations of her and allowed her to be cared for. Some time later there was Thomas, the specializer. Thomas could read at a fourth-grade level and was extremely intelligent. He coped by becoming an expert at breeding and training exotic birds. My current adult client is Jill, the survivor. Jill, a forty-eight-year-old convenience store district manager, has managed to become just competent enough at most everything to allow her to get by. With a reading age at intake of third grade, she set up a color-coded filing system so that all fourteen of the stores in her district were consistent in their filing system. This allowed her to avoid having to read the labels on the files.

Each of these people has brought me a renewed sense of urgency. The time to learn to read is so precious to our children. Although these people lie at the bottom of the reading ranges, we mustn't lose sight of the fact that they are not atypical. There are many at the bottom range. A 1993 U.S. Department of Education study revealed that 42 percent of our school-age children are below basic competency in reading. These numbers are staggering. They're so staggering that it's tempting not to think of them at all. It's tempting to pretend that our children are safe from these frightening statistics, that it will be someone else's child who will have problems, not ours. But there is no assurance of that. Based on the prevailing trend, two in every five children will not learn to read to a level of basic competency. They will become the Jacks, the Tinas, the Thomases, and the Jills. They will fill the spaces of their lives with coping.

Once we move beyond the doubt and accept that the risk to our child is real, it's equally tempting to rationalize our child out of the failed numbers. This is easily done by assigning some level of blame to the failed reader. "Those adults were lazy, troubled, had physical problems that inhibited their reading, came from poor families, went to bad schools," etc. But these rationalizations simply aren't true. In fact the adult nonreaders that I've worked with all came from good homes, and were exceptionally hard working. They were of average or above average intelligence, and they all reported having wanted very, very much to learn to read during their school years. They were not the problem. So what exactly was the problem? And what is the problem? How is it that our society keeps failing its children in the area of reading instruction? Could it be the method of instruction used to teach reading? That line of reasoning is equally tempting to a parent. Simply find out which method produces the best results, save up thousands of dollars, and put your child in a private school that teaches that method. Or, if you can't save up thousands of dollars, find a public school that teaches that method and move halfway across the country into that particular school district. Well, for many or most of us, these are not options. But for those who are actually considering these steps, I suggest a review of the available methods. To do this, let's look at the history of reading in the United States. Let's see if we can find a method that's worth the move from anywhere.

The History of Reading

In the 1700s and 1800s there was one way to teach a child to read. Noah Webster's *Blue-Backed Speller* sold over one hundred million copies in the years from 1783 to the 1890s. *The Blue-Backed Speller* focused on teaching the correspondences between the various English letters and the sounds they were intended to represent. So children learned the sound for each letter in the alphabet and then they practiced reading the sounds and making words. To teach digraphs (two or more letters that represent a single sound) like the two letters **<ai>** in the word 'rain,' the teacher employed rules. For instance, children were taught that generally when two vowels are side by side in a word, it is the sound of the first vowel that is read. So when the child saw the **<ea>** in the word 'meat,' she knew to say the sound 'ee'. She was taught that this sound was a "long **e** sound" as opposed to the "short **e** sound" in the word 'met.' To explain the fact that the **<ea>** in words like 'bread,' 'thread,' 'tread,' 'dread,' 'read' (and others) also represent the "short **e** sound" 'e' like in the word 'met,' she was told that this was an "exception to the rule." So, what the curriculum ended up being was memorization of the twenty-six letter sounds, plus all the rules, plus all the exceptions to all the rules. This phonetic approach of teaching letter-sound correspondences, along with rules for all the exceptions to the rules, soon came to be known as *phonics*. Phonics was a nickname for *phonetics*, which is the term used to describe the sounds of a given language.

In the 1700s, and today, phonics deals in letters and the sounds they represent. This requires memorization of two arbitrary items that are only paired because somebody says they should be. So the letter **<t>,** for instance, represents the sound 't' and the letter **<p>** represents the sound 'p'. This kind of arbitrary memorization of two seemingly unrelated items is called *paired associate learning*. Paired associate learning is very difficult for young children. It is only made easier by somehow making the two items meaningful. Let's look at language acquisition as an example. When your two-year-old fusses for no apparent reason you start trying things. You might say, "Are you hungry?" as you offer an apple. If that doesn't work you might ask, "Do you want a drink?" as you take a glass out of the cabinet. Suddenly baby stops fussing and reaches for the item that you just labeled 'drink.' Now, by having his thirst appeased while getting the two items, the pair (a glass of something nice and the word 'drink'), baby has begun to link the pair of items in memory. This occurred not because he's a genius, as you might suppose, but because the experience of getting the two items (the drink and the word 'drink') together while he was appeased, was very meaningful to him. The problem with teaching the various sounds that letters represent in a pair like this, is that there is no relevance in a sound alone. It has no meaning until it is placed in a word.

Phonics tended, and still does, to teach the sounds of the alphabet for a long time before the learner is taught how to read and spell words with the sounds. So, one problem with phonics is that it relies heavily on paired associate learning, which is difficult for young children unless some relevance is introduced in the learning formula. An additional problem lies in the use of rules to teach the sounds that groups of letters represent. As we've mentioned, the **<ai>** in the word 'rain' would be called a "long **a** sound," and would be explained using the rule that when two vowels are side by side, they represent the long sound of the first letter. This kind of contingent logic is called "propositional logic." It is of the "if, then that" variety that young children simply cannot manage. In fact, you may have even found it confusing when you just read it. It's difficult, and especially so for young children. Not only is the logic difficult to follow, but it is also frequently wrong. In fact, this rule only works in English 40 percent of the time. The **<ai>** "long **a** rule" is wrong in numerous words, such as 'said,' 'again,' 'mountain,' 'captain,' and others. These, of course, would be labeled "exceptions to the rule." So now we have the rule working 40 percent of the time and the exception working 60 percent of the time. As if all this isn't confusing enough, phonics also teaches adjacent consonants as units. So instead of leaving a child alone once he knows the sound to symbol relationship of sounds like 'f' and 'r', it goes on to teach him 'fr', as if it were something altogether different. So now he has three things to remember **<f>**, **<r>**, and **<fr>**.

You might look at the previous paragraph and think, My goodness, this is really confusing. How and why did the instruction become so confusing? Well, phonics evolved from the idea that the English written language is so confusing that it needs rules, regulations, and contingencies, in order to be learned. Never did the innovators of phonics ask if maybe it was the rules that were confusing, rather than the written code. In fact, these rules are so confusing that by the late 1970s, with phonics firmly in place, the illiteracy rate was tottering around 33 percent.

Big Books Take Over Reading Instruction

By the turn of the decade (1980) "whole language" arrived on the scene in a big way. Even the books were big. From "big books" (large-format books that displayed the same old story in large print) to "invented spelling" (the notion that any approximation of a word is acceptable), classroom teachers embraced the principles of whole language from the beginning. With all the rules they had been subject to and had subjected their students to under the phonics regime, it's no wonder they loved whole language. The theory behind whole language was that children do not need to know the code to read the English language. In fact, the inventors of whole language believed that the English written code is too unpredictable to be learned. Whole language innovators believed that children could learn to recognize an infinite number of whole words. Credos like, "We recognize words in the same way that we recognize all the other familiar objects in our visual world—trees and animals, cars and houses, cutlery, cookery, furniture and faces—on sight" (Smith, F., *Reading*, Cambridge University, New York, 1985, p. 57), were taken to heart by teachers everywhere. Literature was used to excite the child about learning to read so that he began to memorize the many words he saw in books. "Integrated curriculum" wove the fabric of each big book into entire units of study across curriculum areas. "Invented spelling" was allowed and even encouraged, as children were expected to "emerge" into literacy. Workshops sprang up around the country, with classroom teachers sharing their ideas and experiences with "language-rich" environments. Teacher creativity was overwhelmingly recognized as the best asset of our classrooms and schools. In addition to workshops, teachers began writing articles for teaching magazines, and even books that laid out their whole language successes. Teachers were, for the first time in the history of mandatory education, not just allowed to be innovative, but actually encouraged to be so. The momentum passed quickly from the colleges to the classrooms, and the teachers became the leaders of whole language innovation.

All that sounds great, but what about the reading scores? Well, the problem with whole language is that it doesn't work. Children do not "recognize whole words like they recognize other familiar objects in their visual world" (Smith, 1985). In fact, reading isn't even based on a visual stimulus, but on an oral one, the sound. It is the sounds that our forefathers were attempting to represent when they invented the written code, not the other way around. Human beings can't even recall that many arbitrary images with no meaningful attributes. It is ludicrous to compare an abstract image like this **house** to one

with attributes and qualities that ground it in meaning like this 

No one confuses this  with this 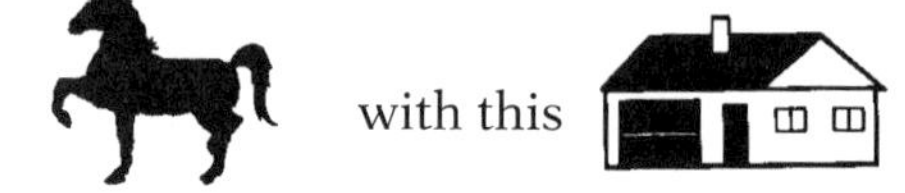

But bad readers are always

confusing this **horse** with this **house**

Despite these facts whole language was all the rage. And what became of phonics? Out with the old and in with the new? Yes and no. When whole language came on the scene around 1980 an entire generation of teachers had been teaching phonics for the previous decade or two, and the newer teachers had been raised on phonics. A survey of teachers conducted by Patrick Groff of San

Diego State University in 1989, and published in the *Orton Annals of Dyslexia* in 1991, reveals that phonics never really left the classroom. Dr. Groff questioned classroom teachers on their agreement or disagreement with various whole language credos. To the statement, "Intensive phonics instruction makes the task of learning to read inordinately difficult, if not impossible" (Weaver, C., *Psychologists and Reading*, Winthrop, Cambridge, MA, 1980), 3 percent agreed, 91 percent disagreed, and 6 percent were undecided. To the statement, "English is spelled too unpredictably for phonics to work" (Smith, 1985), 11 percent agreed, 72 percent disagreed, and 17 percent were undecided.

An independent observational study conducted by the Read America Clinic in 1993 and 1994 found phonics practices well in place and mixed with whole language practices in sixteen out of seventeen randomly selected public schools in five Central Florida counties. Based on these discoveries, it would seem that phonics and whole language have been "mixing it up" eclectically for quite some time now. Yet in the fall of 1996, newspapers and magazines were printing article after article about a return to phonics. At the November 1996 annual meeting of the Orton Dyslexia Society in Boston, Dr. Jean Chall, author of *Learning to Read: The Great Debate* (McGraw Hill, NY, 1967), said that in the previous three-month period she had been interviewed by over twenty national publications on the topic of a return to phonics. So what's all the fuss about? Why are school boards adopting a curriculum that never left the classroom? Why are newspapers writing about the return of a method that never went away? Why don't the headlines just read

PHONICS INSTRUCTION STILL BEING USED
IN CONJUNCTION WITH CHILDREN'S LITERATURE

Because it isn't a very exciting headline, and it doesn't cry out to the public to turn and look and see the change, the innovation, the renewal in our classrooms. Instead, we see headlines like **HARK! PHONICS IS BACK** and **READING CHANGE IN THE AIR** and **PARENTS LEAD WAY IN PHONICS REVIVAL.** So, coming as no surprise to those of us who have been paying attention, phonics is still here or back or, as the kids say, "whatever." At any rate, we currently exist in an educational environment that has eclectically mixed whole language and phonics. What has been gained? According to the U.S. Department of Education bombshell released in

1995, ***not*** percentage points on a reading test. Under the eclectic mix of whole language and phonics, the illiteracy rate has soared to 43 percent!

What Now?

The complaints of the late 1970s are still valid. Phonics is tedious and difficult. The rules associated with phonics instruction are boring and frequently incorrect. New complaints have joined the problems associated with phonics. *We now know, from a twenty-year mountain of research, that phonemic awareness (being able to separate and blend sounds in words), alphabet code knowledge (knowing the correspondence between the sounds and the symbols), and an early start (five years) at learning to read are the three strongest determinants of future reading success, including comprehension.* But now with a new shot at impressing the public, phonics still does not teach phonemic awareness, teaches only about 50 percent of the alphabet code, and teaches that 50 percent using methods that are logically inappropriate to a child under nine years of age. So, why give a failed method another try? Because it's "sort of" right, but then so is whole language, which says read to your kids, suround them with books. So, is the answer this eclectic mix that we seem to be caught in? No! Logically speaking, just because two methods are partially valid does not mean that together they are completely valid. Mixing phonics and whole language assumes that the 67 percent success rate of the last phonics era and the 57 percent success rate of the whole language era, when mixed will equal a 100 percent complete method, all bases covered. In fact what it does equal is an averaged 62 percent success rate. That's not acceptable. Furthermore, it may be that whatever is causing the 33 percent failure rate of phonics and the 43 percent failure rate of whole language is so damaging that it is hurting children, creating Jacks, and Tinas, and Thomases, day by day, year after year, decade after decade.

What exactly is "sort of" right about phonics and whole language? Well, whole language credos which promote the use of literature are great. We should have our kids reading good children's literature as soon as they are able. And integrated curriculum is wonderful. Teachers should strive to make books meaningful across curriculum areas. But first we must teach children to actually be able to read these wonderful "big books." And that's where phonetics comes in. You'll recall that phonetics describes the various sounds in a given language, and that phonics was a nickname for phonetics. Well, phonics was correct in recognizing the importance of teaching the phonetics of the English writing system.

And that is precisely all it was correct about. From that point on, phonics is confusing, often wrong, and developmentally inappropriate to young children.

Phonics begins by teaching children the sounds for all the letters. This orientation from letter to sound, from which phonics comes, is wrong. This is not a matter of opinion. This is fact. The sounds in our language existed long before the letters. The written symbols of our language were invented to represent the sounds we had been speaking for centuries. Phonics instruction is driven from the letter to the sound, as if the sounds exist to suit the letters. This direction of instruction fails to allow the child to use what he already possesses, the sounds. By age five, when somebody starts to teach him to read, he is a master of sounds. He is completely intimate with his language. It is native to him. For him to learn to read, he needs instructional activities which encourage him to learn the symbols that were invented to represent the sounds that, as we've pointed out, he already knows. This knowledge is like a magical key to written language. But phonics throws the key away and starts from scratch, teaching him the sounds as if they were something new.

The wrong direction from which phonics sets out causes problems long after the child has learned all the single-letter sounds. The entire remainder of the code, the double letters which represent sounds, is taught using developmentally inappropriate activities and tedious and inaccurate rules. For instance, the instructional example from Webster's *Blue-Backed Speller* mentioned earlier explains that the first vowel in a vowel digraph is the vowel that should be sounded. Developmental psychologists have known for fifty years that young children (under nine) cannot manage propositional logic. Any parent knows instinctively that children cannot handle contingencies very well. Not only does this line of instruction require the use of propositional logic, but it is often wrong (house, spoon, said, bread). These are called "exceptions to the rule" or "rule breakers." So phonics relies on logic that developmental psychologists know is inappropriate to children, and the information being taught is actually wrong; then why are we harking over the return to phonics, a method which is based upon developmentally inappropriate and inaccurate reasoning?

So What's a Parent to Do?

The method used in this book is Phono-Graphix™. It has been researched and proven to work on children age four to adult nonreaders. It takes what the child knows, the sounds of his language, and teaches him the various *sound pictures* that represent those sounds. It does this through developmentally appropriate lessons that do not rely on propositional and other logic that children cannot understand. Linguistically based Phono-Graphix has been researched and proven to teach reading in one-tenth the time of phonics and with a 100 percent success rate. In a University of South Florida clinical study of Phono-Graphix, thirty-seven learning disabled students and forty-eight garden variety bad readers, subjects were taught to read in just twelve sessions with a 98 percent success rate. Two percent took six to twelve sessions longer (McGuinness, McGuinness & McGuinness, *Orton Annals of Dyslexia*, 1996). In a pilot study conducted at two childcare centers in Central Florida, the same method was used on kindergartners from September 1st to mid-November. After only eleven weeks of exposure, the average reading age of the children on the standardized Woodcock Reading Mastery Test, was first grade, first month. This average score is over nine months above grade level. The worst readers were reading at grade level, and the best readers were reading at first grade, sixth month—over a year above grade level.

In a study conducted at the Millhopper Montessori School in Gainesville, Florida, twenty-four first- and second-graders received Phono-Graphix instruction in reading groups of four to nine children for ten to fifteen minutes per day. At the time of the pretest, using the Woodcock Reading Mastery Test, twenty-five percent of the children were reading below grade level, thirty-four percent were reading at grade level, and forty-one percent were reading above grade level. This group was already well above the national norms, with only twenty-five percent of the children below grade level compared to the forty-three percent that is our national average. After using Phono-Graphix for eight months their scores improved dramatically. At the time of posttesting none of the children scored below grade level, seventeen percent scored at grade level, twenty-one percent were within a year above grade level, and sixty-two percent were over a year above grade level. With children who were in trouble at pretest scoring dramatically above grade level at posttest, these studies not only indicate the invention of a perfect method for correcting reading failure, but indicate that average readers can become super readers!

Now that we've found the perfect method, the really great news is that you needn't save the thousands of dollars for private school, or move halfway across the country. You can teach your child to read in the convenience of your own home. We assume, by the the fact that you've purchased this book, that when confronted with a problem you are a doer, not a wait-and-see type. Well, the first thing to do, now that you know there *is* something that *can* be done, is to follow the lessons in this book *to the letter*, or in this case, *to the sound*. You must read the following, rather technical, explanation of what reading is, and come to understand it theoretically. Why? Because in order to teach someone to do something, anything, you must understand that thing. You must know how to do that thing yourself. I would not presume to teach children to play the piano. I don't know how to play the piano. I did, however, just last week, teach my twelve-year-old how to make wheat bread. The event went fairly well. There were a few things she needed help with. She did not, for example, know what the word "knead" meant. I explained it to her, but soon discovered it required showing her. She caught on quickly. She also needed some instruction in the teaspoon **<t>**, tablespoon **<T>** symbols used in my cookbook. Once I told her what they meant she did fine. Basically, what she lacked was subskill practice and some code knowledge. She had never kneaded before (a subskill of bread making). And she did not know the big **T** / little **t** trick: nothing more than a code. Although it is based on the English sounds, Phono-Graphix's point of departure is a 180 degree difference from phonics. Instead of teaching children the sounds that letters make, we recognize that *letters do not make sounds, they represent sounds*. This is no subtle distinction.

Almost anything you could want to learn or teach has relevant subskills and codes. Subskills are the skills required before you can perform the task. The code is the symbols used to communicate when performing the task. When I was eighteen my cousin took me waterskiing. It was my first trip. I soon discovered that the ability to balance one's body over two planks of wood while being pulled forward by eighty-five Evenrude horses is a subskill I needed lots of practice with. When I finally mastered this subskill and found myself being pulled at a speed I found unnerving, I realized that no matter how many times or how loudly I yelled "slow down," the driver and passengers could not hear me. What I lacked was the code. After I let go, was rescued, and voiced my frustration, they told me the code: a thumb up or a thumb down. It seemed simple once I knew. Later that day, when my legs stopped buckling under me and my frustration had ebbed a bit, it occurred to me that my cousin hadn't thought to instruct me about how to stand or what to do if I wanted to slow down because it was all second nature to him. He and his friends had been skiing expertly for years. For them it was like walking. Watching them ski, I understood that they were on automatic pilot when they did it. They had reached a level of expertise at which they didn't even have to think about what they were doing.

Being able to do the thing you wish to teach is not the only prerequisite of being able to teach it. To teach a thing well, the teacher should understand the processes and subskills involved in doing it. As a parent who wishes to teach your child to read, it's important that you realize that you have reached a level of expertise at reading at which it is second nature to you, just like waterskiing was second nature to my cousin. You are unaware of the subskills needed, and your knowledge of the code is mostly subconscious. The main goals of this book are to:

Teach the subskills and give you ways to help your child practice them
Tell you what the code is and show you how to teach it to your child

Let's look at each of the subskills of reading and as we do, we'll check to be sure that Phono-Graphix is teaching them in a manner that a young child can understand.

SUBSKILLS NECESSARY TO READING

Ability to scan text from left to right. Children of five and older can understand that the code moves in one direction. They may need to be reminded of the particular direction from time to time.

Ability to match visual symbols to auditory sounds, such as the symbol ***<t>*** *= the sound 't'.* Children of five and older can do this paired associate learning as long as relevance is added to the formula. Phono-Graphix teaches only eight sound pictures at a time, using those sound pictures to read and spell real words. By actually using these eight sound pictures to read and spell, children begin to understand why they need to know the code.

Ability to blend discrete sound units into words. As we've proven in our kindergarten study, children of five and older can blend sounds into words, once they have been shown, by example, what it is you expect of them.

Ability to segment sounds in words. Our kindercare study also shows that children of five and older can segment sounds in words once you have shown them, by example what you expect of them.

Ability to understand that sometimes two or more letters represent a sound. For example, sh. Children of five and older can understand that sometimes sound pictures are made with two letters. They cannot understand this by imposition of a propositional rule, but they easily understand that sometimes it just happens. To prove this we asked forty five- and six-year-old children the following questions.

"What's this?" ■

All 40 said, "a square."

"What's this?" ▲

All 40 said, "a triangle."

"What's this?"

All 40 said, "a house."

These six-year-olds easily understood that the two symbols known as "square" and "triangle" could be used together and called something else entirely, "house." So we know that they can also understand that the symbols known as 's' and 'h' can be used together and called something else entirely, 'sh'.

Ability to understand that most sounds can be represented in more than one way. For example, the sound 'ee' can be spelled in several ways: green, team, and happy, and more. Children of six and older can understand and begin to learn this. To provc that six-year-olds understand this logic we asked thirty six-year-olds the following questions:

"What's this?"  All 30 answered, "a flower."

"What's this?"  All 30 answered, "a flower."

"What's this?"  All 30 answered, "a flower."

"Is it okay to have 3 things that look different that are all called flower?"

All 30 answered, "yes."

These six-year-olds easily understood that things can have the same name and not be exactly alike. So we know that they can understand that **<ea>** and **<ee>** and **<y>** could all be pictures of the sound 'ee'. They begin to show consistent memorized recall of the various ways to represent different sounds at about seven or eight years.

7 *Ability to understand that some components of the code can represent more than one sound.* For example, the symbol **<o>** can be used to represent the sounds 'o' as in 'hot,' or 'oe' as in 'most.' Six-year-olds can understand this. To prove this we asked thirty six-year-olds the question, "Name two things this could be." ● All 30 answered, "a ball or a circle." These six-year-olds understood that a single symbol could represent two different things. So we know that they can understand that the sound picture **<o>** can represent the sound 'o' as in 'hot' or the sound 'oe' as in 'most.'

To most proficient readers this might sound a bit excessive. You might be thinking at this point, "I don't think I do all that when I read. I just recognize words as I go." But remember, we're talking about a set of subskills that you learned a long time ago, and that you have become so adept at that you're conscious only of the skill (reading) and not of the subskills. Let's take a look at a typical passage taken from a popular children's book, to see how you read.

> **Th**is me**ss** is so big and so d**ee**p and so t**al**l, **th**e**re**'s no w**ay** to cl**ea**n it up, no w**ay** at **al**l.

If you were really paying attention to what you were doing when you read the passage, the first thing you noticed is that you started at the left side of the line and scanned to the right as you went. Next you analyzed the letter symbols, matching sounds to sound symbols. And you blended as you made your way through the words, pushing sounds together to make words. You also performed analysis as you progressed, processing the **<th>** in 'this' as one sound not two ('t' 'h'). All this might seem simple enough to the experienced adult, but presents numerous challenges for the young child. The word 'this' contains three sounds, yet it's spelled with four letters. That's necessary as there is no single-letter symbol in English for the sound 'th'. Continuing on in the same word, you found the letter symbol **<i>** which could represent the sound 'i' or 'ie' (and a few less common possibilities). How do we know that the second sound in the word is 'i' rather than 'i-e', as in the word 'wild'? We know because 'thīs' is not a word. Even the **<s>** could represent two different sounds, 's' as in 'this' or 'z' as in 'is.' As you can see, the reader is actually balancing three variables when reading this word:

1. When to process one letter **<t>** **<h>** or two letters **<th>** to get a sound
2. Whether **<i>** represents the sound 'i' or 'i-e'
3. Whether **<s>** represents the sound 's' or 'z'

In addition, she has to remember to scan from left to right, and to blend as she goes.

If you continue to analyze the text in our sample passage, you'll see that anytime two letters are bolded they represent one sound. With some thought, you'll realize that these sound pictures are predictable in that they reoccur in text in numerous words. So that's easy, right? **Wrong!** Although the sound pictures reoccur over and over again, like the sound picture **<al>** in the words 'all' and 'tall,' which would also be found in the words 'chalk' and 'talk,' there are frequently numerous sound pictures for one sound. That same 'al' sound in 'talk' is represented with the sound picture **<aw>** in 'fawn,' 'lawn,' and 'awful,' and **<au>** in 'August,' 'fraud,' and 'fault.' To make matters even worse, some of the sound pictures can represent more than one sound. The **<ea>** in 'clean,' for instance, represents a different sound altogether in the words 'great' and 'steak,' and yet another sound in the words 'bread' and 'thread.'

So, even at this simple level our young reader must analyze as she makes her way through each word, making numerous determinations as she progresses, as to whether letters stand alone or work together to represent sounds. This requires combining visual (What do I see and which parts work together?) and auditory (What is the sound it represents?) analysis—no simple task for a six-year-old. In addition, based on our above inventory of challenges, she must sometimes stop and try two or even three sounds in a word before meaning is achieved (as in our **<ea>** example where this sound picture can represent three sounds, such as in 'thread,' 'steak,' 'clean').

For you readers who still insist that you simply breeze over text, instantly recognizing each word as you proceed, we've prepared a special, modified *Cat in the Hat* just for you. Our intention is to increase the level of difficulty, thereby simulating the experience of the new reader. We hope this increased difficulty will slow you down enough to notice that you are performing all the subskills itemized in this chapter.

> This gallimaufry is multitudinously gargantuan, puissantly capacious and ineffably Junoesque and in consequence of such Protean tribulations and in such psychotic contravention of stereotypical consuetudinary hygiene, there exists the infinitesimal exiguity of a satisfactory resolution to this cataclysmic dilemma.

As you can see, when reading this passage it's necessary to track through the word slowly, blending the sounds as you proceed. It's also necessary to stop and determine which letters work together to represent one sound, and which stand alone. In addition, you likely had to try more than one sound for some of the sound pictures in many of the words. You no doubt slowed a bit when you got to the **<au>** in gallimaufry, but your subconscious knowledge of the code allowed you to push on with the sound 'o' in mind. When you got to the **<y>** in that word you might have tried the sounds 'ee' and 'ie', both possible sounds for that particular sound picture. In reading this passage, you likely did not attempt to apply rules.

You might be wondering, "How did I ever learn to read? I wasn't taught all this." We're not saying you can't learn to read when improperly taught. Children try to make order of chaos, and frequently succeed. But this is largely a matter of luck. What we're saying is that Phono-Graphix teaches the subskills of reading in the right order, from the beginning to the end. Unless adults take the time to understand the processes and subskills involved in reading, they should not attempt to teach young children to read. The danger that exists in assuming that children can just be taught to recognize each word as it occurs is considerable. The beliefs of adults affect children's behavior and performance. Comments like, "You *know* that word. Come on, what's it say?" drive the child's performance. The message is, "You've seen that word a few times now. You should have memorized it. Memorizing whole words is what you're supposed to be doing. That's what reading is." And before too long the child begins, consciously or unconsciously, to attempt to memorize whole words. That would be alright if it worked, but it doesn't. The typical person can memorize only about 2,000 to 3,000 words. That's enough to perform at about a first-grade level. That's why so many children can fool their parents and teachers until they get to second grade. If you add in other crutches like using the pictures for clues and trying to guess the story line based on what just happened, the child might be able to fool her significant adults until about the middle of second grade. But eventually her visual memory load will bottom out and the big bad wolf will be huffing and puffing and blowing down a *horse* instead of a *house,* because the words look a lot alike. We call this particular strategy for learning to read "globalizing." The global reader anticipates and guesses, but rarely or never actually decodes text.

As we have already said, the English written code is a sound symbol code, not a word symbol code. That's the game. If you're going to play it you might as well play it right. After years and years of reading we most certainly will end up with a pretty good visual inventory of words. But if we were properly taught, we will also know the code (at least subconsciously), and be able to decode when we encounter new or difficult words, unusual names, etc. Allowing a child to memorize words without teaching him the code actually creates a deficit for him. Imagine that you're six years old and that you are given the choice of memorizing the 20,000 words that you'll use in your daily vocabulary, or memorizing the 134 sound pictures that represent the various sounds used in English. Which do you think would be an easier task? Many children never get that choice. They are taught so badly that they come to think that memorizing words as pictures is what they're supposed to do. It becomes their strategy. One hundred and one of the 193 subjects ages five to sixty-one who were tested by the Read America clinic in a three-year period read the word **horse** as **house**. The attributes are not that dissimilar, *if* you are looking at the word as a word picture. But, if you understand the nature of the written code, and look at the word as a set of sound pictures, things get much simpler. There are, of course, some words in the English language that do not decode properly. My favorite is 'yacht.' In fact, there are about 55 such words. The other 19,950 words that we use and spell daily are predictable and decodable if one knows and uses the English written code.

Many parents who have been working with their young readers instinctively realize the importance of teaching the written English code to their child, and meticulously teach all the single-letter sound pictures but fail to explain to the child that sounds are sometimes represented with two or more letters, what we call the *advanced code*. These children often have the right strategy (sound out words), but lack the advanced code knowledge to be very successful at it. Children who are taught the subskills but not the advanced code develop a one-to-one strategy. One-to-one readers read each letter sound, completely unaware of the advanced code. My favorite example of this was seven-year-old Cybil, who read me a story about a horse named Midnight, which when sounded out one letter at a time sounded like the "'h' 'o' 'r' 's' 'ee' 'm' 'i' 'd' - 'n' 'i' 'g' 't'." By the time a young reader reaches fourth grade, about 60 percent of the text he encounters will be advanced level text. If he doesn't know that part of the code, he will never read above a 40 percent accuracy rate. He may even eventually determine that sounding out words is a waste of his time as he is so often inaccurate in his attempts. That would seem an unnecessary and unfair fate for a child when it is so simple to teach him the entire code.

"It's not so simple," you say, "I've been trying to teach my child and he's still struggling." That's where this book comes in. It's not so hard to teach a child to read when you know exactly what to do. The Phono-Graphix method of reading instruction set out in *Reading Reflex* is a natural method that works in accordance with the developmental capabilities of the learner. It reveals the written language to the child in such a way as to make the code clear and show how that code fits together into meaningful words. This is not just another method. The research conducted on this method (*Orton Annals of Dyslexia*, 1996) reveals it to be the most effective remedial program available, bringing previously failed readers, 40 percent of whom had been previously diagnosed with learning disabilities, to grade level in only twelve sessions. The KinderCare study conducted in 1996 showed that the same principles and techniques used on failed readers effectively teach beginning readers much faster than the national norm. In short, Phono-Graphix is a pure approach to reading instruction—an approach that works for everyone.

Reading Reflex is intended to meet the needs of two kinds of students. It is for young children, age five or so, who are ready to learn to read, and elementary-age children (grades one through five) who are struggling at reading or spelling. If your child is a young child, five or six years old, you will use this book over the next several years, as your child matures and shows the competence to move on to the next activity. If you are working remedially with an older child, you will want to make your way through the lesson plans as quickly as possible so that she can begin reading at grade level and doing well at school.

The following chapter will tell you what you'll need to get started, and will offer some suggestions about setting up your in-house reading school. Chapter two will also give you some helpful information about how children process information and what motivates them. Chapter two also contains four tests which will help you determine which of the reading subskills your child needs help with. Chapters three, four, five, and six are the actual instructional parts of the book. From an explanation of the challenges the chapter brings, to specific lesson plans and word lists, these four chapters will guide you as your child moves toward the *reading reflex*.

A Note to Teachers and Tutors

If you are a school administrator, a classroom teacher, or a reading therapist working clinically, we invite you to call us at 1-800-732-3868 or at 352-735-9292; fax us at 352-735-9294; write to us at P.O. Box 1246, Mount Dora, FL 32776; e-mail us at RAchat@aol.com, or visit our Web site at www.readamerica.net. There are numerous support materials such as our classroom supplement, classroom curriculum, more coded stories, games, and computer programs that can be used in conjunction with the materials in this book. Read America operates a training institute offering our certification course in Orlando, Florida, and London, England. In addition, Read America maintains an international membership organization and distributes our membership publication *ParenTeacher Magazine*. For a free copy please call us.

Since the writing of this book Phono-Graphix has been implemented in many classrooms and districts around the country, Canada, the U.K., Australia, and New Zealand. An update is offered in the preface.

CHAPTER TWO

GETTING STARTED

As you prepare to teach your child to read and spell, it's important to take the time to accomplish a few things before you get started. Please do not make the mistake of plunging into the lessons unprepared. One dad we worked with expressed frustration while working in Chapter four. "He (his six-year-old) made a mistake reading the word 'frog,'" he explained. "He read it as 'fog.'" When I asked him how he handled it, hoping he would give me the correction as it is explained in the lesson plan, he said, "Well, I reminded him that, 'ef' 'ar' says 'fr'." When I explained that he should be referring to the symbols by sounds, not by letter names, and that his son should be saying each sound separately, he looked baffled. Later he confessed he hadn't read Chapter one, two, or three, but had plunged right in to the lessons in Chapter four.

We suggest that you read the entire book. If you haven't read the introduction and Chapter one, please go back and do so now. After you've read this chapter and gotten all the materials you'll need, continue on to Chapter three and then just after reading it begin the lessons with your child. When she is accomplished at these lessons, read Chapter four and then work with her on the lessons in that chapter. Continue through the book in this way, reading each chapter even if your child's tests do not indicate a need for her to work in this chapter. Each chapter contains information about reading that you need to understand.

We hope the following sections will answer your questions and address your concerns.

"I've never taught anyone before. How can I teach my child to read?"

In providing reading lessons for your child, your role will be that of a mentor, and your child's role will be that of a learner. The learner-mentor relationship is as old as mankind. It should not be new to you as a parent. You've taught your child many "tricks," to walk, to talk, to use a toilet, to use silverware, to ride her bike. The lessons in this book will offer you the expertise to teach her to read. That's been made easy for you. The harder part is establishing the role of mentor in a new situation, reading teacher. You'll need to work at this, to show her that you mean business, that together you are going to accomplish the goal of learning to read and spell.

There are many different kinds of children. You know as well as we that they come in many shapes and sizes, with different interests, likes and dislikes, and different experiences behind them. You may be the lucky one whose child is excited and happy to spend some time with you, doing reading or anything else you so desire. Or, you may have the worst case of avoidance on record since Sam. Sam was a client of mine about two years ago. At that time Sam was eight years old, almost nine. He is the one I think of as I write about the importance of maintaining control of the learner-mentor situation. In a way he was a composite of all the different kinds of clients I had had before and after him, because, well, he tried absolutely everything in order to get out of lessons. At the first session he was quiet and thoughtful. It was clear that he had other things to be doing, places to go and many, many other more interesting people to see. He didn't say this, but he let me know with his posture and the gentle but firm roll of his eyes at appropriate times. I carried on just the same and presented him with the prescribed lessons. When I walked him out to the waiting room his mother looked apprehensive. "How did it go?" she asked with trepidation. That's when I knew I was in trouble. At the next session Sam seated himself at my table and waited. As I began our second lesson he proudly proclaimed, "This is so dumb. I already know how to read. I don't need to do this." Well, I had heard this "I already know how" thing before (and now you have too) so with all the sincerity I could muster I answered, "Oh good, then this should be easy for you. We'll be able to get through it all in no time." Then I said, "I work with lots of kids who can already read. Their parents just want it to be really easy for them. So my job is to teach them some tricks that make reading and spelling super easy for them." Kids like things to be easy, so this usually works.

The role of the mentor is a very powerful one. He is the expert, the exemplar. He knows everything about the topic he teaches. This makes him above reproach, beyond question. Your child will not doubt you in this role, as she knows you are an accomplished reader. Once you've established yourself as the mentor, the actual lessons are easy. Everything you need to know is written in each lesson plan. As you use the lessons to their full advantage, it's very important that you also use the mentor role to *its* full advantage. When you direct your child in her reading lessons, your directions are not negotiable. There is no room for whining or argument. Your demeanor and verbal directions will help you to establish yourself as the mentor. You should be confident and certain in your directions to your child. It's all written down so there is no need to hesitate. If *you* do not hesitate in *your* work, *she* will follow suit. Your work together is important work. It is the work of learning to read, a very grown-up thing to do. It should be presented in a serious light and it will be taken seriously.

One of the jobs of the mentor is to offer examples for the learner that are intended to become the learner's automatic response to the task being taught, her strategy for reading and spelling. This requires patience. A new client I recently started working with (Darcy, age twelve), is what we call a "part word reader." She looks at a word and uses any of the letters in any order to try to construct meaning. So, for example, at our second session she read the word 'multiply' as 'mul' (they usually get the first syllable right) and then 'it' (reversing the letters **<ti>** to construct the word 'it'), and then 'fly' (disregarding the fact that there is a **<p>** and not an **<f>** in this word). She looked at me and said, "'mull-et fly.' Is that a fishing thing?" In situations like this it's tempting to jump in and try to get the right word happening as soon as possible. But as the mentor, that's not your job. Your job is to redirect the learner one step at a time. So in this situation I started out by saying, "You got the first chunk (my word for syllable) right. After 'mul,' you said 'it.' Check that please." Once that issue was straightened out I said, "Good, so what have you got so far?" She answered with the appropriate 'mul ti.' Then I asked, "And what's next?" getting the correct response of 'ply.' All this took lots of patience. The actual issues are the easy part. They are written down in the lesson plan. It's the patience that's tough. Remember that if your response as your child's mentor is to hurry, to rush through the lessons, you will be setting your child up to do the same. If your response is to become frustrated, your child will learn to express frustration when the task gets challenging. If your response is to take it slow, perform the desired steps in the correct order, and start fresh when an error occurs, your child will learn patience with herself and perseverance with the task at hand. Each lesson plan offers specific steps for handling any error that your child may make. By following the steps provided and starting over when an error occurs, you are giving her the message that, "This is important work. I really want you to learn to read and spell. I love you and together we can accomplish this."

So in addition to acting as exemplar, the mentor must offer this critical guidance through the lessons necessary to learn the task. According to Webster, to guide is to "point out the way for." Pointing out the way is no easy task. It is often much easier to just take one to the point of destination, skipping the necessity to lay out the course. How many times have you said "Never mind, I'll just do it myself"? In the case of reading instruction, this is the beginning of the end. In the lesson plans, the steps are clearly laid out. Your job as the mentor is to follow, not skip, them. To effectively guide the new reader, the mentor must point the way, help the learner see the way. This means that every single step you expect of your new reader must be made completely explicit to her. With each error you must point out what happened, as the lesson plans indicate, and redirect her toward what you wanted to happen.

"Will my lessons with my child interfere in her natural process of learning to read?"

There is nothing natural about learning to read. The written code is an invention and the process is in no way native to children. Your child will learn to walk without your help, but she will not necessarily learn to read. Occasionally a teacher will find a child who does just get it and start reading spontaneously. The risk you run in waiting to see if your child is one of those few is great. By the time you discover that she isn't one of those literary prodigies we've all heard tell of, you'll have a remedial reader on your hands rather than a new reader. The other, and worse, possibility is that she may actually start to read, but in the wrong way. Many bright children with a high visual memory start to memorize whole words if no one teaches them that this is not how we read. Or, like Darcy did, they might adopt a part word strategy. Six-year-old Josh, a client several years back, was a child who appeared to his teacher to just get it and start reading spontaneously. But as the school year went on, his mother became alarmed by some of his mistakes. At his first session he read the word 'oxen' as the two words 'on next,' and the word 'earn' as 'end red.' Clearly he was treating words as if they were an anagram to be solved. In that situation you've got a remedial reader with a bad habit on your hands. In all, the safest bet is to start early and teach her the right way from the beginning.

"My house makes Grand Central Station seem peaceful. How will my child learn to read in that environment?"

Walk through your home and give some thought to the proper location for your reading lessons. In order to avoid confusion and organizational chaos, lessons should be given in the same spot each time. This is very important as it sets the stage for your child to be the learner and to respect you as the mentor. Moving around the house from lesson to lesson may disrupt the development of this critical learner-mentor relationship. I worked with one parent who continually complained that she was having trouble maintaining control over the lessons. I went to the house to observe the next lesson, and was shocked to find that the lesson was being carried out on the pool patio in glaring sunlight with two younger siblings splashing and screaming nearby.

In choosing the perfect spot for lessons, try to find somewhere that is consistently quiet. Avoid a location where you would be at the mercy of other family members. If you have other children who may have needs during the lesson, make arrangements for them ahead of time. They can visit grandma or maybe grandma can come over and spend some time with them at your house. I advise you not to choose the same spot where your child does her homework. There are several reasons behind this advice. The reading lessons will not be anything like your child's homework. They are directed lessons, with the mentor taking the lead role. When helping your child with her homework, she takes the lead role, not you. Also, if your child is struggling, homework time may conjure up negative feelings for her. Avoid using your child's room for lessons. Your child is in charge in her room. It's her turf. You must be in charge during lessons. One place you might consider for your lessons is your room. For the family with a modest home, that might be the only spot that offers the appropriate privacy you will need.

"Will I need special materials?"

Once you've decided on the perfect location for lessons, you will need to prepare it before you can get started. You will need a table or desk you can work on. It should have a flat, level surface, about two to three feet wide and two feet deep. It should be free of other materials that might distract your child. It should be situated so that you can sit across from your child rather than beside her. This gives you more control. It also allows you to see her face so that you can better determine what she is doing wrong when she makes errors. For instance, this morning I was working with a six-year-old first-grade boy named Zachary. Zachary was reading the following sentence: "The boy next door was mean to his sister." He did fine with "The boy" but when he got to "next" he faltered. I watched his mouth to see what he was attempting and saw that he was sounding the letter name 'en' rather than the correct sound 'n' for the sound picture **<n>**. I simply pointed to the **<n>** with my pencil and said 'en' is two sounds 'e' 'n'. This (pointing to the **<n>**) is just 'n'. If I had been beside Zachary I would not have seen his little lips forming the sounds 'e' 'n'. I wouldn't have known why he couldn't read the word 'next.' By seeing what he was doing I was able to offer the appropriate feedback to correct the error in a meaningful way.

The specific corrections are offered throughout the lesson plans. That's the easy part, assuming you have set up the work space correctly. Being across from your child also allows you to use your finger or pencil point to indicate word parts from above the text rather than below it which might obscure her vision of the word or part of the word. Being across from your child during lessons is not an option, but a necessity. If you can't locate a perfect desk or table that allows this, you may have to invest in a card table. Some of the large budget department stores sell folding tables about three feet wide by two feet deep. These are perfect for your lessons because they are long enough to offer sufficient work space, but not so deep as to be difficult to reach across. Do not give up and use the floor or a floor table of any sort. A proper table is a must.

You will also need comfortable upright chairs. Make sure that your child can reach the table with ease. She may need to sit on something to get her up high enough to see what's going on. She should not be at an odd angle to the text. This may confuse her vision of words. It may also cause glare from overhead lighting. I frequently hear from parents that they can't get their children to sit while doing their homework. This is usually remedied by an appropriate table and chair arrangement that allows the child to reach and to see what she's doing.

Your chair needs to be comfortable as well. You do not want to be rushing through lessons so that you can seek out a more comfortable location. I am frequently asked to observe parent and child working together for home schooling evaluations. On one such occasion the parent kept reaching across her chest with her left arm and rubbing her right shoulder. It was clear that she was tired and stiff. About ten minutes into the lesson the child said, "Mommy, if your back hurts we can do this later." It's best to avoid situations where your discomfort is supplying your child with excuses to stop the lessons. Part of my written recommendations were to replace the stool she was using for lessons with a proper straight-backed chair with a full seat.

I had a similar situation occur during a damage control observation. I was asked to observe a client working with his nanny. Gary, an otherwise compliant and sweet child, was cranky and miserable when doing his lesson with his nanny. The lessons were given in his father's study about an hour before Dad got home from the office. This seemed a good idea as that space was considered sacred ground, eliciting Gary's respect. Everything started out fine. The nanny seemed to understand the material and gave clear directions. But about five minutes into the lesson Gary started to squirm and fuss. "I'm thirsty. I'm hungry. I'm tired. I have to go to the bathroom." Name a body function and he had to do it. After a few minutes she dismissed him to go to the bathroom. I moved over to where Gary had been sitting to chat with her about him and the problem became clear. His dad's desk lamp was angled in such a way that it shone on the mahogany surface and reflected up into Gary's face. It would have made anyone fussy. At well over six feet tall, it wasn't a problem for Gary's father. But, for little Gary and his little reading therapist (me) the desk lamp was a big problem. I quickly adjusted the lamp and had a drink of water waiting for Gary when he got back from the bathroom. The lesson continued with no fussing. His nanny said it was his best lesson to date. Always make sure the lighting is good in your work environment. Test the chair where your child will be sitting (from the height at which she will be sitting) to make sure there isn't a glare. Too much light is as bad as too little. Also avoid lighting that is behind her head that might cast a shadow over her work area.

You will need a few items for your work with your child. You will need about seventy small envelopes, 4" x 5" or 6". These are for storing the word building puzzles in, as well as the auditory processing puzzles. To store the envelopes, you'll need a shoebox. You will also need a supply of paper and pencils with good erasers, as well as a pencil sharpener. Standard wide-ruled notebook paper is the best. I really don't like the special beginning writer papers that some schools use. They are expensive and tear easily. They smudge when you use an eraser on them. And for most children, they are too wide-ruled. Most children write smaller, not larger than adults. I find that the larger the printing, the greater the room for crooked lines and square circles. It is easier to write small than it is to write large. I encourage you to encourage your new writer to scale down her printing. Special pencil grips are not necessary, but if your child is used to one, allow her to use it for your lessons. While you're in the paper department, pick up some colored pencils. They add a bit of novelty when writing begins to get boring. Be sure to get the ones that erase. These are the ones that have erasers on the ends. You may have to go to an art supply store to find the erasable colored pencils. Some school supply stores have them. Buy colors that are fairly dark and show up nicely on paper. Red, medium blue, green, purple, and orange are best. Avoid pink, light blue, and yellow. Colored pencils should be used one at a time. Kids like to write every other word and sometimes every other letter in a different color. The rainbow effect is okay for art class, but distracting during reading lessons. Remember, you're in charge. Your child can pick a pencil and write. Every now and then you can let her pick a new color, but not for every other word. Also available at most school supply stores, is a dry erase board. Don't let the sales person talk you into a big wall model. You need a small (9" x 12") table top model. To write on this you will need two medium point dry erase markers in different colors and a dry eraser.

While we're on the topic of writing, a note about cursive. Many second and third graders are trying their hand at cursive writing. Your lessons are not the time or place for this. There are two reasons why. If cursive is new to your child, she will be focusing on style rather than the lessons. In addition, the intention of many of the lessons is to separate sounds in words. This is difficult when the entire word is connected. I simply tell the children that I can't read cursive upside down (you're supposed to be sitting across the table from her). Do not negotiate on this point. Cursive is not an option for your lessons.

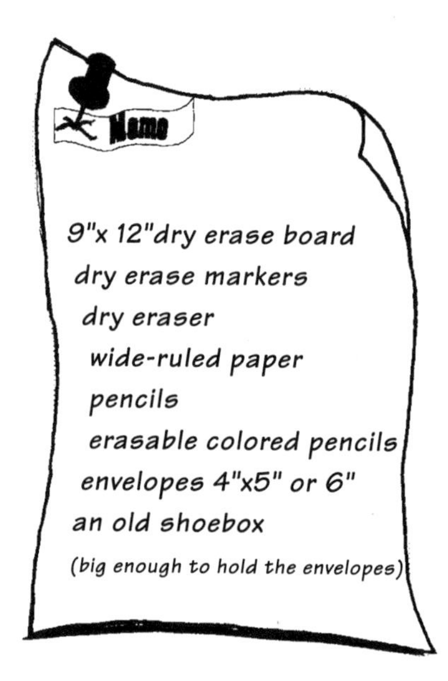

Name
9"x 12"dry erase board
dry erase markers
dry eraser
wide-ruled paper
pencils
erasable colored pencils
envelopes 4"x5" or 6"
an old shoebox
(big enough to hold the envelopes)

Organizing your materials is important. If you can't leave your work table set up between lessons, find a nice box or drawer you can keep everything in. Don't store the materials too far out of reach. If you need a ladder to get them down, or you have to go down to the basement to find them, you'll tend to postpone your lessons. Set aside the time to set up the environment before each lesson. If you invite your child to a messy desk and start pushing things out of the way and searching for materials, she will have a hard time respecting you as the expert. Imagine coming to a staff meeting at your job only to find that your boss is badly prepared and terribly disorganized. Always make sure that the materials for your lesson are the only things on your work table.

Do not allow your child to help herself to the materials between lessons. She should think of the materials as your property, not hers. If she shows an interest in having a dry erase board of her own, buy her one. Remember, it is important that you are in charge of the lesson, the environment, and the materials. Allowing her to use the materials between lessons may threaten your authority as the reading mentor. You may question and doubt this advice. You may even think us rigid and authoritative. You're right. We are. Remember, the relationship you strive for in regard to teaching your child to read is a clinical one. When a child walks into my office she immediately knows, by the order of the materials and the demeanor I display, that this is sacred turf. This is my place, my stuff, my game. By establishing that early, I can get her to do things, lessons, she would not normally commit to without a struggle. I had a client who was an absolute terror with his mother during his home lessons. After a month she offered to bring him to me twice as often if I would let her off the hook on the home assignments. "I'll pay you, of course," was her pleading message. Even when clients come to our office for reading therapy I feel it's important for parents to do home lessons with them, so I offered to come out and observe the situation. It was clear on sight, before the lesson even began that nine-year-old Michael had complete control of the environment. The dry erase board had to be fetched from his bedroom. The pencil, lying in wait on the table, was an eighteen-inch candy cane with a bell on the end. Matchbox cars were stored inside the eraser box, instead of markers. When it was time to get started Michael's mother asked him to turn off the TV. "Why?" he asked, which I took as an indication that it was generally left on during lessons. The simple act of asking him to turn it off was her first mistake. It implies that he, and he alone, has dominion over the TV. This was clearly Michael's party.

An analogy that comes to mind on the matter of maintaining control of the space and the things in it, is the doctor's office. Our society places importance upon doctors. Why? Well, one reason is that they are considered experts. If, as a parent, you can be the reading expert, you will get similar respect from your child. We also treat doctors with reverence because they have a bunch of neat stuff that we are only allowed to touch with express permission. The blood pressure monitor is wrapped around our arm for us. The thermometer gets put in our mouth, not handed to us. If my dentist asked me to please turn on the drill, I might respond like Michael, "Why?" or Gary, "I'm thirsty. I'm hungry. I have to go to the bathroom." Once your child begins to succeed at various steps in the process, she'll discover, as Gary and Michael did, that it's fun to succeed, that it makes her life easier and that, in the long run, it allows her more time to play, because she can get her homework done more quickly.

"How can I motivate my child to want to read?"

As a parent about to embark on the task of teaching your child to read, do not make the mistake of confusing wants with *motives*. If your child doesn't want to do her reading lessons it doesn't mean she isn't motivated to be able to read. Wants deal with immediate behaviors with no regard as to *why* the behavior is wanted. Motives concern themselves with the "why" of behavior. I may want to go for a picnic on Tuesday, but the behavior I actually choose is to go to work instead. My behavior is motivated by the fact that I must earn money to buy food and pay for my son's college tuition. Your child may want to watch TV or any number of activities more fun than reading lessons, but still be motivated to be able to read. She's motivated to because she knows she *must*. It's one of those things that everyone does in order to become grown up.

We talk to hundreds of parents and teachers about motivation. It is a common question. But when you really listen, the question isn't about motivation at all. It's about "wants" and attitudes. We all know we can get children to do their work. We are bigger than them, and smarter. We have ways of making the little people do what we want them to do. What parents and teachers are really talking about when they talk about motivation, is attitude. What they're really saying is, "I wish my child had a better attitude about his reading." What they sometimes fail to understand is that what makes a child have a good attitude about reading is being a good reader. If you can't proceed until the attitude is better, this becomes a catch 22 situation. The only solution is to work with the not-so-great attitude until you can improve the reading.

A study conducted by Dennis Kear and Randolf Ellsworth of Wichita State University (*Reading Research Quarterly*, 1996). examined children's attitudes about reading from first to sixth grades. They looked at excellent readers, average readers, and poor readers. They found that children had the best attitude about reading when they were in first grade, regardless of how well they were doing. After first grade the attitude of the average and poor groups declined significantly, with only the excellent readers maintaining a good attitude about reading. These results were consistent across sexes and ethnic groups. The results of this study offer three important implications to how a parent proceeds:

> If the only way to make your child have a good attitude about reading is for him to be among the top readers, you better stop worrying about whether or not he's motivated and *get busy with the lessons*.
> Attitude about reading dropped significantly by second grade, so *get busy fast*.
> Average just isn't good enough, even for the kids, so *get busy now*.

"My child isn't really interested in reading." Interest and Other Myths

Last week we received a call at the clinic that is typical of what we hear from parents regularly. It went something like this. "My daughter is having some trouble at school. She (who it turned out was a second grader) is just not really interested in reading. She likes school. She loves her new teacher (it's early September) and has lots of friends. But she has a lot of reading and spelling homework, and frankly, I can't get her to work on it for longer than about ten minutes. She's really struggling with the reading. She's just not really very interested in it. Whenever I try to help her she whines and we end up in a power struggle. I heard about your program (referring to our one-on-one clinical services) and I'm interested in enrolling her." Clearly, this parent, in her current mind set, would fail if we sold her this book and encouraged her to teach her child to read and spell at home. Well, let's have a look at the problem, and see if we can adjust her perspective just a bit.

"My daughter is having trouble at school."

As the conversation continued it appeared that she wasn't having trouble *at school* at all. She "liked school," "loved her new teacher," and had "lots of friends." As it turned out, when her father got involved and "made her study her spelling words" she did much better.

"She has a lot of reading and spelling homework."

This started out as the child's problem and at some point became the parent's problem. As long as she isn't allowed to play or watch television until her homework is done, the problem remains hers. It is only when you give in or give up that it becomes yours.

"I can't get her to work on it for longer than ten minutes."

The problem here is not that Mom can't "get" her to work on homework. The problem is that Mom thinks she needs to want to work on homework, that she necessarily must be "interested" in working on homework. For hundreds of years, children have accomplished school work. Interest is not the issue. The issue is obligation. If school is preparation for life, we must teach our children that they have an obligation to do their homework. It is her job. It is her work. Just like Mom and Dad have work, she too has work that must be done to the best of her ability. Just imagine what would happen in America's work places if employers had to "get" their employees to do their work. "Now Miss Jones, I really need this report turned in by 3:00. It's already 1:30 and you've just been goofing around for hours."

Although this sounds ludicrous, it is no more ludicrous than expecting your child to always be interested in her homework. With a bit of luck, Miss Jones might be interested in half the projects assigned to her. The other half get done because it is her job. She is obliged to do them. Yes, it is true that some fortunate people work at careers that truly move them. As parents we hope that our children will grow to discover their vocations and find great rewards in it. These people may be cancer researchers on a mission to find a cure in their lifetime, in their lab. Or they may be novelists who spend hours weaving plots and bringing interesting characters to life. But whoever they are, they have some portion of their job that is less desirable than that portion which they *live* to do. And it is very doubtful that they came to that career with no sense of obligation, no self-discipline. They were not children who got to choose which assignments to do and when to do them. They worked hard for the knowledge that gave them the power of choice.

"Whenever I try to help her she whines."

That is my personal favorite, Wow, whining, that's scary! I have a theory that nature makes babies cry a lot so that their parents will get used to it early on. My twenty-year-old son whined his way through high school. Now he's at Florida State and he still whines about school. I think he's gotten used to his own whining now. His roommate doesn't whine much at all. In fact, he doesn't do much studying. I guess it's because his Mom isn't there to "get" him to do it. My twelve-year-old daughter is an interesting case. She whines the most before a grade of A. We can always tell when she's going to get a poor grade on a test, because she didn't whine much when studying for it. Getting used to hearing yourself whine about your work is something that we all must accomplish. In fact, I don't think I could work without that constant drone of my own sweet whine. Right now for instance, it's Saturday morning, September 7th. My birthday was this past Wednesday. We didn't celebrate because I had clients until 7:30 p.m. It was decided for me that we would celebrate today. My family is asleep. When they wake we are to head off for a beach picnic. But, we promised our editor that we would send her this chapter on Monday morning. So, I've been up since 6:30 a.m. working and whining. As you proceed with your lessons, if you just can't get used to the whining, try to find solace in the facts revealed by the previously mentioned University of Wichita study. It is the *best* readers who have the *best* attitude about reading.

"Whenever I try to help her, we end up in a power struggle."

And of course there's the ever popular power struggle. Do not ever engage in a power struggle with a child. You cannot win unless you are willing to do physical battle. Power struggles occur because somebody got the idea that there was an option, a choice. So the struggle ensued to move from your choice to theirs. Never let this happen with a child. Homework is not an option. There are no choices here. Your child can have lots of choices in life, what flavor ice cream, what shirt to wear, what to name the new puppy, what to do when she finishes her homework, and what to be when she grows up, lots and lots of choices. But homework is not one of them, and neither is her reading lesson. Let her whine. You'll both get used to it in time. But get the lessons in this book done, and the homework too. Waiting around for your child to be interested in this book is like standing at the side of the road she just ran into and waiting for a car to hit her. You would never do that. If she were in danger you would take rapid, firm action. Well, she is. With an illiteracy rate of 42 percent hanging over her head, she is in grave danger. With statistics that show she will only be a happy reader if she is the best reader, she is in grave danger indeed. Your power as her parent is in her youth. When she is older, she will just be a statistic. Right now, she is a child. And you are her parent. Her parent who, with this book, has been empowered to save her from the danger of a lifetime of illiteracy.

"Should I offer my child incentives to get her to do her work?"

Ralph Waldo Emerson once wrote, "The reward of a thing well done is having done it." Emerson's words would be proven by motivation researchers fifty years after he wrote them. Research (Butler, R.A., "Incentive conditions," *Journal of Experimental Psychology*, 1954) shows us that rewards such as stickers (smelly or otherwise) are a waste of our time. In fact, according to some studies (Deci, E.L., *Intrinsic Motivation*, Plenum, New York, 1975), they may even have the opposite effect of demotivating the learner. Another researcher (Brown, R.A., *A First Language: The Early Stages*, Harvard University Press, Cambridge, MA, 1973) found that young children learning to speak changed their incorrect speech patterns to correct ones in order to match the speech of the adults in their lives. Rewarding these changes had absolutely no effect on the rate of improvement. For these reasons, I strongly urge you not to get caught up in the rewards game as part of your reading lessons.

When your child shows progress, offer her lots of verbal praise, "You're doing a great job!" is worth fifty grape smelly stickers. "You should be proud of yourself!" is one of the most powerful things a parent or teacher can say to a child. It is a natural incentive that leaves the message, loud and clear, that the learner should feel good about *herself* because of what *she* did. This empowers the learner, giving her the means to feel good about herself whenever she chooses, by simply performing the same appropriate task. Another natural incentive that you can offer your child is to share the burden of the work. Even at the clinic we will take turns reading word lists or every other sentence in a story. When she's really struggling, the most precious gifts you can offer your child are your continued effort and your patience. Let her know by what you say and what you do, that you will help her get through this. The lessons are clear and concise. As her parent, your job is to get the message across that you're not going to give up on her. I've found that one thing that can really help bridge the gap between the time when it's a struggle until the time it gets easier, is simply saying, "It's okay, this is hard stuff." Children who are struggling appreciate knowing that what they're working on isn't as simple as they imagine it to be. Remember what Jack's teacher told him, "You're going to end up digging ditches." Just imagine how it might have changed his life if she had said, "I know this is hard, Jack. But I'm going to help you get through it."

"My child is a visual learner. Will this book work for him?"

It is true that there are individual differences among learners. We all have our strengths and weaknesses, which tend to mold our particular learning style. And learning styles are very relevant to many things that we learn, like science and history. Adding as many senses to instruction of these subjects helps children to learn about them. When I was a classroom teacher years ago, I offered children opportunities to hear, see, smell, and even taste history. But reading is a little different. It comes from a specific direction. As we mentioned in Chapter one, it is a visual code for sounds. So, it originates as an auditory thing, but we represent it visually (in writing). Given this, we must address both the visual and the auditory aspects of reading. If you rely too heavily on the visual, you run the risk that you will give your child the mistaken idea that she can memorize endless strings of whole words. Even children with remarkably high visual memories can only memorize about five thousand words. This may seem like a lot, but it will only get her to about third grade level. By the time she is swallowed up by a crack, she has received four years of reinforcement of her high visual tendencies, and no reinforcement of her auditory skills, which, being the weaker of the two, is what she actually needed more practice with. Reading is what it is, it is a visual representation of spoken words. Phono-Graphix addresses that, in every lesson plan. Stick to the lesson plans and you'll do fine.

"Will my child get confused because they use a different method at school?"

We would love to tell you no, but the truth is that she might. You've read Chapter one. We've already shown you how confusing phonics can be. You've seen that although what whole language teaches is important, it is all about literature and not literacy. So the obvious answer is yes, your child may well be confused. However, it will not be Phono-Graphix that will confuse her. Phono-Graphix will be her anchor, her guiding light. The secret is to provide it for her quickly, before she gets led astray by other information. On the surface it may seem wrong to teach your child something different from what she's learning at school, but until the schools can improve on the current 42 percent illiteracy rate, you have no choice. And the 33 percent illiteracy rate we saw during the last phonics era isn't good enough. Your only way to improve upon those odds is to intervene with something that has been proven to work, consistently, not half of the time, or a third of the time, but always. Remember, your goals and her teacher's goals are the same. We find that when teachers learn about Phono-Graphix they love it. "It's so easy." "It makes perfect sense," are common remarks. Buy her a copy of *Reading Reflex* for Christmas.

"How much and how often?"

Much of your work with your child is intended to establish an automatic response to text. With post-kindergartners, that might involve breaking bad habits such as trying to memorize whole words, or trying to sound each letter instead of each sound picture, 'h' 'o' 'u' 's' 'e', instead of 'h' 'ou' 'se'. This requires lots of time and lots of repetition. On the other hand, you don't want life in your house to become a reading drudge. If your child is hard to corner, we suggest you take advantage of the situation once he is cornered, by doing a full hour of lessons. If your child is fairly easy to corner, but easily distracted, you might go for the more often and shorter plan, say thirty minutes three or four times per week. You will need to experiment with the schedule until you find the perfect plan for you and your child. Obviously, the more you do the lessons the faster she will learn. As a minimum we recommend two hours per week for children six or older, and ninety minutes per week for kindergartners. Avoid late nights when you and your child are tired. Also avoid times of the day that are too rushed and stressful. If you tend to be distracted before work, don't try to squeeze in a reading lesson with your child. It won't go well. It's always best to come up with a schedule and stick to it each week. That way everyone knows what's expected of them. At all costs, avoid long periods of time when you don't do any lessons. Your child will forget the drill and you'll both be starting over. Even in a busy time, you should not go longer than a week without some practice.

"Will I understand the lesson plans? What if I don't get it?"

The lessons have been laid out for you. We're going to walk you through one so that you'll understand how simple they are. The first section of each lesson plan is the *readiness* section. This tells you whether you should do this particular lesson with your child, and when. For instance, the Sound Bingo Game in Chapter three says, "This lesson is intended for young children up to about first grade, sixth month." If your child is older than that and still needs work in sound to sound picture correspondences, you can do this lesson as additional practice. So for instance, if your child is in second grade and can't read a word, but knows the sound to sound picture correspondence between all the Sound Bingo sounds shown, don't bother doing this with her.

Once you have done a lesson with your child it's alright to move ahead to the next lesson. Don't wait for perfection before you progress. You should also be working at numerous lessons at a time, so in one sitting you might do word building and auditory processing, and in the next you might do both of those and three-sound word reading. You might also work between chapters. For instance, your child might be able to *read* the four-sound words in Chapter four, while she is still working at *spelling* three-sound words in Chapter three. In general, you can move backwards at any point and out of sequence, but never move ahead out of sequence.

The next section is the *goals* section. This section tells you exactly what the goals for this lesson are. So a goal for a lesson in Chapter five might say, *"To cause your child to analyze the sound pictures in each word to teach her that this is how we read, rather than by memorizing whole words. To cause her to notice the various ways that the sounds are spelled. For example:* ***<ai>*** *represents the sound 'a-e' in the word 'train.'"* This section is very important. It serves to remind you throughout the lesson, "What am I doing here? What is my purpose in this lesson?" The goals of the lessons overlap. So the goal of *creating an automatic response to text* may appear in numerous lesson plans. This doesn't mean you can do just one of those lesson plans or some of them. The more exposure your child has to lessons that encourage a certain reading behavior, the faster she will begin performing that behavior.

The next section is the *materials* section. This section tells you exactly what materials you will need to perform the lesson. This gives you an opportunity to get everything ready ahead of time.

The actual *presentation* is the next section of your lesson plan. This section is laid out in steps. Step 1 generally directs you to lay out the materials in a specific manner. If there is anything difficult, a picture is provided. At each step specific language is offered to help you in communicating directions to your child. Please don't think of these as scripted lessons. Your own words will be more natural to you and to your child. However, be careful not to change the intent of the directions. For instance, *"What's the first sound you hear in 'cat'?"* verbalized the fact that this is a listening activity, by using the word *'hear.'* When we use the words *sound picture* we are attempting to make the child think of letters and letter groups as pictures of sounds. The presentation also offers direction on using your pencil or finger to indicate word parts to your child. The presentation walks you through the lesson as if nothing goes wrong. The next section deals with errors your child might make.

The final section is *correcting problems*. In this section every possible error is discussed, with directions on how to correct the error. This is probably the most important part of the lesson plan. If you think of mistakes as opportunities, herein lie the secrets to your child's success.

Another tool available to you as you use the lesson plans is the glossary of terms and techniques on pages 347–354.

"How will I know which lessons to do with my child?"

If your child is in the sixth month of first grade (or younger) she is a new reader for the purposes of this book. We've called in our little friend Sound Doggy to guide you through the lessons. The Sound Doggy symbol in the top corner of the page means that the lesson or materials are appropriate for new readers (first grade, sixth month, or younger). If you follow Sound Doggy's advice, you will be fine. When your child has completed these new reader lessons and materials, you can continue on to the other materials, but we suggest you wait until she has started second grade, or maybe toward the end of the summer before she starts second grade before you move past the lessons.

If your child is older than the sixth month of first grade, or has been retained in first grade, you should start in Chapter three and make your way through the book, including the Sound Doggy lessons. There are just a few lessons which are not necessary for most children older than first grade, sixth month. These are indicated in the *readiness* section.

"What's the pretest all about?"

Before you start working with your child, it's important to know exactly what her problems are. If your child is in the sixth month of first grade or older, or has been retained in first grade, give her all of the tests at the back of this chapter.

The Code Knowledge Test is a test of your ability as well as your child's. If you have trouble accessing the sounds from our example words on the score sheet, you should consider the audio tape from Read America before you begin working with your child.

The composite score sheet following the tests will tell you whether or not your child is currently ready for curriculum at her grade level. The composite score is offered to give you an overall idea of where your child stands, and to give you a single number that you can use to gauge her improvement. This score is not normed, but is merely an interpretation based on the clinical and diagnostic experience of the authors, and the type of curriculum used in schools. If your child's composite score is 89 or lower, she is not ready for her current grade.

This does not mean that you should retain her at school. Recent research indicates that retention is not usually helpful, merely delaying the problem for another year. It is also important to understand that there is likely nothing that is going to occur in that repeated year that will improve her score. She will be in the same school with another teacher who has similar training. There is no reason to assume that she will suddenly be taught to blend, to segment sounds in words, or be taught the English written code. These skills are not commonly taught in today's schools.

If she scores 90 or above she is ready for her grade, but that does not necessarily mean she will integrate all of the skills on the test and do well. Working at *Reading Reflex* will still be your assurance of that. It will teach her to efficiently use all of the subskills measured on the test, increase her fluency (speed of reading) and her accuracy and comprehension, and make her a great speller. It will move her from the average reading group to the highest reading group which, according to the aforementioned University of Wichita study, will assure that she will enjoy reading.

The test results will also forewarn you of what chapters she will need to work extra hard at. As we've mentioned, we suggest that you start at the beginning and make your way through each chapter, rather than skipping Chapter three, for instance, if her scores indicate that she's doing well with three-sound words. This is recommended for two reasons. It's always nicer to start easy and get harder gradually rather than jumping in at a level she can't manage at all. Also, working in Chapter three will make explicit for her exactly how our written language works—*we use sound pictures to represent sounds, and we build words with sound pictures.*

If your child is younger than the sixth month of first grade, give her all of the tests except the *auditory processing test*. This test is not developmentally appropriate to young children. When testing a young child under first grade, sixth month, you'll need to give her lots of direction and examples in order to get her to understand what it is you want her to do on each test. We also suggest that you stop the test when she reaches a point of failure. If she can't give you a correct answer on three consecutive attempts, stop the test at that point. The answers she's gotten correct so far are her total score.

"What pace should I take? What about pacing my child?"

Parents worry that they need to memorize the steps and language of the lesson plans. That's not necessary. In fact, keeping the book open and referring to it for direction will actually work to your advantage in two ways. It will help you slow down and take one step at a time, and it will offer you an appeal to authority if your child argues about what you're doing. "It says here in the book that you need to do this" may work when other attempts have failed.

Pace is very important when you're working with your child. Just last night I got a call from an independent reading therapist in Gainesville, who uses Phono-Graphix. She has a thirteen-year-old client who speed reads, very badly. "I can't seem to slow her down," she complained. "It's like a race. And I find myself rushing too." That's exactly what happens when someone hurries. They actually get us hurrying too. Don't fall into this trap. You set the pace. Slow way down. If she reads too quickly, ask her to read the passage again. Tell her you just can't follow along at that pace. If she has to read it twice, she'll be inconvenienced and find it easier to read it slowly the first time.

"What should I expect of my child's literacy development?"

Children are all different. That's what makes them special, and it's what makes them such a challenge. Your child might do fabulously at age five and just absorb every lesson you offer. Or your child might take longer than the average child to learn the principles and practices of reading and spelling. But in general, there are some goals you should have for your child's literacy development. These are presented in the Literacy Growth Chart on page 44. We suggest that you view this as a set of goals, rather than norms. Remember, you want your child to be reading above grade level.

Trust Yourself

As a parent, you know your child better than anyone else does. As you proceed with your lessons together, trust yourself, and by all means, cut yourself some slack, lots of it in fact. It's not easy working with your own child. I had the supreme pleasure of having both of my children in class with me over the years and I know the challenges very well. But the fact is no one else cares as much about her literacy as you do. And no one will work as hard as you will toward that end. You and your child have a unique bond. You know when she's getting it versus just going through the motions. You know when she's really going to throw up versus trying to get out of a lesson. You know whether she means "rabbit" when she says "wabbit." You know whether she's not having a good lesson because she was up too late last night. You know her. Use that bond to your advantage, and to hers, as you work together toward the *reading reflex*.

LITERACY GROWTH CHART

10 Years Reading one fiction and one nonfiction book per month. Subscribes to two age-appropriate magazines.

9 Years Reading three-syllable words with consistent accuracy. Spelling two-syllable words with consistent accuracy. Reading one fiction or nonfiction book per month. Subscribes to one age-appropriate magazine.

8 Years Reading two-syllable words with consistent accuracy. Spelling single-syllable words with consistent accuracy. Reading two to three short books per week. Subscribes to one age-appropriate magazine.

7 Years Knows the advanced written code with an accuracy rate of 90%. Reading single-syllable words with consistent accuracy. Reading two-syllable words with very few errors. Spelling single-syllable words with very few errors. Reading one to two short books per week orally to a parent.

6 Years Knows the advanced written code with an accuracy rate of 70%. Reading single-syllable words with very few errors. Spelling single-syllable words fairly well. Reading orally to a parent for ten to fifteen minutes each day.

5 Years Knows the basic code perfectly. Can read any three-sound word. Beginning to read and spell words containing adjacent consonants.

4 Years Beginning to learn the basic code. Beginning to read and spell three-sound words with accuracy.

BLENDING TEST

Do not allow your child to see the test. Tell your child that you are going to say some sounds, and that she should tell you what word it sounds like. Sit near enough that she can hear you clearly, and see your mouth. Explain to her that you can say the sounds only once and so she should listen and watch carefully. Say each sound in the first word, with a one-second interval between each sound 'p' 'i' 'g'. Do not repeat the word. Write down her first response.

PART ONE	
p i g	✓
b u g	✓
h a t	✓
p i n	✓
r a t	✓
b **ir** d	✓
sh e **ll**	✓
f i **ve**	?
b **oa** t	✓

PART TWO	
f r o g	✓
g r a **ss**	✓
s t i **ck**	✓
p r i n t	✓
c r u n **ch**	✓
p l a n t	?

13

Interpretation of Scores 14+ = good -14 = low moderate -11 = poor

Less than a perfect score on part one indicates that your child has trouble blending or pushing together the sounds in three-sound words. This will require lots of work in Chapter three.

Less than a perfect score on part two indicates that your child has trouble pushing together sounds in four- and five-sound words. This will require lots of work in Chapter four.

PHONEME SEGMENTATION TEST

Do not allow your child to see the test. Explain to your child that you want her to tell you all the sounds in the word 'dog.' If she offers a letter name say, "That's a letter. What's the *sound*?" If she persists at responding with letter names, mark those responses wrong. Put a check for each correct answer in the corresponding space. If she omits a sound, mark it wrong, EX: 'frog' = 'f' 'o' 'g'. You would mark these responses like this **✓ X ✓ ✓**. If she gives the wrong sound, mark it wrong, EX: 'frog' = 'f' 'r' 'a' 'g'. You would score these responses like this **✓ ✓ X ✓**. If she blends two sounds together, mark both sounds wrong, EX: 'frog' = 'fr' 'o' 'g'. You would mark these responses like this **X X ✓ ✓**. 'f' 'ro' 'g' would be marked like this **✓ X X ✓**.

PART ONE	
dog	___ ___ ___
hat	___ ___ ___
pin	___ ___ ___
pot	___ ___ ___
rat	___ ___ ___
nut	___ ___ ___

PART TWO	
frog	___ ___ ___ ___
black	___ ___ ___ ___
nest	___ ___ ___ ___
trip	___ ___ ___ ___
milk	___ ___ ___ ___
drum	___ ___ ___ ___

Interpretation of Scores 40+ = good - 40 = low moderate - 36 = poor

Offered a letter name more than 2 times, EX: 'dog' = 'dee' 'oe' 'gee'. Your child may not understand that letters are symbols for sounds. She may be trying to recall the sound of the letter by thinking of the letter name, an unnecessary step requiring a translation. This will require lots of work in Chapters three and four.

Omitted vowel sound or chunked it to a consonant sound 2 or more times, EX: 'dog' = 'd' 'g' or 'do' 'g' or 'd' 'og'. Your child may have a vowel sound hanging on the end of her consonants and may need retraining in the pronunciation of consonant sounds. This will require lots of work in Chapter three.

Chunked consonants together or omitted one of them more than 2 times, EX: 'frog' = 'fr' 'o' 'g' or 'f' 'o' 'g'. Your child may be having trouble isolating the separate sounds in words, causing her to leave sounds out and add sounds that aren't there. This will require lots of work in Chapter four.

Repeated the wrong sound 2 or more times, EX: 'frog' = 'f' 'r' 'a' 'g'. Your child may have a low auditory memory. This will require lots and lots of work at the basic code level (Chapters three and four).

AUDITORY PROCESSING TEST

The results of this test are not reliable for children under age six.

Do not allow your child to see the test. Ask your child to say the word 'pig.' Now ask her to say 'pig' without the sound 'p'. If she has trouble doing this, offer an example. Say, "OK, if I wanted to say 'dog' without the 'd' it would be 'og'." Continue with all the words.

PART ONE

say **pig** w/o the **'p'** _________ **(ig)**

say **pog** w/o the **'g'** _________ **(po)**

say **sip** w/o the **'s'** _________ **(ip)**

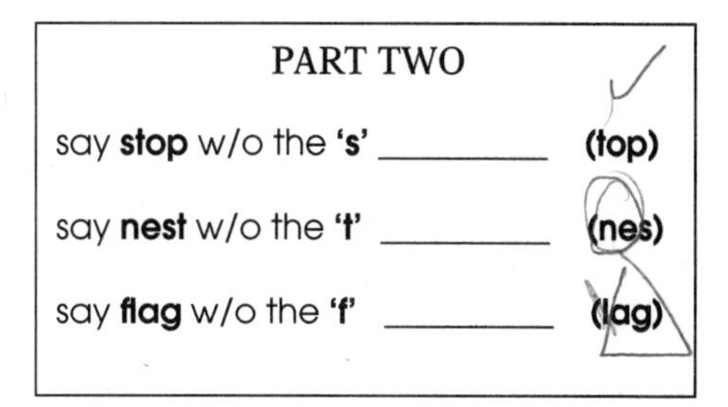
PART TWO

say **stop** w/o the **'s'** _________ **(top)**

say **nest** w/o the **'t'** _________ **(nes)**

say **flag** w/o the **'f'** _________ **(lag)**

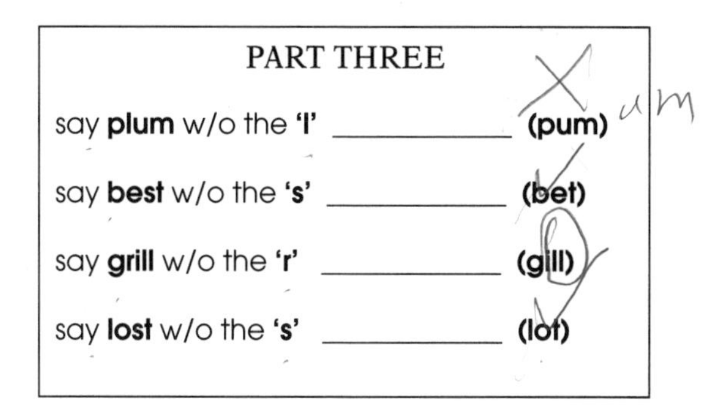
PART THREE

say **plum** w/o the **'l'** _________ **(pum)**

say **best** w/o the **'s'** _________ **(bet)**

say **grill** w/o the **'r'** _________ **(gill)**

say **lost** w/o the **'s'** _________ **(lot)**

Interpretation of Scores +8 = good +5 = low moderate -5 = poor

Was unable to score correctly on all of the first 3 test items. Your child is experiencing difficulty segmenting and isolating single sounds in simple words. This requires lots of work in Chapter three.

Removed the adjacent consonant to the target sound in part two or three, EX: flag without the 'f' = 'ag'. Your child is experiencing difficulty segmenting adjacent consonant sounds. This requires lots of work in Chapter four.

Unable to perform (no correct responses). Your child is having difficulty understanding the nature of sounds in words. Extensive work in Chapters three and four is needed.

CODE KNOWLEDGE TEST

This page is the key for the code knowledge test on the next page. Use the next page as the cue sheet to test your child. Do not let your child see this page. Place a barrier between this page and the next. A piece of cardstock or a clip board will do. After each sound is a word or words containing that sound or sounds. This is to assist you if you are uncertain of the sound or sounds that the sound picture represents. For example, the sound picture **<ie>** in the last column can represent the sound 'ie' as in the word 'd<u>ie</u>' or 'ee' as in the word 'ch<u>ie</u>f.' Indicate the first sound picture and ask, "If you saw this in a word, what sound would you say?" If she offers any of the correct sounds, mark her answer as correct. If she offers a letter name, tell her, "That's a letter. I want to know what sound it stands for." If she proceeds to offer letter names, you must mark these answers incorrect. Only the sounds are correct answers. Keep track of the number of correct and incorrect responses. The total correct times two is the percentage of code knowledge your child has at this time.

__ b	boy	__ y	yes / happy / fly	__ oa	boat
__ c	cat / city	__ z	zipper	__ ow	now / snow
__ d	dog	__ i	rip	__ igh	night
__ f	fat	__ e	net	__ eigh	eight / height
__ g	got / gentle	__ a	mat	__ ay	play
__ h	hop	__ o	mop	__ ie	die / chief
__ j	job	__ u	nut	__ aw	saw
__ k	kid	__ sh	ship	__ ee	seen
__ l	lap	__ ch	chip	__ ey	key / they
__ m	mop	__ th	this / Thursday	__ ue	blue / cue
__ n	nod	__ ck	duck	__ ew	few / new
__ p	pat	__ qu	quick 'kw'	__ au	August
__ r	rat	__ ce	nice	__ oo	wood / moon
__ s	sat	__ ai	rain	__ ui	suit
__ t	top	__ ou	out / group /	__ oy	boy
__ v	give		touch	__ oi	soil
__ w	with	__ ea	each / steak /		
__ x	fox 'ks' / exit 'gz'		bread		

Interpretation of Scores

Raw score times 2 equals percentage of correct answers.

	<u>good</u>	<u>low moderate</u>	<u>poor</u>
6 years old	60-100%	50-60%	-50%
7 years old	70-100%	60-70%	-60%
8 years old	80-100%	70-80%	-70%

If your child falls in the low moderate to poor range, extensive work in Chapter five will be needed. If she scores in the good range, you should still complete the lessons in Chapter five, but your child will move through them with much greater ease.

CODE KNOWLEDGE CUE CARD

b	x	oa
c	y	ow
d	z	igh
f	i	eigh
g	e	ay
h	a	ie
j	o	aw
k	u	ee
l	sh	ey
m	ch	ue
n	th	ew
p	ck	au
r	qu	oo
s	ce	ui
t	ai	oy
v	ou	oi
w	ea	

COMPOSITE READING SCORE

Date of test________________

Total number correct from Blending Test ______ X 6.66 = _________

Total number correct from Segmenting Test ______ X 2.38 = _________

Total number correct from Auditory Processing Test ____ X 10 = _________

Total number correct from Code Knowledge Test ____ X 2 = _________

Total score of the above four tests _________ divide by 4 = __________

Enter the above total score in the grade your child is currently in, or if it is summer, the grade your child is entering in the next school year.

1st grade	score X 1.10 __________
2nd grade	score X 1.05 __________
3rd grade	score X 1.00 __________
4th grade	score X .95 __________
5th grade	score X .95 __________
6th grade	score X .90 __________
7th grade	score X .90 __________
8th grade or older	score X .90 __________

Interpretation of Scores

90 or above indicates a readiness for the reading material your child will encounter in her current or upcoming grade.

89 or lower indicates that your child is not ready for the reading material she will encounter in her current or upcoming grade.

CHAPTER THREE

TEACHING THE BASIC CODE

The information in this chapter, as well as the lesson plans and activities at the end, are intended for young children just learning to read, and children in the sixth month of first grade and older whose test scores in Chapter two indicate a need for these lessons.

Specifically, this chapter deals with the *basic code*. By basic code, we mean the most common sounds, and those sounds that are represented by only one letter. Teaching your child the reading mechanics needed to manage the basic code will establish the way she responds to all future text as well. This first step is very important to all that will follow. The goals of this chapter are numerous. They're laid out here with an explanation of each, and some discussion of what can go wrong if the specific goal is not met.

Goal #1. That your child understands that letters are pictures of sounds

The first step in learning to read is understanding the nature of our written code. There are symbols that represent sounds. Each time we see one of the symbols, we are supposed to say the sound that it represents. We make our way through the word and when we get to the end we have meaning. At the basic code level, all the sounds are represented by a single-letter sound picture. There is no sound 'sh' in the basic code, as this sound picture has two letters. So the words, 'cat' and 'big' and 'sad,' are all words that we can work with in this chapter, because each sound in these words is represented by only one letter. In addition, we do not, in this chapter, address any of the overlap in the code. The sound picture **<a>** represents only the sound 'a' as in 'hat,' even though you and I know it can also represent the sounds 'a-e' as in the word 'paper' and the sound 'o' as in the word 'want.' It's important to limit the introduction of the code in this way, to establish the goals of this level before moving on to the goals of the subsequent levels.

Many children fail to understand that letters are pictures of sounds. At some point in their literacy development they espouse the notion that letters "make" sounds. This thinking is precisely the reverse of our goal. It's confusing to children because it implies that the letter has meaning in and of itself, and that they must be stupid because they just don't get it. What we want them to understand is that the sound picture (the letter) is a symbol for a sound which they need to remember. It helps if they understand the nature of symbols, that they are arbitrary, that they stand for something else just because we agree that they will. As parents, we can help our new readers to establish a clear understanding of the sound picture nature of text by avoiding certain language when we work with them. "What does that say?" can be replaced with, "Do you remember what we say when we see that?" The term *sound picture* was developed at the Read America clinic and been found to be a very powerful and descriptive term which gently forces the logic we seek.

If letters could read...

Another common mistake that some parents and teachers make that children find confusing, is the use of letter names in referring to the sound pictures. If we refer to 'see' and 'tee' and 'ef', etc., in helping our young readers, we are forcing them to learn two names for each symbol, the letter name and the sound. This is completely unnecessary. Many children can't do this easily and end up remembering only the letter name. They are forever trying to access, or remember the sound, by cueing off some part of the letter name,“‘ef’ um ‘e’?, no um ‘f’?” Although this translation step is completely unnecessary and confusing, it does work for some letters. The sound that corresponds to the letter ‘tee’ **<t>** is found right at the beginning of the letter name. But what about ‘see’ **<c>** which usually represents ‘c’, not ‘s’, and ‘em’ **<m>** which represents ‘m’, not ‘e’, and ‘wie’ **<y>**, which usually represents the sound ‘ee’ as in the word ‘happy,’ and never represents the sound ‘w’? If you take the time to analyze the alphabet names and sounds you realize why so many children have trouble. We recommend that you never use letter names when working with your child. Always refer to sound pictures by the sound they represent, not their letter name. The futility of letter name instruction is proven over and over again with every adult nonreader who can recite the alphabet with ease. When posing a question for your child in which you feel inclined to use a letter name, for example, “What sound does ‘tee’ represent?”, you can easily sidestep the letter name by simply indicating the letter with your pencil or pointer finger, and saying, “What sound does *that* represent?” By mastering this and other techniques explained in the lesson plans you can avoid letter names altogether and help your child avoid reading failure from letter name interference.

One child in particular comes to mind when we think of the problems that teaching children the letter names can bring on. Stella is a really cute and super confident six-year-old girl. She has beautiful flaming red hair and a freckled nose. Stella's mother brought her into the Read America clinic in mid-September of her first-grade year. In kindergarten Stella had spent hours forming letters and eventually writing some short words, which she would proudly present to her mother, telling her what they said. She would read off the letter names “‘see’ ‘ae’ ‘tee’” and then say the word ‘cat.’ Her mother attributed her early start at reading and spelling to Stella's obvious intelligence, and to her own hard work at teaching Stella the letter names and how to form all the letters. This certainly showed itself, as Stella had remarkable penmanship for a six-year-old, and indeed she did know each letter by name.

Stella had a lot of trouble identifying sounds. This was revealed by a code knowledge test which told us that Stella's first response to text was consistently letter names. So **<c>** was ‘see,’ and **<f>** was ‘ef,’ and **<w>** was ‘double you.’ When prompted further with the query, “Yes, that is an ‘ef’, but what *sound* do you say when you see it?" Stella responded with, " 'f'." But when asked, "And this is a 'double-you,' but what *sound* do you say when you see it?" Stella responded with, "'dub', um no it's 'd'." Aside from the 'dub', which left Stella's mother's mouth agape, this is a typical response from children of Stella's age. Stella thinks the sound that corresponds with this sound picture is 'd' because the letter name (double-you) begins with the 'd' sound.

Fortunately for Stella, she was a quick learner and remediated within just twelve sessions. During that time, Stella was retrained to understand that letters are pictures of sounds and that they represent those sounds, not the letter names. Considerable effort was spent during the first half of her therapy in teaching her to respond primarily with the sounds and not the letter names.

Stella's particular reading problem is quite common. She is not alone in making the assumption that what an adult tells her about a symbol is what she should try to remember.

We received a call from Stella's mother about a month after she had finished reading therapy. Stella had so impressed her teacher with her improvement, that her teacher, the chair of the school's in-service committee, had asked Stella's mom if she could arrange for me to provide an in-service training session for the teachers at Stella's school. We accepted, happy to have an opportunity to share our insight with a group of teachers. Quite ironically, the event went well, right up until I told the teachers that they should teach sounds, not letter names. "Oh, but they have to know their letter names!" was the overwhelming consensus. We went round and round for a while. We explained that children will learn the names of the letters easily in time. We explained that I've worked with scores of adult nonreaders, who all knew the letter names, yet couldn't read. We explained that letter names confuse children and cause interference when they are trying to sound words out. But they still insisted. Then we got tough. "Okay! Let's play a game," we said. "The game is called Introductions." We went round the room and assigned each of them a fictitious name and a nickname. "This is Pat, but you can call her Harriette. This is George, but you can call him Tom. This is Tammy, but you can call her Sally." After we had so dubbed all twenty-two of them, we took three of the teachers to the front of the room and lined them up. "Okay, can anyone tell me who this is?" I asked, pointing to the first one. "Do you mean her name, or what we're supposed to call her?" one of the teachers asked.

"What you are supposed to call her?" I responded. "I don't get it," commented another. "Why do we need two names if you just want us to remember one?" "Our point exactly," we said.

The teachers might have been able to recall the information if I had only given them the important part. But with all the extra names, they didn't have a chance. Yet, that's exactly what we do to our children when we teach them the letter names and the sounds at the same time. Or worse still, the letter names and *then* the sounds. When you teach a child anything, start with the important part. Make sure they know it intimately before you move on to the less important part. In the case of reading it is the sounds that she will need to know. If you feel you must teach letter names, do so *only* after the sounds have been firmly established. Our point is a simple one, elaborately made. Teach your child what will be the most useful bit of information to help her learn to read.

Goal #2. That she knows the correspondence between all the sounds and sound pictures that make up the basic code

If your child is very young (under six) expect her to take a long time to learn the correspondence between all the sounds and sound pictures that make up the basic code. Young children have more difficulty learning the distinctions between many of the sound pictures. Children under six, for instance, often lack the left to right orientation needed to distinguish between the sound pictures **<d>** and **<b>**. Similar sounds are also confusing to young children. The sounds 'i' as in 'pig' and 'e' as in 'peg,' may take longer to learn than 'a' as in 'pat' and 'o' as in 'pot,' which are more auditorily distinguishable.

It's important that you teach the sound to sound picture correspondence within the context of words. Use the lesson plans provided at the end of this chapter. Do not try to teach the code in isolation, "This is 's' and this is 'p' and this is 't'." This kind of drill gives children the impression that letters exist for their own sake, rather than as components of words. It's also harder to learn the sounds in isolation. As we explained in Chapter one, learning the correspondences between symbol and sound is paired associate learning, the pairing of two items that only go together because someone says they do. Just like any other name, I am Carmen because my mother said I would be Carmen. The letter **<p>** is 'p' because somebody, a long, long time ago, said it would be 'p' and we all agreed to go along with that. Paired associate learning is facilitated by relevance or meaning. By teaching the sound to symbol correspondences in the context of words, your child will see how they work to build words and she will find relevance in that. The letter **<p>** is one of three parts to **<pig>**. It represents 'p', the first thing you hear in the word 'pig.' The letter **<i>** is another part of **<pig>**; it represents the second thing you hear in the word 'pig.' The letter **<g>** is another part of 'pig;' it represents the last thing you hear in the word 'pig.' By using the lesson plans, your child will learn the sound picture to sound correspondence in a shorter time, because they will be tools she can use to build words. Once she knows even a few she can begin to spell and read words. When she encounters a sound picture she doesn't know, you can help her by telling her what sound it represents.

When teaching your child the basic code vowel sounds please do not make the mistake of telling her that the sounds are short sounds. Phonics programs do this and children find it very confusing. When children think of short and long, they think in terms of length, not sounds. In addition, there is nothing intrinsically shorter about the sound 'a' as in 'hat,' or 'a-e' as in 'rain.' So why bring it up at all. What your child needs to know is that there is the sound 'a' and then later, in Chapter five, we will introduce the sound 'a-e', and all the various sound pictures for that sound.

Another thing we need to caution you about is the use of "key words" to teach the sound to symbol correspondence. This is common practice among phonics programs. So the child is taught to access the sounds like this—she sees **<a>**, she says 'ay'...'apple'...'a'.

This use of a key word is intended to help her remember the sound that the letter represents. But what it actually does is add yet another step to the process. So now the child has even more to remember. By using key words, we are also running the risk that the child will start to believe that it is only the first sound in a word that is important. We've retrained many children whose strategy was to look at the first letter in the word and start guessing as many words as they could think of that start with that sound. This is the most common strategy that we see at the Read America clinic among first graders.

Now, we've mentioned that young children take a long time at learning the correspondences between symbols and sounds, but we haven't mentioned older kids who are having reading troubles. Older children may know the correspondences between symbol and sound, but not use the information when they read. They may have learned any or all of the bad habits we've just discussed, when they were younger. These children need lots of reinforcement to change those habits. In many cases it takes longer to break old habits than to learn new ones. In order to break old habits you must replace them with new ones that work. When your child stumbles in a word, she needs to be asked, "What sound is that?" When she doesn't know, she needs to be told, and the lessons for that sound should be practiced again. This kind of questioning and supplying of information interferes with her attempts to use the wrong information to figure out what the words say. For instance, if she is looking at the word **<train>** and has just said 'tree' and you say "No," she has not been redirected. So she will continue to guess another word that starts with the sound 't'. But if instead, you ask her, "What sound is this?" as you indicate the **<ai>** with your pencil point, she will stop the guessing and start thinking about what she needs to know in order to read this word. If she doesn't know what sound **<ai>** represents, simply tell her. Then later you can practice the lessons that teach the various ways to represent the sound 'a-e'. These techniques are covered in the lesson plans. If you stick to the lesson plans, you'll be fine.

Goal #3. That she understands that spoken words are made up of sounds

The first step in coming to understand written language is understanding spoken language. In working with your new reader, you must never lose sight of the fact that written language is merely a visual representation of spoken language. You can help your child to understand this through your approach to spoken language. For young children just learning to read, we encourage use of the sound games at the back of this chapter. Ask your child what's the first thing she hears in various words. Start with very short words of two and three sounds. Optimize your time together by integrating these games into your regular activities. When you're walking on the beach with your new reader, and she discovers an interesting seashell, ask, "What's the first sound you *hear* in 'shell'?" Make sure she understands that it's what she *hears*, not what she *sees* that you are interested in. When you're riding to school or day care together, ask her to think of a word that begins with the sound 'p'. When you're at the grocery store and she asks for a pack of gum, ask her to tell you the three sounds she hears in the word 'gum.' If she's young, and can't tell you all the sounds, ask for the first sound she hears. Teach her to take words apart. Children who lack this kind of intimacy with oral language have a much harder time at learning to manage written language. Research shows that they will not read as well, that their vocabularies will suffer, and that their written and oral comprehension will not be as high as that of their peers.

Older children who are working at correcting reading problems may not be willing to play sound games. Their problems can be corrected using other lesson plans. The goals are the same for many lesson plans. Each lesson plan tells you who you should do the lesson with. If you follow this advice strictly, you and your child will do well.

Some children have more difficulty than others at being able to isolate sounds within words. They appear to be able only to hear the word as a unit, 'cat,' and have a lot of trouble hearing the individual sounds, 'c' 'a' 't'. In psychological and educational parlance, this is called an *auditory processing deficit*. I caution you not to get caught up in this. Like all deficits, it simply means that your child isn't currently very good at this task. No assumptions can be made about why she isn't very good at it. It could be as simple as the fact that she hasn't been taught to do it. Before you worry too long and hard over her struggling with this skill, I will tell you that in over four hundred remediations, the Read America clinic has never had a client who couldn't be taught to hear isolated sounds in words. This includes clients with hearing aids and hearing implants. Giovani was one such client. At eighteen months of age, he had lost his hearing to spinal meningitis. At three he received a hearing implant. At six he is reading. In fact, he is beginning to express interest in learning Italian, his mother's native tongue.

Goal #4. That she understands that written words are made up of sound pictures which represent the sounds in words

There are three things that young children are very good at. The first, which any parent will attest to, is getting what they need or want. Whether it's a candy bar, a cold drink, or a new toy, children will find a way to maneuver it into their possession. Another thing they're good at is labeling. At eighteen months of age, children label, or name five to seven new items each week, and by age five, they have learned five to ten thousand words. Think of the memory load that must be required to input that much information in so short a time. Another thing they're good at is sorting or categorizing. At eighteen months, my daughter met my neighbor's new eight-week-old kitten. In an effort to have her treat it gently, I told her it was a baby cat. She frowned deeply at me, sorted it by how many legs it had, compared and contrasted it to her prototype of baby, and quickly labeled it 'doggy.' As she had no prototype of cat to work with, she had used her existing prototype of attributes, and was able, in seconds, to match up this four-legged minibeast to a dog rather than a baby, which has but two legs. Young children have a remarkable capacity for sorting attributes. Research has shown that from birth, infants begin sorting faces into three categories, beloved, familiar, and unfamiliar.

These skills will work to your child's advantage as pictures of the sounds are added to the sound game activities mentioned in the last section. Her desire to have what she wants and needs will move her in the direction you choose for her. As we've illustrated in Chapter two, she knows she *needs* to learn to read, and with a bit of luck, she even *wants* to learn. Her natural ability as a labeler will help her to learn the sound for each of the sound pictures. And her adeptness at categorizing and sorting will assist her as she notices the attributes of sounds and sound pictures.

If you take the time to sensitize your child to oral language, but fail to introduce her to the code (the sound pictures that represent the sounds), much of your efforts will be wasted. Her pronunciation may be better than that of her peers, but it will never help her read. She must know the code. Start early and apply your efforts frequently. Your hard work and her natural inventory of skills will pay off.

Goal #5. That she understands that the sound pictures in written words occur in a sequence from left to right

We speak to parents all the time who are worried about their child's reading and writing development because of letters written backwards and words that run from right to left. We always remind parents that the left to right orientation of written English is completely arbitrary. It might just as easily have been right to left, like Hebrew, or top to bottom, like many oriental languages. There is no natural reason why it is left to right. Your child does not possess a left to right gene that is not functioning properly. Also, parents should remember that young children have not fully established their own internal awareness of this side and that. Many children even have difficulty with top and bottom.

All of this is completely normal to an age and to a point. We expect to see top to bottom awareness established by about age five. Left to right orientation takes a little longer. It is not uncommon to see letter reversals until about age eight. Generally, the older the child, the less blatant the error. For instance, a five-year-old might do something like this:

with a reversed **<b>**, a reversed and tipped **<a>**, **<t>** which is running away from the rest of the word, and going uphill. But at seven years old that same child should have established a level base plane, and might only reverse letters that look like other letters, like **<b>** and **<d>**.

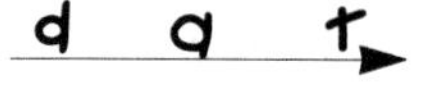

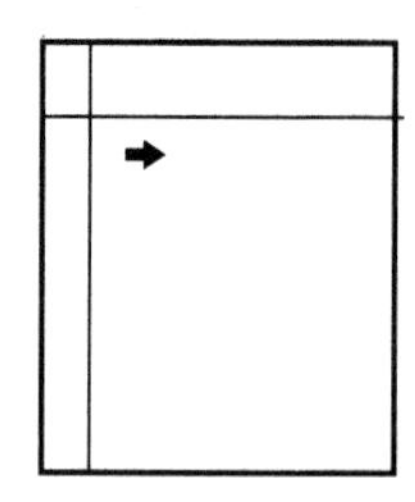

Helping your child with these issues is merely a matter of orienting her and offering her repetition. Children who consistently write from the right side of the paper to the left should be given a point of reference as a starting place. A little arrow in the left column pointing to the right may be all she needs to get her going in the right direction.

When your child reverses individual letters, try using very specific language to explain the problem. For example, in the case of the dat error above, try this as a simple but descriptive correction, "You've put the line on the wrong side of the circle." Instead of having her erase the entire letter, have her erase the line only and then put it on the other side of the circle. Telling her exactly what she's done will help her realize that there are two sides of the circle and that one is the correct side and one is incorrect. Having her erase just the line and then move it will help her see specifically what's wrong. The most important thing is to understand that it's perfectly normal to reverse letters up to seven and even eight years old. Don't worry about it. Try the tips we've offered here, and relax.

Goal #6. That she is able to segment the sounds in spoken words

When we speak of segmenting sounds in words, we are speaking of the ability to unglue and separate the smallest units of sound. For instance, in the word 'big,' the first sound we hear is 'b', and then 'i', and then 'g'. In the word 'train,' we hear 't', then 'r', and then 'ae', then 'n'. Remember, we are speaking of sounds, not letter names.

The ability to separate the sounds in words is the highest correlator to reading success. According to a University of Texas study (Juel, Connie, et al, *Acquisition of literacy, Journal of Educational Psychology,* 1986), segmenting ability also correlates to reading comprehension as well as oral comprehension. Children who learn to read without having established good segmenting ability are at much greater risk of having trouble with longer words, reading slowly, and having difficulty comprehending. This is very powerful information. Do not underestimate the importance of segmenting. The segmenting test at the back of Chapter two has told you whether or not your child needs to improve on her segmenting ability. After you complete the activities at the back of this chapter, you can retest her to see what progress you've made. As you work on segmenting with her, remember it is not just her ability to sound out words that is at stake, but also her ability to comprehend what she hears and reads to the best of her ability.

When doing the lessons at the back of this chapter, be diligent in making sure that your child's segmenting is clear. Do not allow overlap in her segmenting. The word 'sip' for instance should be 's' 'i' 'p'. Some children tend to run sounds together when segmenting:

'si' 'p' or 'si' 'i' 'p' or 'si' 'i' 'ip'

Just because all the sounds are included doesn't make these responses correct. What we seek is nice, clear segmenting. Each sound must stand alone, with no overlap, and no chunking sounds together.

In addition to overlap and chunking, another typical error that parents tend to allow when teaching segmenting is what we call sloppy 'u'.

EX: "sip" = 'su' 'i' 'pu'

The sloppy 'u' happens because individual consonant sounds, without vowels, are not very loud. It is the vowels in our language that give it volume. By adding the sloppy 'u' vowel sound to consonants, we make them more audible. The problem is that we also make them sloppy. So, 'su' 'i' 'pu' doesn't even sound like a word. We end up with a sort of Latin-sounding nonsense word. Another problem with sloppy 'u' is a spelling issue. If we want to spell the word 'tub,' for instance, and we think of 'tu' when we write **<t>**, the only remaining sound we need is 'b'. And of course we end up with this **<tb>** instead of this **<tub>**. Each of these errors is discussed in detail in the lesson plans, with examples of correction techniques.

Of all the skills that we ask parents to practice with their children, segmenting seems to cause parents the most difficulty, and we don't assume that you (the parent) are able to segment with ease. Many adults cannot. We recently had a child in the program whose mother called me during her second homework session with her son. "He's just not getting it," she complained. He thinks there are three sounds in 'choose.'" Well, as there are, in fact, three sounds in 'choose,' I began to wonder if Mom was getting it. When I asked her to tell me what the sounds in 'choose' are, she said, "'choo' and 'oose'." Not only did she fail to give the correct answer, 'ch' 'oo' 'z', but she also had some overlap in her answer. We hear the 'oo' sound affixed to the back end of the 'ch' sound and to the front end of the 'z' sound. We worked with Brandon's mom for about thirty minutes and cleared up this issue altogether. At Brandon's last session his mom confessed to me that she had never been a great reader, but that since I showed her how to segment, she was reading more often and with less difficulty. For parents who are having trouble segmenting themselves, please take a few moments and practice this basic segmenting activity. Say each word, and then say the sounds to the right of the word one at a time.

h **ou se**	'h' 'ow' 's'	f r **ow** n	'f' 'r' 'ow' 'n'
g r **ea** t	'g' 'r' 'ae' 't'	s m i l e	's' 'm' 'ie' 'l'
s i t	's' 'i' 't'	s t a l e	's' 't' 'ae' 'l'
s a t	's' 'a' 't'	t a b **le**	't' 'ae' 'b' 'l'
f l **oa** t	'f' 'l' 'oe' 't'	s n o b	's' 'n' 'o' 'b'
d r i p	'd' 'r' 'i' 'p'	**ch oo se**	'ch' 'oo' 'z'

Goal #7. That she is able to blend the sounds in words

Learning to push sounds together or *blend* them into words is the last goal of this chapter. Accomplished adult readers tend to take the notion of blending for granted. They don't realize that for many children this is a very difficult task to understand and to perform. The first step for your child is understanding what happens when sounds occur in sequence. The best way to help her understand is by example. The language you would have to use to explain this is too confusing for a child. It's best to show her how this works by saying segmented sounds in sequence and then saying the word. Remember, say sounds, not letter names.

'c' 'a' 't' 'cat'

This sort of example will help her see and hear what's happening.

It's not uncommon for young children six and under who are just starting to blend to have trouble remembering all the sounds in a three-sound word. They will frequently say all the sounds 'c' 'a' 't' and then blend just the last two leaving the first sound off entirely: 'at'. The best way to help them through this is to teach them to blend the first two sounds and then add on the third: 'c' 'a' 'ca' 't'...'cat.' This reduces the memory load. Once sounds are linked, or blended, they become a unit, so your child has only one thing to remember and then the last sound gets added on. When you use this aid, do not teach 'ca' as if it were a new sound to learn. Some phonics programs try to teach all the possible consonant-vowel combinations and call the combinations "word families." This is very confusing to children. They end up with more to learn than is necessary. If she already knows 'c' and 'a', she doesn't need to learn 'ca', she only needs to learn to push the sounds together before adding on the last sound. Simply teach her to blend the first two first and then add the last. This is what good readers do subconsciously and very quickly. This drill allows her to practice the process, while demonstrating for her that this is what reading is, pushing sounds together to make words.

Another typical mistake that children make is to say all the sounds and then guess a similar word. For example, 'p' 'o' 't'...'top' or 'm' 'a' 'p'...'tap.' The same procedure explained in the previous paragraph will help alleviate this problem. You can also add a bit of simple language like this, "If this (indicate the word) was 'tap,' this (indicate the **<m>**) would be a picture of 't'. But it isn't. It's a picture of 'm'. Try again, please." As we've mentioned, each of these errors is covered in the lesson plans that follow. Please read each lesson plan carefully and take a few minutes to practice the steps before you begin working with your child.

When your child starts blending words with success, it's important to help her realize that she is reading. Some parents fail to acknowledge this accomplishment because the process of saying a sound, a sound, a sound and then pushing the sounds together to make a word, sounds more like an automaton than a child reading. If you fail to acknowledge this early accomplishment, you're cheating your child out of her right to feel good about herself. In time she will be reading with the fluency you both seek. For now, she needs to practice with meticulous care the skills she has learned so far. You should allow and encourage her to take it slow, sounding each sound and blending as she needs to. New readers should be told that adults read quickly because they took the time to practice slowly as children.

As we've mentioned in Chapter two, if your child is a new reader, in first grade, sixth month, or younger, just follow the Sound Doggy symbols throughout the book, regardless of her test scores. In this chapter, lessons are set out in three sets: Fat Cat Sat, which teaches the sound pictures **<f>**, **<c>**, **<s>**, **<a>**, **<o>**, **<m>**, **<p>**, and **<t>**; Bug On Jug, which teaches **<b>**, **<d>**, **<u>**, **<g>**, **<j>**, **<i>**, **<h>**, and **<r>**; and Ben Bun, which teaches **<e>**, **<n>**, **<v>**, **<w>**, **<z>**, and **<l>**. This order is intended to establish the sound to sound picture correspondence of the sounds in each set, and how we use these to read and spell, before moving on to the next set. So you should present all the Fat Cat Sat lessons in the order they appear before moving on to the Bug On Jug lessons, and then present all the Bug On Jug lessons before moving on to Ben Bun. If your child is older than the sixth month of first grade and has been retained in first grade, you, too, should follow the Fat Cat Sat, Bug On Jug, and Ben Bun lessons as described above.

If your child is older than first grade, sixth month, and is in second grade or beyond, do all of the lessons in the book, including the Sound Doggy lessons, unless the readiness section says that the lesson is not necessary for your child.

Whether your child is a new reader or an older child, you can *do more than one lesson in a sitting*. We find that the biggest mistake that parents make with their children is that they fail to do the lessons repeatedly. Remember, if you are working with a young child, she needs lots and lots of repetition to learn the material. If you are working with an older child, she needs repetition in order to break old habits and replace them with new, more effective ones. *Repetition is the key*. Even when you progress to new lessons, you can *keep practicing previous lessons*. You will know your child doesn't need to continue working on a lesson when she is performing with fairly consistent accuracy.

THE BLENDING GAME

Readiness

This activity is for children ages four and older. You needn't do this lesson with your child if she scored perfectly on the blending test.

Goals

To encourage the child to think about sounds in words.

To cause the child to blend isolated sounds in words.

Materials

There are no materials needed for this activity. Do this activity orally, only. Do not use sound pictures with this lesson. This game is supposed to be casual and fun. Once you have tried it and succeeded at home at your work table, you can start playing it when you're out and about. It's especially fun for car trips.

Presentation

1. Tell your child that you're going to play a sound blending game.
2. Think of a three-sound word. Say the sounds in segmented fashion 'r' 'e' 'd'.
3. Have your child guess the word.

Correcting Problems

When she blends them there is something wrong, for example, 'm' 'a' 'p' comes out as 'mop.'

Repeat the sounds, accentuating and extending the sound she got wrong. EX: 'm' 'aaaa' 'p'.

Variation on Presentation

If your child is able to segment with some success, you can take turns being the segmenter.

FINDING SOUNDS AROUND US

Readiness

This is an activity for children ages four and older. You needn't do this activity with your child if she scored perfectly on the segmenting test.

Goals

To encourage the child to think about sounds in words.

To cause the child to isolate the first sound from the rest of the word.

Materials

There are no materials needed for this activity. Do this activity orally, only. Do not use sound pictures with this lesson. This game is supposed to be casual and fun. Once you have tried it and succeeded at home at your work table, you can start playing it when you're out and about. It's especially fun for car trips.

Presentation

1. Tell your child that you're going to play a sound game.
2. Tell her you're thinking of an animal. Tell her what the first sound you hear in the word is. EX: 'p'.
3. Encourage her to guess what animal you're thinking of.

Correcting Problems

She guesses a word that does not start with the target sound.

For example, you have told her that you're thinking of an animal that starts with the sound 'p'. She responds with 'cat.' Say, "The first sound in 'cat' is 'c'. The first sound in the animal I'm thinking of is 'p'."

Variation on Presentation

Have your child think of the animal and give you the clue. You can take turns being the clue giver.

THREE-SOUND WORD BUILDING

Readiness

Do this lesson with any child. If your child is younger than first grade, sixth month, she should be doing the segmenting game (the lesson before this one) with at least minimal success before you attempt this lesson.

Goals

To cause the child to understand the sight to sound relationship of text.

To cause the child to understand the left to right relationship of text.

To cause the child to consciously understand how she can represent sounds in words.

To create an automatic spelling strategy.

Materials

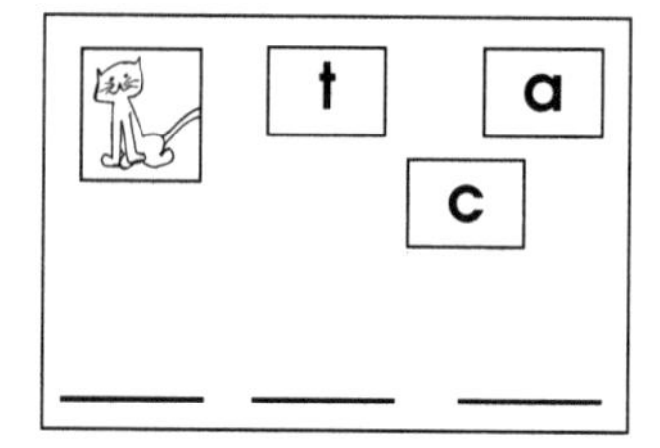

The word building puzzles following this lesson plan.

Your dry erase board.

One envelope for each word puzzle and picture.

One shoebox.

Cut up word puzzles ahead of time. Write the name of each puzzle on the inside flap of the envelope. Store puzzles in envelopes in your shoebox.

Presentation

The word 'cat' is used as an example. The lesson is the same for all of the three-sound word building puzzles.

1. Explain that there are three sounds in the word you're going to spell. Make three lines on your dry erase board. Being careful not to reveal the word on the envelope, lay out the sound pictures from the puzzle marked 'cat.' Say,

Three-Sound Word Building, continued

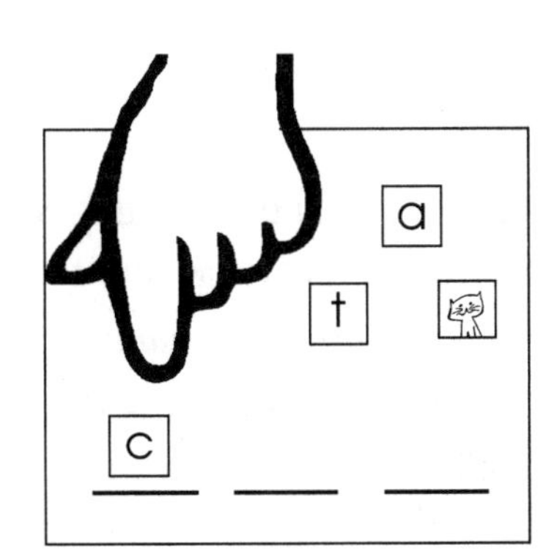

"What's the first sound you hear in 'cat'?" Run your finger along the three lines as you slowly say 'cat.' Do not segment the sounds in the word. That's your child's job. But say the word very slowly as you move your finger along the lines, so that she can hear all the sounds and understands that they should be represented in sequence.

2. After she tells you what sound she hears first, invite her to find the corresponding sound picture. Make sure she says the sound as she puts the sound picture on the first line. Once she has placed the first sound picture say, "Good, what's the next sound you hear in 'cat'?" Once again, you should run your finger along over the lines as you slowly say, 'cat.' Make certain that she says each sound as she locates the corresponding sound picture and places it in sequence.
3. After all sound picture cards have been placed, have her say each sound as you point to its sound picture in sequence. Once all the sound pictures have been placed, have her map the word on a piece of lined paper. When mapping she should say one sound at a time as she writes the sound picture for that sound. Mapping should be clear, concise, and completely segmented.

After this lesson proceed on to the other Fat Cat Sat lessons through Reading Stories in Basic Code, before doing any Bug On Jug or Ben Bun lessons.

Correcting Problems

The child links two or more sounds, when asked to give the sounds in a word.

EX: 'ca' 't' or 'c' 'at'

Say, "'ca' is two sounds. What's the first sound in 'ca'?" Accentuate your mouth and the changing of the sounds as you question. Do not separate the two sounds for her.

continued

Three-Sound Word Building, continued

Her sound production is bad. She adds a sloppy 'u' sound after consonants.

EX: 'cat' = 'cu' 'a' 'tu'.

Simply repeat the sound correctly and say, "'c', not 'c...u'" (accentuating the difference in the two sounds in 'cu').

The child uses letter names. "The first sound in 'cat' is 'see.'"

Simply say, "No, that is the letter name. Letter names won't help you learn to spell or read. What sound do you hear? Tell me what you hear, not the letter name." Do not ask the question "What sound does 'see' make?" This wrongly reinforces the strategy that letters make sounds. They do not, people do.

FAT CAT SAT WORD BUILDING

For use with Three-Sound Word Building. Cut word building puzzles and store them in envelopes. Store envelopes in a shoebox.

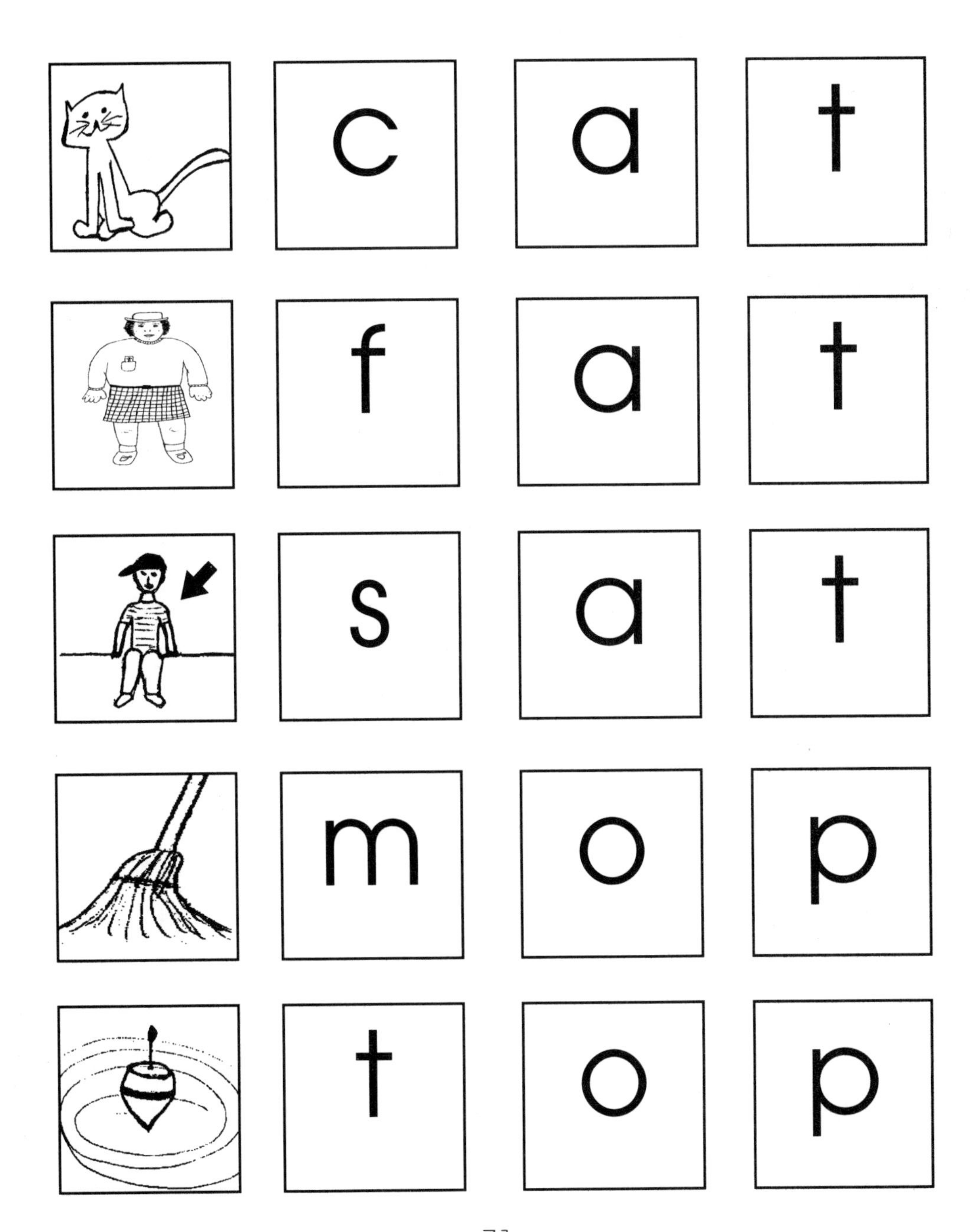

cat

fat

sat

mop

top

FAT CAT SAT WORD BUILDING

For use with Three-Sound Word Building. Cut word building puzzles and store them in envelopes. Store envelopes in a shoebox.

cop

map

tap

pop

BUG ON JUG WORD BUILDING

For use with Three-Sound Word Building. Cut word building puzzles and store them in envelopes. Store envelopes in a shoebox.

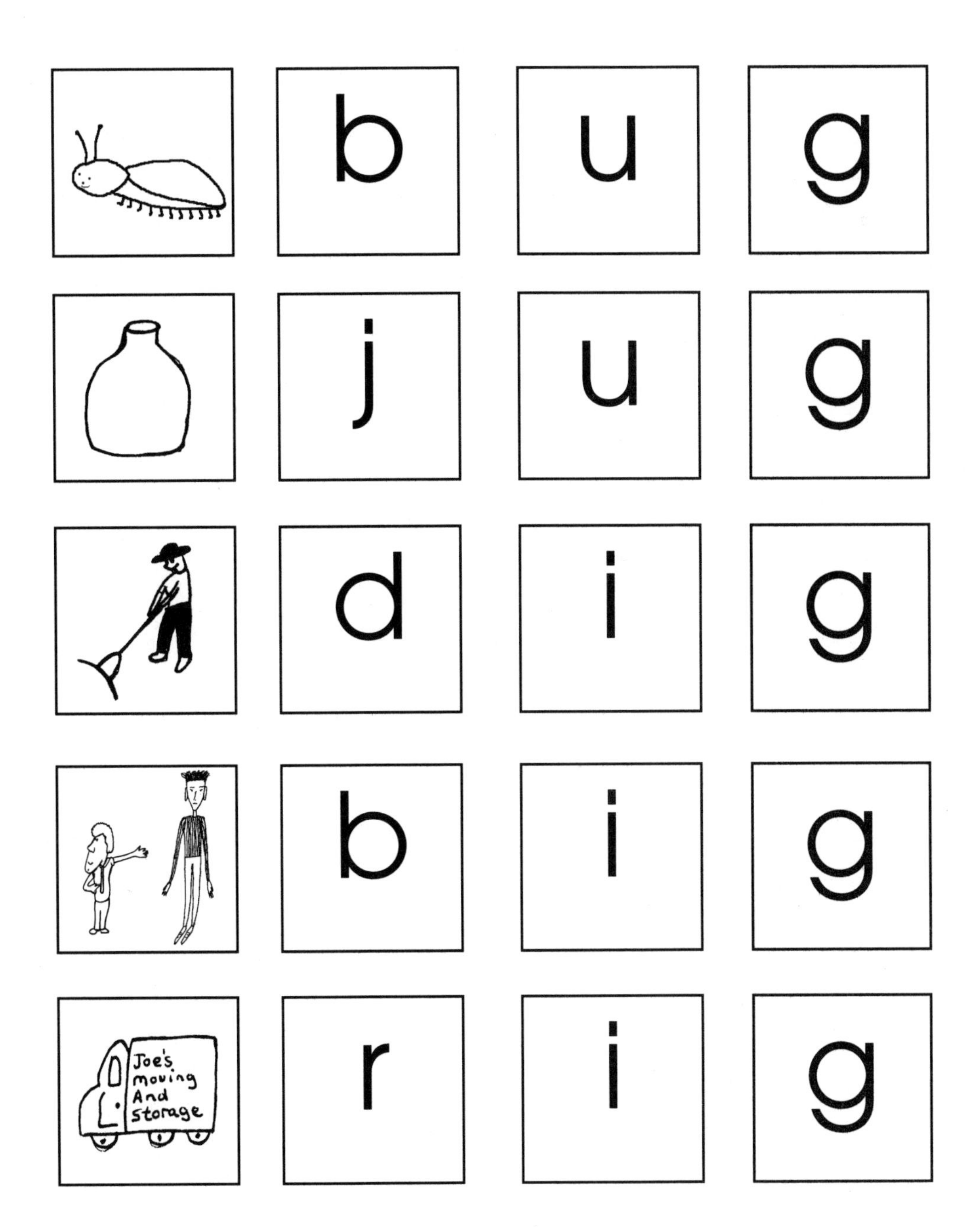

bug

jug

dig

big

rig

BUG ON JUG WORD BUILDING

For use with Three-Sound Word Building. Cut word building puzzles and store them in envelopes. Store envelopes in a shoebox.

	r	u	g
	h	u	g
	j	i	g
	d	u	g

rug

hug

jig

dug

BEN BUN
WORD BUILDING

For use with Three-Sound Word Building. Cut word building puzzles and store them in envelopes. Store envelopes in a shoebox.

wet

zip

web

mutt

bun

BEN BUN WORD BUILDING

For use with Three-Sound Word Building. Cut word building puzzles and store them in envelopes. Store envelopes in a shoebox.

buzz

net

vet

bell

THREE-SOUND AUDITORY PROCESSING

Readiness

Do this lesson with any child. If your child is younger than first grade, sixth month, she should be doing Word Building (the lesson before this one) with at least minimal success before you attempt this lesson.

Goals

To cause your child to consciously understand how she can manipulate sounds to create and change words.

If she doesn't already know the sound picture to sound correspondence, this will help her learn it.

Materials

The auditory processing puzzles following this lesson plan.

One envelope for each auditory processing puzzle.

Cut up auditory processing puzzles ahead of time. Write the name of each puzzle on the inside flap of the envelope. Store puzzles in envelopes in your shoebox.

Presentation

This lesson plan describes Fat Cat Sat, the first set of sounds you will work with, but the lesson will be the same for all three sets of sounds.

1. Lay out the sound pictures from one of the auditory processing pouches.

2. Hold the calling card 

in your hand so that your child cannot see the answers.

continued

Three-Sound Auditory Processing, continued

3. Say, "I'll go first. I'll spell 'cot'." Use your pointer finger to slide the sound pictures one at a time into position to spell 'cot.' Say each sound as you line up the corresponding sound picture. Do this on the first set of lines, a few inches below the line of sound pictures.
4. Now, use your pointer finger or a pencil to point to each sound picture as your child says the corresponding sounds. If she is still learning the corresponding sounds, say each sound and then have her repeat it after you. Make sure she is looking at the sound pictures as she says the sounds, and not at you.
5. Now say, "If that spells 'cot,' let's spell 'pot.' Use your pointer finger or a pencil to slowly move across the word 'cot,' as you say the new word, 'pot.' This will help bring her attention to the location of the sound picture that must be changed. Do not say the sounds separately, but as slowly as you can. This causes her to have to segment the sounds. Be very careful to make sure your pencil or pointer finger is in the correct location, over the corresponding sound as you slowly say the word.
6. Continue with each change, offering help as needed. After each change, point to each sound picture and have her say each sound in the word, as shown in step 4.

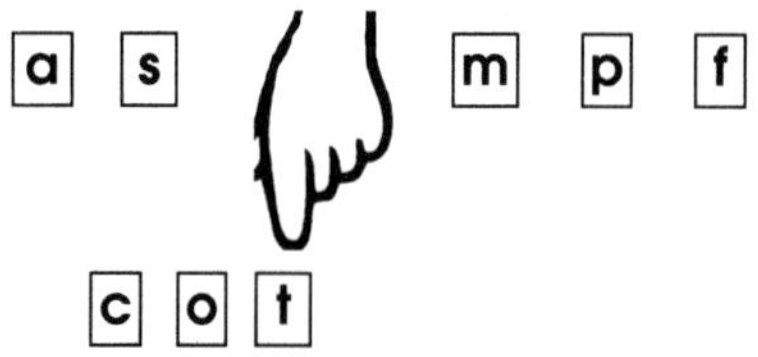

After this lesson proceed on to the other Fat Cat Sat lessons through Reading Stories in Basic Code before doing any Bug On Jug or Ben Bun lessons.

Correcting Problems

The child chooses the wrong sound picture.

EX: change 'cot' to 'pot' = 'mot'

If she gets the wrong sound picture, tell her what she's got. Say, "That says 'mot,' we want 'pot.'" Try this first without segmenting the sounds. Use your

Three-Sound Auditory Processing, continued

pointer finger or pencil to indicate the sounds as you say the word. If after two or three tries, your child does not make the correct change, you will need to segment the sounds for her. Say, "We need to make 'cot' say 'pot,' 'p' 'o' 't'," as you move your pencil or pointer finger over each sound picture as you say the sounds.

She can't segment the sounds when you say the words.

EX: You say 'cot' and she simply cannot tell you what the first sound is.

Are you sure you are saying the word very slowly? If you are, and she still can't do this, you need to stop the lesson and practice the previous lesson until she is showing more consistent success.

FAT CAT SAT
AUDITORY PROCESSING

For use with Three-Sound Auditory Processing. Cut auditory processing puzzles and store them in envelopes. Store envelopes in a shoebox.

cot	tap
pot	cap
pat	map
fat	mop
mat	sop
cat	cop
sat	top
sap	pop

o	t	p
c	a	f
m	s	p

BUG ON JUG
AUDITORY PROCESSING

For use with Three-Sound Auditory Processing. Cut auditory processing puzzles and store them in envelopes. Store envelopes in a shoebox.

rug	big
bug	jig
dug	jug
dig	hug
rig	

	b	u
r	g	h
j	i	d

BEN BUN
AUDITORY PROCESSING

For use with Three-Sound Auditory Processing. Cut auditory processing puzzles and store them in envelopes. Store envelopes in a shoebox.

let	but
wet	buzz
vet	bun
net	Ben
nut	bell

ll

e

e t w

l u b

n v zz

SOUND BINGO

Readiness

Older children who know the sound to sound picture correspondence of these letters needn't do this lesson, but they can if they want to.

Goals

To practice the sight to sound correspondence between the basic code sound pictures and the sounds they represent.

To offer practice forming the basic sound pictures.

Materials

The Sound Bingo sheets following this lesson plan. There are two different cards provided. One is for you and one is for your child. There are three sets of each so that you can play the game three different times.

The corresponding auditory processing sound pictures from the three sound auditory processing materials. If you are doing Fat Cat Sat Sound Bingo, use the Fat Cat Sat auditory processing sound pictures.

Colored pencils.

Presentation

This lesson plan describes the Fat Cat Sat Sound Bingo lesson. It will be the same for Bug On Jug and Ben Bun.

1. Take out the sound pictures from the Fat Cat Sat auditory processing activity. Turn them upside down on your work table. Tear out two of the game sheets. Make sure they are not the same. Give one to your child and keep one for yourself.
2. Choose a sound picture but don't let her see it. Tell her the sound. Give her an opportunity to find the appropriate sound picture on her bingo card. If she doesn't know which sound picture the sound represents, you can show her the sound picture calling card you picked, and then turn the card back over again while she searches her card for matching sound pictures. By

Sound Bingo, continued

turning the card back over, you are training her visual memory to recall the picture.

3. When a match is found, the player should trace over the corresponding sound pictures using a colored pencil, and say the sound as she traces the sound picture. We do this instead of covering the sound picture with chips as is generally done in bingo, as it gives your child practice at forming the sound picture as she says the sound.

Note: Some parents like to let the child win. They control the progress of the game by pretending to miss a sound picture that they have on their card when it is called. Other, more competitive parents play to win.

After this lesson, proceed on to the other Fat Cat Sat lessons through Reading Stories in Basic Code before doing any Bug On Jug or Ben Bun lessons.

Correcting Problems

After revealing the sound picture to your child and then turning it over, she still doesn't find the match on her card.

Tell her she does have a match and show her the calling card again. Allow her to see the calling card until she locates the match.

FAT CAT SAT SOUND BINGO

For calling cards, use the sound pictures from the Fat Cat Sat Auditory Processing materials.

f	f	p	m
p	p	m	c
a	s	a	s
m	f	s	a
s	a	c	f

FAT CAT SAT SOUND BINGO

For calling cards, use the sound pictures from the Fat Cat Sat Auditory Processing materials.

a	f	o	t
f	a	f	m
f	a	t	m
c	c	m	a
p	p	c	m

FAT CAT SAT SOUND BINGO

For calling cards, use the sound pictures from the Fat Cat Sat Auditory Processing materials.

f	f	p	m
p	p	m	c
a	s	a	s
m	f	s	a
s	a	c	f

FAT CAT SAT SOUND BINGO

For calling cards, use the sound pictures from the Fat Cat Sat Auditory Processing materials.

a	f	o	t
f	a	f	m
f	a	t	m
c	c	m	a
p	p	c	m

FAT CAT SAT SOUND BINGO

For calling cards, use the sound pictures from the Fat Cat Sat Auditory Processing materials.

f	f	p	m
p	p	m	c
a	s	a	s
m	f	s	a
s	a	c	f

FAT CAT SAT SOUND BINGO

For calling cards, use the sound pictures from the Fat Cat Sat Auditory Processing materials.

a	f	o	t
f	a	f	m
f	a	t	m
c	c	m	a
p	p	c	m

BUG ON JUG SOUND BINGO

For calling cards, use the sound pictures from the Bug On Jug Auditory Processing materials, and Fat Cat Sat Auditory Processing materials.

u	p	a	t
g	u	o	s
p	s	j	c
r	h	b	d
b	p	u	m

BUG ON JUG SOUND BINGO

For calling cards, use the sound pictures from the Bug On Jug Auditory Processing materials, and Fat Cat Sat Auditory Processing materials.

f	r	s	m
a	b	t	o
g	f	j	i
p	b	m	s
j	d	u	p

BUG ON JUG SOUND BINGO

For calling cards, use the sound pictures from the **Bug On Jug Auditory Processing** materials, and Fat Cat Sat Auditory Processing materials.

u	p	a	t
g	u	o	s
p	s	j	c
r	h	b	d
b	p	u	m

BUG ON JUG SOUND BINGO

For calling cards, use the sound pictures from the Bug On Jug Auditory Processing materials, and Fat Cat Sat Auditory Processing materials.

f	r	s	m
a	b	t	o
g	f	j	i
p	b	m	s
j	d	u	p

BUG ON JUG SOUND BINGO

For calling cards, use the sound pictures from the Bug On Jug Auditory Processing materials, and Fat Cat Sat Auditory Processing materials.

u	p	a	t
g	u	o	s
p	s	j	c
r	h	b	d
b	p	u	m

BUG ON JUG SOUND BINGO

For calling cards, use the sound pictures from the Bug On Jug Auditory Processing materials, and Fat Cat Sat Auditory Processing materials.

f	r	s	m
a	b	t	o
g	f	j	i
p	b	m	s
j	d	u	p

BEN BUN SOUND BINGO

For calling cards, use the sound pictures from the Ben Bun, Fat Cat Sat, and Bug On Jug Auditory Processing materials.

u	p	e	t
g	n	w	i
l	z	j	c
r	h	b	d
b	p	n	v

BEN BUN SOUND BINGO

For calling cards, use the sound pictures from the Ben Bun, Fat Cat Sat, and Bug On Jug Auditory Processing materials.

f	r	w	m
e	l	t	o
g	f	j	i
p	b	v	s
j	d	u	z

BEN BUN SOUND BINGO

For calling cards, use the sound pictures from the Ben Bun, Fat Cat Sat, and Bug On Jug Auditory Processing materials.

u	p	e	t
g	n	w	i
l	z	j	c
r	h	b	d
b	p	n	v

BEN BUN SOUND BINGO

For calling cards, use the sound pictures from the Ben Bun, Fat Cat Sat, and Bug On Jug Auditory Processing materials.

f	r	w	m
e	l	t	o
g	f	j	i
p	b	v	s
j	d	u	z

BEN BUN SOUND BINGO

For calling cards, use the sound pictures from the Ben Bun, Fat Cat Sat, and Bug On Jug Auditory Processing materials.

u	p	e	t
g	n	w	i
l	z	j	c
r	h	b	d
b	p	n	v

BEN BUN
SOUND BINGO

For calling cards, use the sound pictures from the Ben Bun, Fat Cat Sat, and Bug On Jug Auditory Processing materials.

f	r	w	m
e	l	t	o
g	f	j	i
p	b	v	s
j	d	u	z

THREE-SOUND DIRECTED READING

Readiness

Do this lesson with any child. Your child should be fairly accurate with the sound to sound picture relationship of the sound pictures before you attempt this lesson.

Goals

To learn that sounds blend together to make words.

To offer practice at blending three sounds to read a word.

Materials

The word lists following this lesson plan.

The dry erase board, or a piece of lined paper.

An envelope for storing the words.

Cut words up. Store each set separately. Write the name on the envelope.

Presentation

1. Show the child the first word.
2. Ask her to read the sounds.
3. Encourage her to say the blended word.
4. Have her map the word onto a piece of lined paper or your dry erase board. Make sure she says each sound as she writes the corresponding sound picture.

After this lesson proceed on to the other Fat Cat Sat lessons through Reading Stories in Basic Code, before doing any Bug On Jug or Ben Bun lessons.

When you reach the Ben Bun words, you will notice that a few words have double letter sound pictures, and that the double letters are bolded and close together. EX: b e ***ll****. Simply tell your child that this is just another way to represent the sound 'l', that it is another picture of that sound.*

continued

Correcting Problems

The child does not know one of the sounds.

EX: For the word 'map,' she says, "'m' 'a' 'b'...'mab.'"

Tell her the correct sound. Point to the sound picture **<p>** as you offer the correct sound 'p'.

The child reads all the sounds correctly, but when she blends them there is something wrong. EX: 'm' 'a' 'p' comes out 'cap.' This is especially common with children who are developing or have developed a guessing strategy.

Say, "You said all the sounds, but when you blended them you read 'cap.'" Use your finger to indicate the sounds as you say the word. Then say, "If this was 'cap,' this (indicate **<m>**) would be the sound 'c'. But it isn't. It's 'm'. Try again, please."

The child has great difficulty blending sounds. She says all the sounds correctly, but really can't seem to blend them together to get the word.

Teach her to blend as she goes. EX: For the word 'map,' have her stop and blend the first two sounds and then add on the last sound 'm' 'a'... 'ma'...'p'...'map.'

Variation of Presentation

Some children are simply unable to blend for a long period of time. This is especially true of young children. If this is the case with your child, try this variation before going on to the above presentation. Knowing what the word says and then blending it will help your child to understand what blending is, and to hear the word happening as she blends it, by already knowing what the word is.

1. Show your child the first word. Say, "This is 'cat.' Let's say all the sounds in 'cat.'"
2. Use your finger to indicate each sound picture as your child says the segmented sounds. "'c' 'a' 't'."
3. Have her map the word onto a sheet of lined paper. Make sure she says each sound as she writes the corresponding sound picture.

FAT CAT SAT WORD LIST

For use with Three-Sound Directed Reading and Three-Sound Spelling Practice

cat	sat
pop	mop
cot	sap
cop	sop
pot	tap
cap	sap
pat	top
map	Sam

BUG ON JUG WORD LIST

For use with Three-Sound Directed Reading and Three-Sound Spelling Practice

rug	rig
hug	bud
bug	big
hag	jig
dug	mug
bag	jug
dig	tug
bad	mud

BEN BUN WORD LIST

For use with Three-Sound Directed Reading and Three-Sound Spelling Practice

be**ll**	win
let	bu**zz**
Ben	wit
net	fu**zz**
bun	wet
nut	fun
bin	web
but	zip

THREE-SOUND SPELLING PRACTICE

Readiness

Do this lesson with any child. Your child should be fairly consistently accurate at reading the words (the lesson before this one) before you attempt to have her spell them.

Goals

To give the child practice spelling words with three sounds.

Materials

The word reading lists preceding this lesson plan.

Lined paper or the dry erase board.

Something to write with.

Presentation

1. Explain that you're going to play a spelling game.
2. Give your child a piece of lined paper, or you can use the dry erase board.
3. Explain that she should say the sounds as she writes the sound pictures.
4. Using the words from the list preceding this lesson, call out one word at a time and encourage her to say each sound as she writes the sound picture that represents that sound.

After this lesson proceed on to the other Fat Cat Sat lessons through Reading Stories in Basic Code, before doing any Bug On Jug or Ben Bun lessons.

Correcting Problems

The child doesn't say the sounds when spelling the words.

continued

Three-Sound Spelling Practice, continued

Do not allow your child to spell silently. She may be spelling by letter name rather than sounds. Many children memorize whole words by making the letter names into a kind of song..."see, ay, tee...'cat.'" This undermines your efforts to help her learn to spell and read. Make her say each sound as she spells the words.

READING STORIES IN BASIC CODE

Readiness

You should begin this lesson once your child has begun to read three-sound words with consistent accuracy. If your child is an older child who might find the stories silly, skip this lesson and move on to Chapter four.

Goals

To practice reading basic code in stories.

Materials

The Fat Cat Sat, Bug On Jug, and Ben Bun stories following this lesson plan.

After your child has completed all other lessons in the chapter, she can read the last three stories, Mad Cat, Missing Cat, and Fun in The Sun.

Presentation

1. Explain to your child that you are going to read a story together.
2. Show her the story and encourage her to read the words. Use your finger to redirect her and to correct problems as needed, just as you would if she were reading isolated words.
3. After each phrase or sentence say, "Yes, very good," then reread the phrase or sentence to her. This will assure that she follows the theme of the story despite any difficulty she has had in reading the words.
4. If your child doesn't want to read every sentence, you can take turns. You can read one sentence and she can read one sentence. When it's your turn, you should read slowly, modeling how you want her to say each sound and blend them into words.

continued

Reading Stories in Basic Code, continued

Correcting Problems

All problems can be corrected in the same way as if she were reading isolated words. See the Three-Sound Directed Reading lesson plan earlier in this chapter.

FAT CAT SAT STORY

For use with Reading Stories in Basic Code.

Fat cat sat on mat.

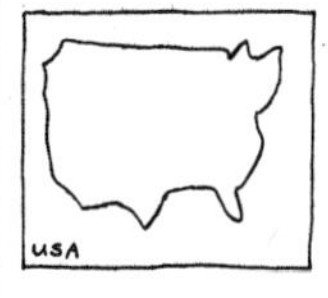

Fat cat sat on map.

Fat cat sat on mop.

Fat cat sat on cop.

Fat cat sat on Pat.

BUG ON JUG STORY

For use with Reading Stories in Basic Code.

Big bug dug.

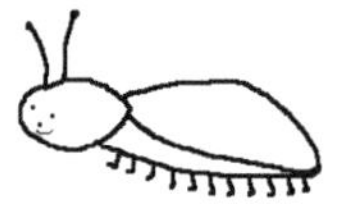

Big bug dug jug.

Big bug did hug jug.

Big bug did jig jug.

Big bug sat on jug.

BEN BUN STORY

For use with Reading Stories in Basic Code.

Ben Bun is wet.

Buzz...
Ben Bun got bit.

Ben Bun is in net.

Ben Bun at vet.

MAD CAT

Directions: Have the child read the story. Offer help as needed.

Difficult words: 'to' 'a' 'hiss' 'hill' 'is'

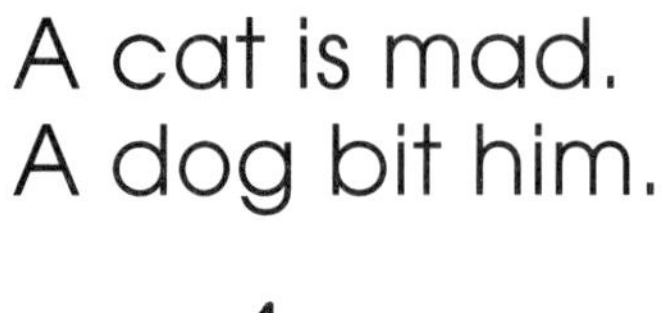

A cat is mad.
A dog bit him.

It is bad to nip
at a cat.

1

A dog ran. A
cat ran.

Get a dog!
Get a bad
dog!

2

It is not a bad
dog. It is a pet.
It is Dan's pet. It
is Sal. "Get on
Sal!"

3

Sal got on. It is
a hi**ll**. It is a big
hi**ll**.

4

Dan and Sal
got up a hi**ll**.

5

On top is Mom.

6

Mom is mad at
a cat. It is bad
to hi**ss** at Sal.

7

The End

8

MISSING CAT

Directions: Have the child read the story. Offer help as needed.

Difficult words: 'a' 'hill' 'hiss' 'is' 'his' 'box'

Jan had a nap on a bed.

Jan is up.

1

Jan is sad. Tom cat is not on his mat. Tom cat is not on his cot.

2

It is a bad cat. It did not get a nap. It got o**ff** his cot.

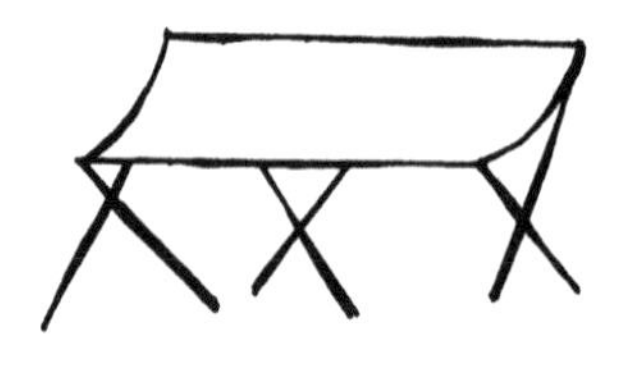

3

Jan got on. Jan got up a hi**ll**.

4

"Tom ! Tom cat !" It is a hi**ss**. It is a cat. It is Tom.

"Bad cat did not get a nap."

5

Jan got Tom cat in a box.

6

Tom cat is sad in a box.

7

Jan got Tom on his cot. "Get a nap Tom. Get a nap on a cot."

8

FUN IN THE SUN

Directions: Have the child read the story. Offer help as needed.

Difficult words: 'a' 'off' 'kiss' 'is' 'his'

Jan is in bed. It is Mom. "Get up Jan !"
1

"Sun is up ! It is fun."
2

Jan sat up. Sun is up.
3

Tom sat up. Tom got off his cot. Get a sip Jan.
Get a sip Tom. "Yum!"
4

"Tom, it is a
bad dog and
his kid. It is a
dog that bit
Tom."

5

Jan hid Tom in
a bag. Tom is
sad. It is bad in
a bag.

6

Sal did ki**ss**
Tom. It is not a
bad dog, it is a
bad bag.

7

Dan and Jan
and Tom and
Sal did run in
sun. It is fun !

8

What Now?

Congratulations! You've completed your first reading lessons with your child. If your child is a new reader, younger than first grade, sixth month, you should continue on and do the lessons in Chapter four that have a Sound Doggy on them. If she is very young, a kindergartner or younger, you may want to wait a few months before you continue on to Chapter four. If she did very well during the Chapter three lessons, you can try moving on to Chapter four and see how she does. But be aware that the ability to blend words with adjacent consonants is somewhat developmental. If she has a lot of trouble with it, you should back off and just keep practicing three-sound reading and spelling. And then try again in two to three months. Do not stop her lessons entirely. She is young and will forget what you have taught her so far. In addition to practicing the lessons in this chapter, here are a few bright ideas you can do together in the meantime. These are just a few ideas. I'm sure you'll think of more.

- Buy early readers and take turns reading. Have her read all the three-sound words while you read the harder words.

- Write her short notes in three-sound words. Leave them around for her.

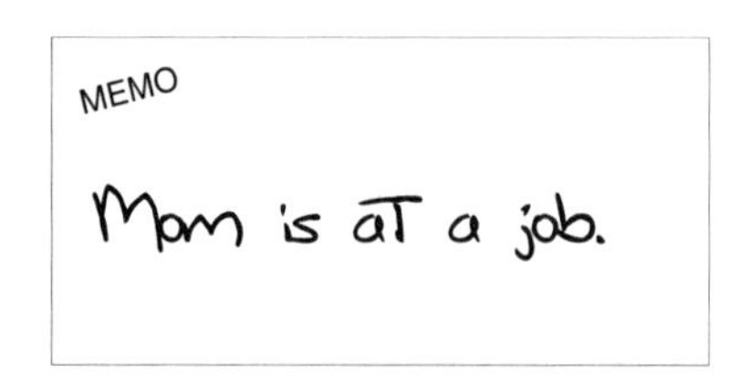

- Get some card stock and have her start labeling all the three-sound items in your home.

If your child is older than first grade, sixth month, she might enjoy these activities too. But, you will also need to move on to the lessons in Chapter four.

CHAPTER FOUR

ADJACENT CONSONANT SOUNDS

By the time you reach this chapter, you've accomplished a great deal. By now your child should be able to recognize these sound pictures.

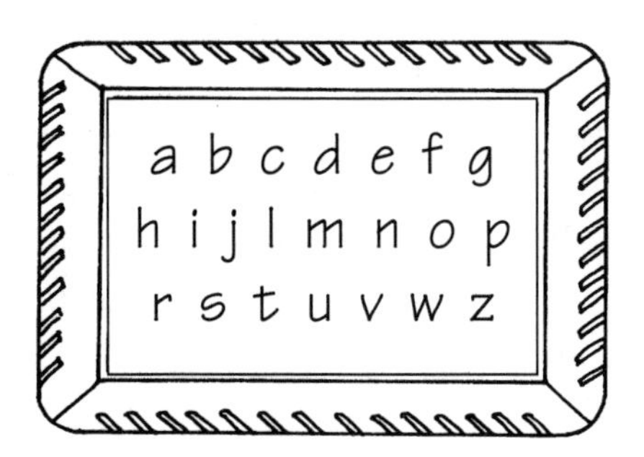

a b c d e f g
h i j l m n o p
r s t u v w z

He should be able to blend these sound pictures into words when they appear in three-sound words. And he should be able to segment and represent these sounds in order to spell three-sound words. He has also been exposed to some words that contain double consonants. He should understand that these doubled consonants are just another picture of the same sound.

Basically, he is an expert at reading and spelling words with a consonant sound–vowel sound–consonant sound (CVC) configuration such as in the words **<cat> <bell>** and **<sip>.**

Your next challenge is to help your child stretch these same skills that he uses to read and spell CVC words to include reading and spelling words that contain two adjacent consonants representing two different sounds. These might be a vowel-consonant-consonant (VCC) configuration like the word **<and>**, or a consonant-vowel-consonant-consonant (CVCC) configuration like in the word **<past>**, or a consonant-consonant-vowel-consonant (CCVC) configuration like in the word **<frog>**. These are often referred to as "blends." Although this term is commonly used by reading teachers, it is confusing and tends to focus the instruction in the wrong direction. It's confusing because, after all, don't all sounds in words blend? Once the word has been read, and the sounds blended into a word, they are blends. The sounds in **<cat>**, for instance, are blended just as much as the sounds in **<frog>**, even though **<cat>** contains none of what are referred to as blends. Yet, many reading programs and teachers tend to focus on these adjacent consonants, the blend, rather than the real instructional issues of this level. Let's see how they do that and why we want to avoid making those same mistakes.

To Blend or Not to Blend

In phonics programs children learn 'br' and 'st' and other blends as if they necessarily went together. This gives children the idea that they have to remember these blends like a picture. If your child can recognize the sound picture **<b>** and the sound picture **<r>**, why should he have to learn **
** as if it were something different? With nearly one hundred possible consonant-consonant combinations, memorizing them all would only serve to overload his visual memory. And what rationale could we offer for doing this when they are the same, when there is no new information, only two consonant sound pictures that he already knows, side by side? And finally, if we have children memorize all the possible consonant-consonant combinations, why shouldn't we have them memorize all the possible consonant-vowel combinations, like the 'ca' in 'cat,' or the 'ig' in 'big'? Unfortunately, many phonics programs do just that. The next section explains why this is unnecessary and ineffective.

Pink Elephants, Flying Pigs, and Word Families

Many phonics programs drill children in lists of words with like beginnings or like endings. They call these "word families." Children are taught to read these similar words in chains. So there would be the 'pi' "word family" with 'pin,' 'pig,' 'pit,' 'pip,' and the 'ag' "word family" with 'bag,' 'gag,' 'tag,' 'rag.' There are numerous problems with this kind of drill. It teaches the child to memorize parts of a word as if they were a unit, when in fact these parts are two distinct sounds. If we teach them as units, we will have to teach the approximately one thousand possible consonant-vowel and vowel-consonant combinations. This would seem an inexcusable waste of time when your child already knows all of these sounds individually. Another obvious problem with this kind of instruction is that it teaches the child not to decode the whole word. If, by hint of the previous word, he knows that the last two sounds are 'ag', he need only assess the first sound to get the correct answer. Eventually, he will stop reading the whole word and learn to look only at the first sound picture.

We must also remember that we are teaching children to read so that they can read stories. In the real world, words do not occur in families, they occur in meaningful sentences. The concept of word families is sweet, but it just doesn't happen. When is the last time you found a string of words that rhyme, making up an entire story? By drilling children with word families, we are setting them up to think that reading is a rhyming game rather than something we do to acquire meaning.

We've had many children who suffered from this kind of instruction, but one in particular comes to mind because of the severity of the problem. David's mother contacted us as a result of his teacher's warnings that she would have to hold him back to repeat the first grade. "David is very lucky," his mother explained during her initial call to our clinic. "He attends the best private school in the area," she continued. "His brother learned to read there with no problem. I just don't know what's wrong with David." A further interview with David's parents revealed that the school was using a popular phonics method, combined with a good children's literature program. David, now in the spring of his first-grade year, was reading at first grade, second month, on the standardized Woodcock Reading Mastery test. His segmenting score was 36 of 63 attempts. On this test, he chunked every single adjacent consonant, as if they were one sound. He said that the first sound in 'frog' was 'fr' and the first sound in 'stop' was 'st', and so on. Occasionally he even chunked the next two sounds, so that he named the next sound after the 'st' in 'stop' as 'op'. On the blending test, he got a perfect score. His auditory processing score was 6 of 10. For instance, when asked to say 'flag' without the 'f', his response was 'ag'.

Seven-year-old Tessa is an extreme example of the failure of word families as an instructional technique. Her intake responses on the Woodcock Reading Mastery test were noteworthy and merit mention here as a firm warning against the use of word families in teaching reading. The child is expected to read the words on a pallette. The fourth word on the test is 'not.' Tessa read this correctly. The next five words are 'red,' 'box,' 'look,' 'do,' and 'big.' After 'not,' Tessa read 'rot,' 'bot,' 'lot,' 'dot,' and 'bot,' It was obvious to us, and confirmed by Tessa's parents, that Tessa's school was teaching word families in their phonics program. Tessa got fixated on 'not,' and then used the first sound in the next five words to create the 'ot' family.

Perhaps the most powerful argument against teaching adjacent consonant sounds as units, and teaching consonant-vowel word families, is that the written language was not intended to be used this way. Our written language was intended as a sound picture code, not a word family code to be memorized in little arbitrary chunks. So, instead of wasting precious visual memory on redundant information, we teach children to blend sounds together, not to remember them as a unit. It is important, however, to remember that when we ask children to read words with two adjacent consonant sounds, we are asking them to perform a more difficult version of the same skill they can already perform with three-sound words. There is no new information. They already know all the sound pictures, but it is still more difficult. Let's look at the goals of this level to find out why.

Goal #1. To be able to perform the basic reading skills while articulating adjacent consonant sounds

Linguistically speaking, blending a consonant and vowel presents fewer challenges to the reader than blending two consonant sounds. After all, your new reader has had practice at this since babyhood in such words as 'Ma ma ma ma' and 'da da da da.' Even after his speech developed past the consonant-vowel stage, he had some trouble with consonant-consonant words. Words like 'cracker' got abridged to 'cacker,' and 'blankie' sounded more like 'bakie.' His speech was conspicuously devoid of consonant blends. By the time a child is about three, he has learned to fit adjacent consonants into words. But isn't it natural to expect him to have trouble with this old skill anew, as he begins to learn to read? After all, we are asking him to perform numerous tasks at once. This is the case with any new skill we learn. When I was one year old I learned to stay upright. When I was five my sister put skates on me and I had to learn to stay upright with wheels on my feet. My son learned to ride a tricycle when he was three or four. When he was seven, we bought him a two-wheeler and he had to learn to steer while balancing. Whenever we add to our inventory of skills, we must relearn a bit of the old ones. This is called adapting. After several bruises and a wounded ego, I learned to stay upright with wheels on my feet. And after spending Easter weekend with Mom holding on to his bicycle seat my son was able, finally, to steer while balancing. Learning to fit adjacent consonants into words presents a similar challenge. Your job, as your child's reading mentor, is a lot like my job when I balanced my son's bike for him while he learned to steer all over again.

When you're working with a young child just learning to read it's important to allow him lots of time to make his way up to words that include adjacent consonant sounds. Offer lots of practice, and exercise lots of patience. This is often a difficult step for young children. The lesson plans in this chapter offer several instructive tips for helping your child through this level. If you're working remedially at this level, with an older child, you'll need to be a bit more demanding. It is important to move through this level and on, so that he can achieve grade level as soon as possible.

Goal #2. To be able to recall all the sounds in longer words when blending

Most words containing adjacent consonant sounds are longer than three-sound words. There are a few three-sound words containing consonant blends such as 'and,' 'act,' and 'elm,' but most words containing consonant blends have four or five sounds like 'past,' 'frog,' and 'plant.' For the new reader this presents a short-term memory challenge. If your new reader is still having to think about the sound that each sound picture represents, there may be a bit of a time lag between sounds. This time lag can serve to cause him to forget what he had so far. For instance, he sees **<frog>**. He says 'f' and then, ever so slowly, 'r'. Then he says 'o' and finally 'g'. It's no wonder that the 'r' sound tends to get lost and he says 'fog.' The more fluent he is in decoding the sound pictures, and the more practice he gets at doing this, the faster he will say each sound and the less likely he will be to lose one or two of them as he goes. If you are working with a young child who is taking a very long time between sounds, you probably need to spend more time on the lessons in Chapter three, learning the basic code.

Goal #3. To avoid the tendency to add sounds to words

If you are working remedially with a child who has been taught that adjacent consonant sounds are units, you may get a lot of extra sounds coming your way. Children who have been drilled in 'st','bl','fl','tr', 'gr', and the other one hundred and ninety-five or so possible consonant combinations, tend to want to pronounce every word with a blend. 'Fog' becomes 'frog' and 'back' becomes 'black' and 'sick' becomes 'stick,' and so on. It's as if the two sounds get irrevocably stuck together. We worked with a fourth grader about two years ago who had the worst case of this we've ever seen. I observed Robby and the reading therapist who was working with him, and took these notes:

> *Robby is reading a book about how maple syrup is tapped from trees. He has just read, "Men trap trees to get slap." I'm assuming he means, "Men tap trees to get sap."*

The following week I sat in again and heard all about a boat trip in the fog. But it came out as "a bloat trip in the frog."

Although Robby was an extreme case at the age of nine, this kind of adding of consonants is quite common among younger children who have been taught to chunk adjacent consonants. If your child is in this situation, you will need to do lots of retraining. He will need to do oral segmenting of words with adjacent consonant sounds. He will need to map words with adjacent consonants, and he will need to do auditory processing activities. Each of these lessons is explained in detail at the back of this chapter.

So we see by the goals of this chapter, that although there is no new information for the child, although the sounds and the sound pictures are the same as in Chapter three, the words are longer, making the work much harder. We suggest that you follow the lesson plans in the order they are presented. Do all the lesson plans using the vowel-consonant-consonant (VCC) words, then the consonant-vowel-consonant-consonant (CVCC) words next and then consonant-consonant-vowel-consonant (CCVC) words last. This is suggested because it represents the order of difficulty. Children have the most trouble with adjacent consonants at the front of words. As in chapter three, you can do more than one lesson plan at a sitting. As in Chapter three, we urge lots of repetition. Old habits are hard to break, and new ones are hard to establish. *Repetition is the key.* Remember to keep practicing old lessons after you have moved on to new ones. A good format for your sessions is to warm up with old lessons for a few minutes and then move on to the newer ones.

If your child is a new reader, younger than the sixth month of first grade, you should keep following the Sound Doggy, skipping the first lesson, Auditory Processing with Adjacent Consonants. If your child is older than first grade, sixth month, you should do all of the lessons with him.

AUDITORY PROCESSING WITH ADJACENT CONSONANTS

Readiness

This lesson is not appropriate for children in first grade, sixth month, or younger. Do this lesson with children older than that age.

Goals

To cause the child to consciously understand how she can manipulate sounds to create and change words containing adjacent consonants.

To spell by sounds. This lesson uses nonsense words so the child who guesses a lot must spell by sounds.

Materials

The auditory processing cards and cue cards following this lesson plan.

An envelope to store each puzzle in and a shoebox to store the envelopes in.

Presentation

1. Lay out the sound pictures from one of the auditory processing puzzles.

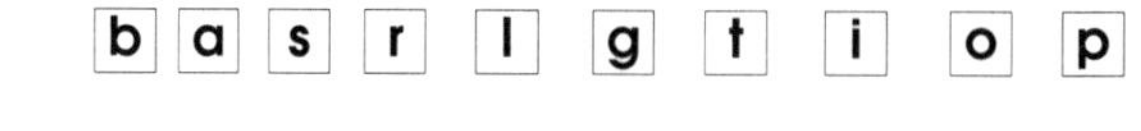

2. Hold the calling card

rap	lost
brap	gost
brip	got
bip	lot
bipt	slot
bopt	sot
bot	sop
blot	sob
lot	stob

in your hand so that your child cannot see the answers.

3. Say, "We're going to spell some made-up words. I'll go first. I'll spell 'rap.'" Use your pointer finger to slide the sound pictures one at a time into position to spell 'rap.' Say each sound as you line up the corresponding sound picture. Do this on the first set of lines, a few inches below the line of sound pictures.

continued

Auditory Processing with Adjacent Consonants, continued

4. Now, use your pointer finger or a pencil to point to each sound picture as your child says the corresponding sounds. If he is still learning the corresponding sounds, say each sound and then have him repeat it after you. Make sure he is looking at the sound pictures, and not at you, as he says the sounds.
5. Now say, "If that spells 'rap,' let's spell 'brap.' Use your pointer finger or a pencil to slowly move across the word 'rap,' as you say the new word, 'brap.' This will help bring his attention to the location of the sound picture that must be changed. Do not say the sounds separately, but as slowly as you can. This causes him to have to segment the sounds. Be very careful to make sure your pencil or pointer finger is in the correct location, over the corresponding sound as you slowly say the word.

6. Continue with each change, offering help as needed. After each change, point to each sound picture and have him say each sound in the word, as described in step four.

Correcting Problems

The child chooses the wrong sound picture.

EX: Change 'brap' to 'brip,' child spells 'brop.'

You want to find out if he heard the sound 'o' when you said 'brip,' or if he thinks the sound picture **<o>** represents the sound 'i'. Say, "What sound is this (indicate the **<o>**)?" If he says 'o' say, "Yes, that's right. So this is 'brop.' We need 'brip.'" Try to accentuate the 'i' sound as you repeat the word.

The child omits a sound.

EX: brap is spelled bap.

Say, "You've left out a sound. Let's see what's missing." Run your finger over the word as you say the word slowly. Do not segment the sounds. Your child will

continued

learn best if he is encouraged to detect the sounds on his own. By running your finger over the word as you say the sound, you are giving him an opportunity to hear something that he has failed to represent visually, and to discover his own mistake.

He indicates a sound picture and says two blended sounds.

EX: **<b>** = 'br'.

Say, "You said 'br' for this (indicate the **<b>** sound picture). But 'br' is two sounds. What are the two sounds in 'br'?"

AUDITORY PROCESSING WITH ADJACENT CONSONANTS

For use with Auditory Processing with Adjacent Consonants. Cut auditory processing puzzles and store them in an envelope in a shoebox.

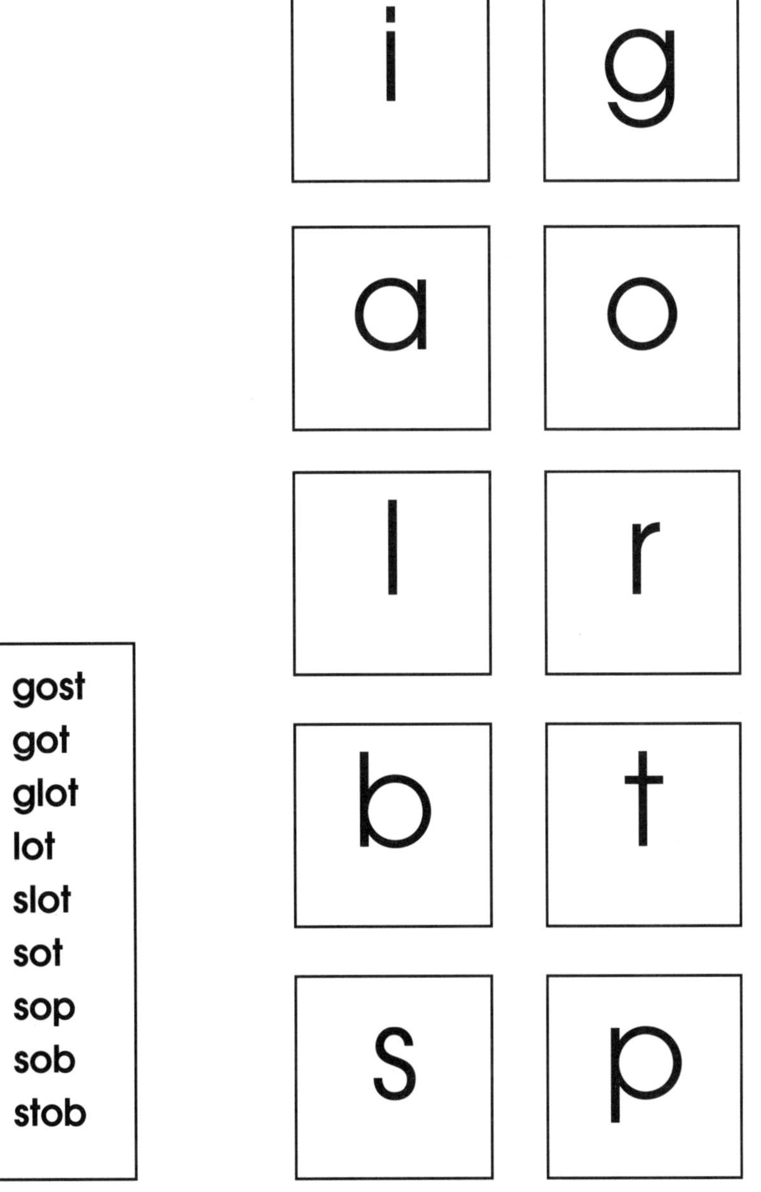

AUDITORY PROCESSING WITH ADJACENT CONSONANTS

For use with Auditory Processing with Adjacent Consonants. Cut auditory processing puzzles and store them in an envelope in a shoebox.

o	s
g	g
i	w
r	a
t	f

og	**trif**
gog	**trig**
grog	**twig**
trog	**swig**
tog	**swag**
stog	**swaf**
stof	**saf**
tof	**gaf**
trof	**graf**

AUDITORY PROCESSING WITH ADJACENT CONSONANTS

For use with Auditory Processing with Adjacent Consonants. Cut auditory processing puzzles and store them in an envelope in a shoebox.

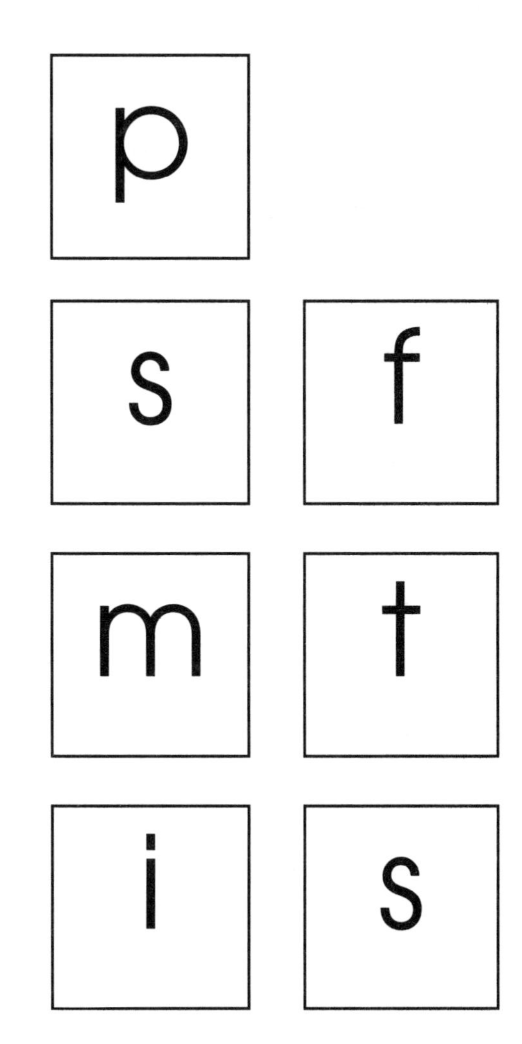

stip
sip
sips
sisp
sis
sif
stif
tif
tifs
tis
tisp
isp
misp
mip
smip
smit
smis
stis

WORD BUILDING WITH ADJACENT CONSONANTS

Readiness

Do this lesson with any child. Be sure your child has had sufficient success with the lessons in Chapter three before moving to this level. If your child is younger than first grade, sixth month, try this lesson and see how he does. If he has a lot of trouble and doesn't respond to any of the error corrections after several attempts, discontinue lessons in this chapter for about two months and then try again.

Goals

To cause the child to understand the sight to sound relationship of text.

To cause the child to understand the left to right relationship of text.

To cause the child to consciously understand how he can represent sounds in words.

To create an automatic spelling strategy.

To offer the child experience and practice doing all of the above using words that contain adjacent consonants.

Materials

The VCC, CVCC, or CCVC word building puzzles following this lesson plan.

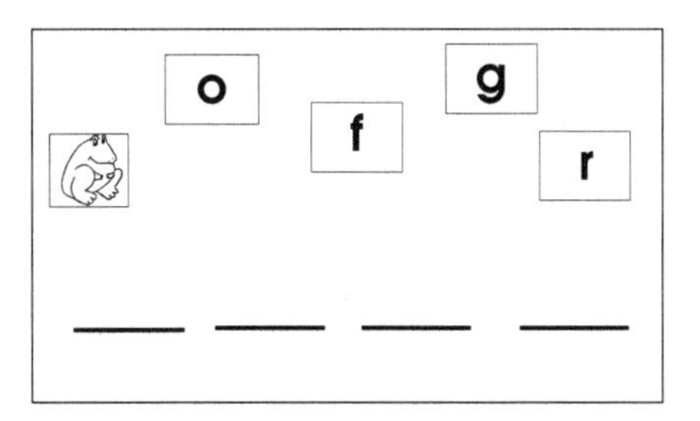

One envelope for each word puzzle and picture.

One file shoebox large enough to store envelopes.

Cut up word puzzles ahead of time. Write the name of each puzzle on the in-side flap of the envelope. Store puzzles in envelopes in your shoebox.

continued

Word Building with Adjacent Consonants, continued

Presentation

The word 'frog' is used as an example. The lesson is the same for all of the adjacent consonant-sound word-building puzzles.

1. Draw a line for each sound along the bottom of your dry erase board. Being careful not to reveal the word on the envelope, lay out the sound pictures from the envelope marked 'frog.' Say, "What's the first sound you hear in 'frog'?" Run your finger along the four lines as you slowly say 'frog.' Do not segment the sounds in the word, but say the word very slowly. 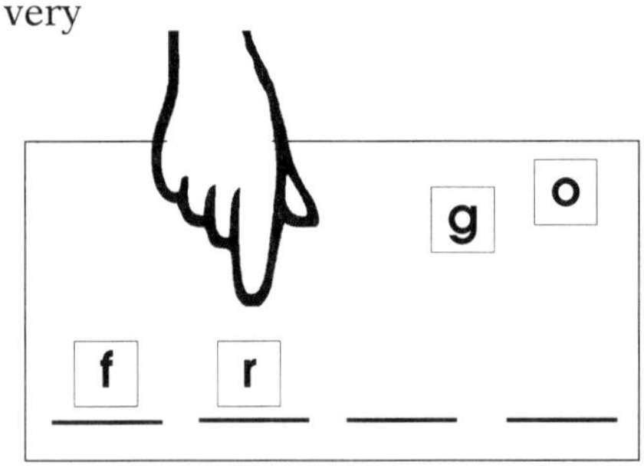
2. After he tells you what sound he hears first, invite him to find the corresponding sound picture. Make sure he says the sound as he puts the sound picture on the first line. Once he has placed the first sound picture say, "Good, what's the next sound you hear in 'frog'?" Once again, you should run your finger along over the lines as you slowly say, 'frog.' Make certain that he says each sound as he locates the corresponding sound picture and places it in sequence.
3. After all sound picture cards have been placed, have him say each sound as you point to its sound picture in sequence. Once all the sound pictures have been placed, have him map the word on a piece of lined paper. When mapping he should say one sound at a time *as* he writes the sound picture for that sound. Mapping should be clear, concise, and completely segmented.

After this lesson proceed to the other VCC lessons before going on to CVCC and then CCVC.

Correcting Problems

The child links two or more sounds when asked to give the sounds in a word.

EX: 'fr' 'o' 'g'

Say, "'fr' is two sounds. What's the *first* sound in 'fr'?" Accentuate your mouth and the changing of the sounds as you question. Do not separate the two sounds for him.

His sound production is bad. He adds an 'u' sound after consonants.

EX: 'frog' 'fu' 'ru' 'o' 'gu'

Simply repeat the sound correctly and say, "'f', not 'f...u'," (accentuating the difference in the two sounds in 'fu').

He uses letter names. "The first sound in frog is 'ef'."

Simply say , "No, that is the *letter name.* Letter names won't help you learn to spell or read. What *sound* do you *hear*? Tell me what you *hear,* not the letter name." Do not ask the question "What sound does 'ef' make?" This wrongly reinforces the strategy that letters make sounds. Letters do not make sounds, people do.

VCC WORD BUILDING

Cut word building puzzles and store them in envelopes. Store envelopes in a shoebox.

elk

elm

ant

alp

asp

VCC WORD BUILDING

Cut word building puzzles and store them in envelopes. Store envelopes in a shoe-box.

aft

elf

amp

and

CVCC WORD BUILDING

Cut word building puzzles and store them in envelopes. Store envelopes in a shoe-box.

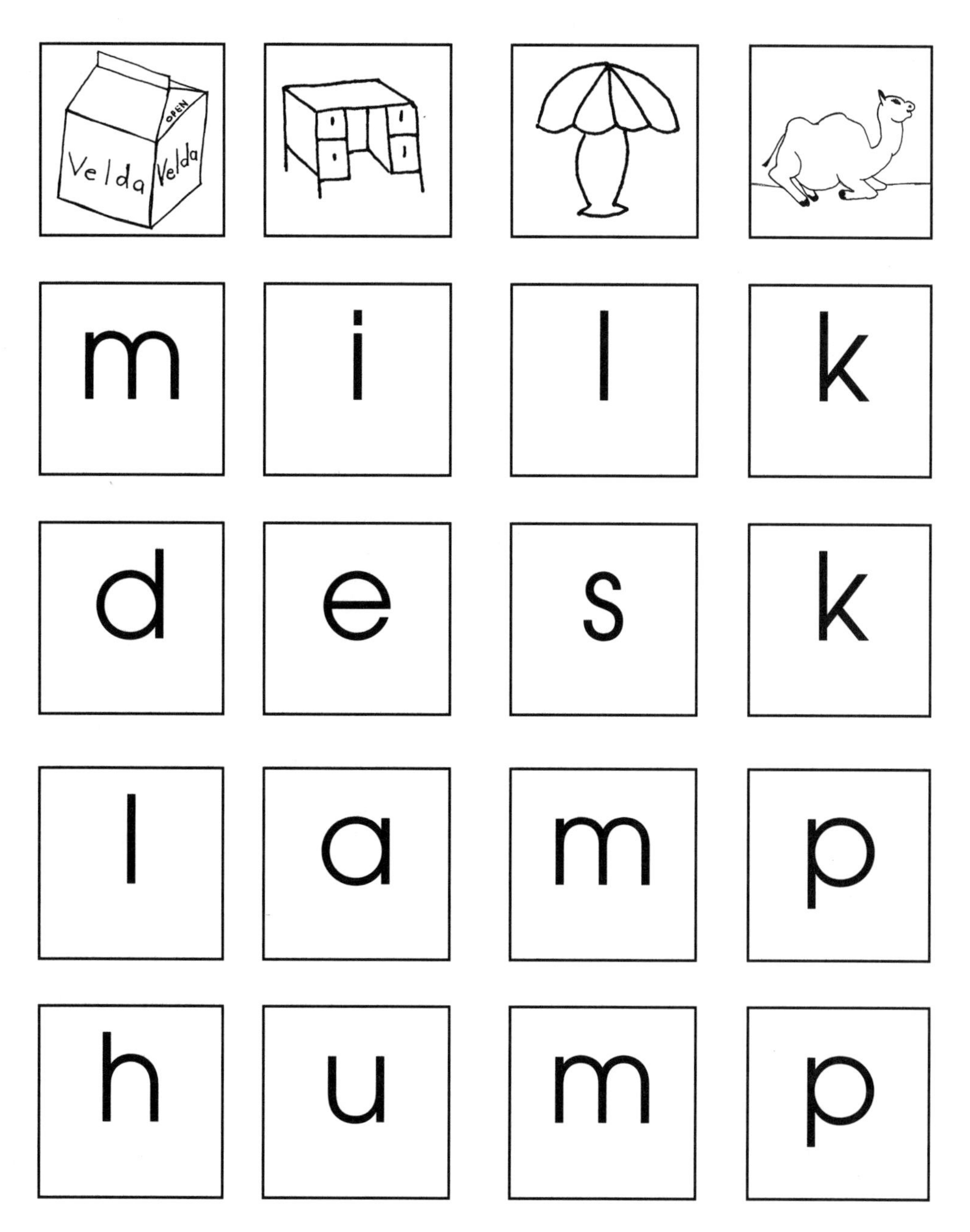

hump lamp desk milk

CVCC WORD BUILDING

Cut word building puzzles and store them in envelopes. Store envelopes in a shoebox.

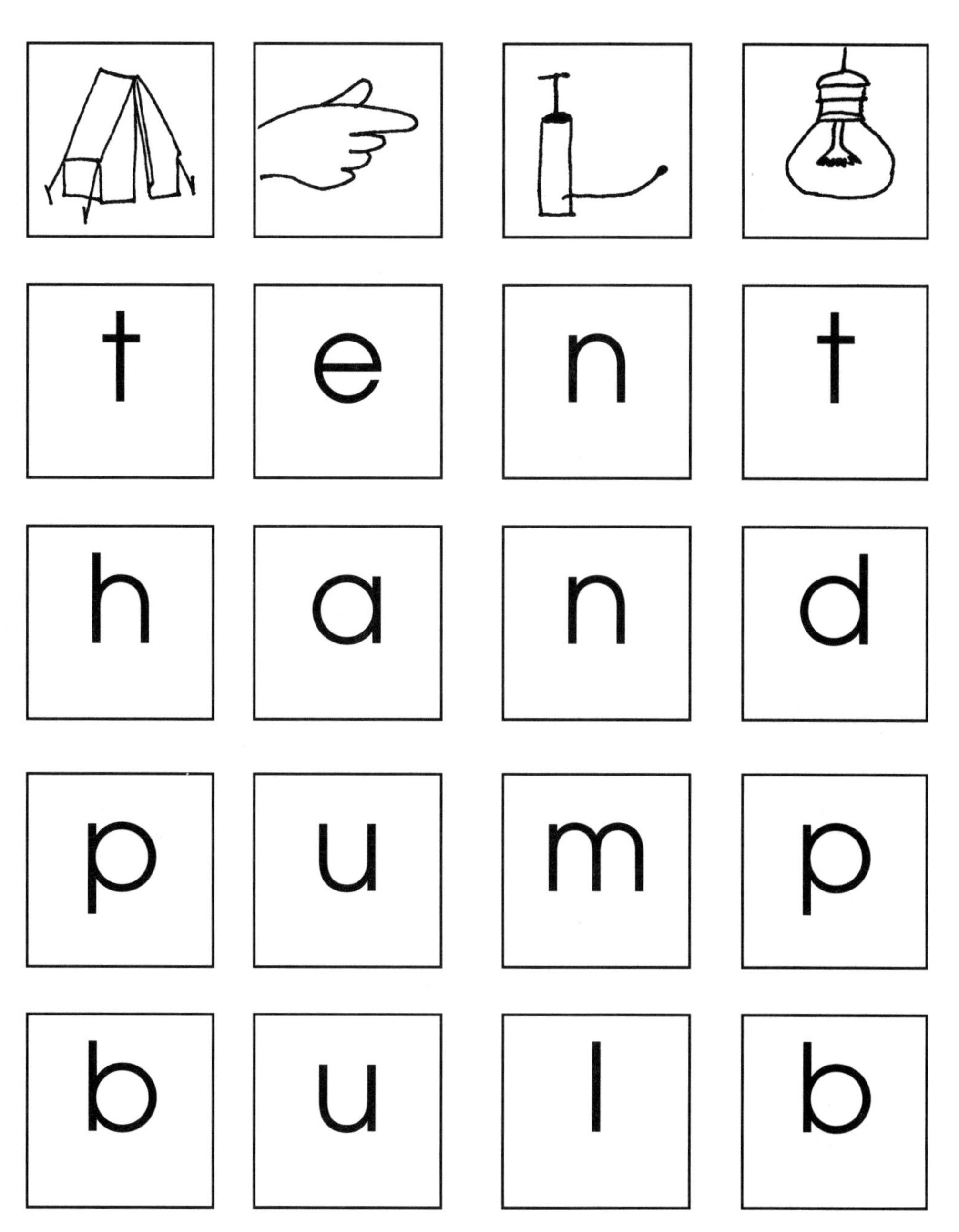

bulb pump hand tent

CCVC WORD BUILDING

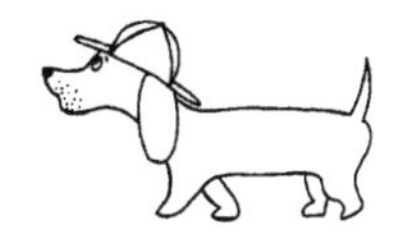

Cut word building puzzles and store them in envelopes. Store envelopes in a shoebox.

			2+2
s	t	o	p
f	l	a	g
f	r	o	g
p	l	u	s

plus flag frog stop

CCVC WORD BUILDING

Cut word building puzzles and store them in envelopes. Store envelopes in a shoe-box.

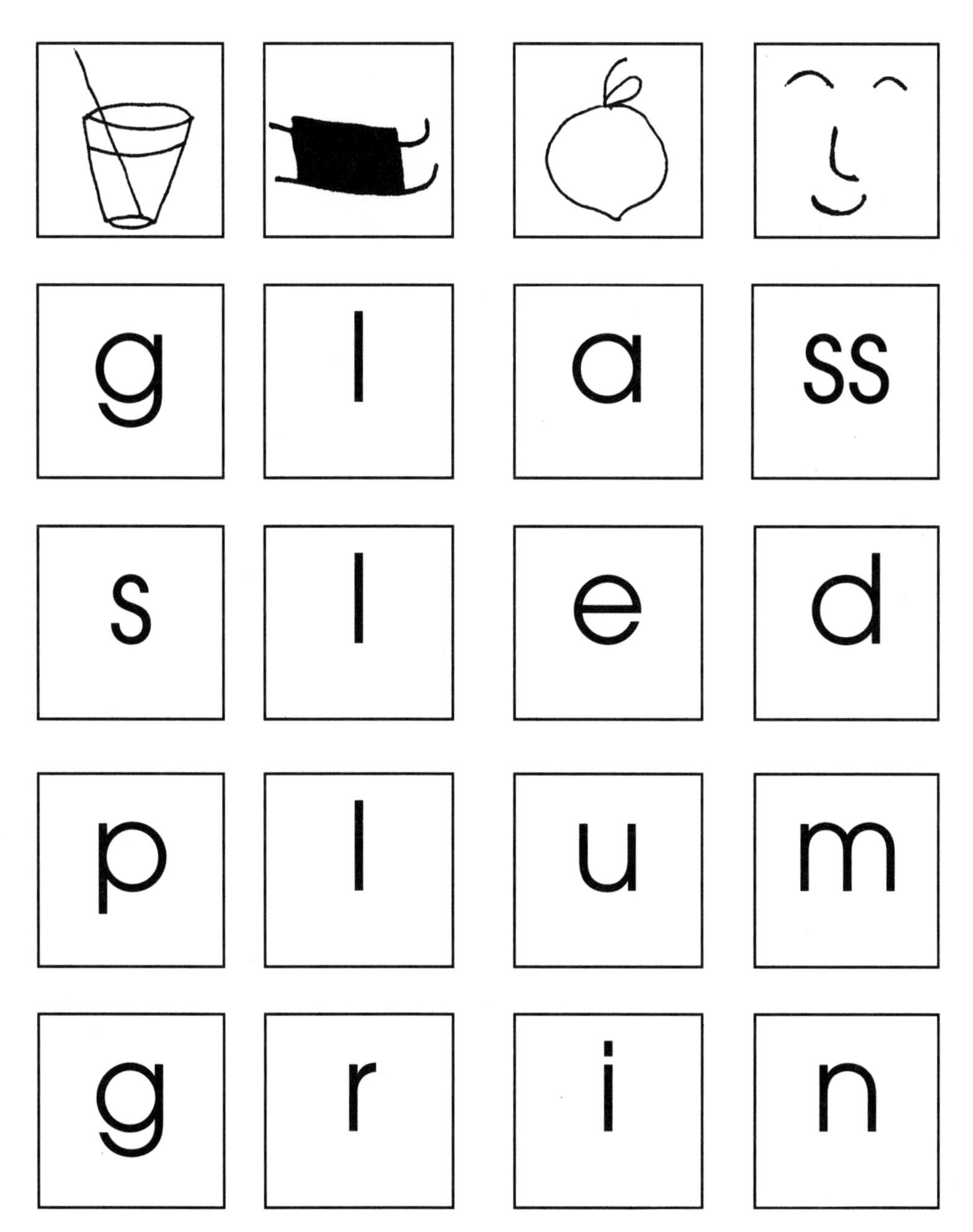

grin plum sled glass

DIRECTED READING WITH ADJACENT CONSONANTS

Readiness

Do this lesson with any child. Be sure your child has had sufficient success with the Word Building with Adjacent Consonants lesson before moving to this lesson. If your child is younger than first grade, sixth month, try this lesson and see how he does. If he has a lot of trouble and doesn't respond to any of the error corrections after several attempts, discontinue this lesson and continue to do the adjacent consonant word building lesson with him, along with lessons in Chapter three. Try this lesson again in a few weeks.

Goals

To learn that sounds blend together to make words.

To offer practice at blending sounds to read a word that contains adjacent consonants.

Materials

The word lists following this lesson plan. These can be cut up and stored in an envelope.

The dry erase board, or a piece of lined paper.

Presentation

1. Show the child the first word.
2. Ask him to read the sounds.
3. Encourage him to say the blended word.
4. Have him map the word onto a piece of lined paper. Make sure he says each sound as he writes the corresponding sound picture.

Correcting Problems

The child reads all the sounds correctly, but when he blends them there is something wrong. For example, 'c' 'l' 'a' 'p' comes out 'cap.' This is especially common among children who have developed a guessing strategy.

continued

Directed Reading with Adjacent Consonants, continued

Say, "You said all the sounds, but when you blended them you read 'cap.' You left out the 'l' sound. Try again, please."

The child has great difficulty blending sounds. He says all the sounds correctly, but really can't seem to blend them together to get the word.

Teach him to blend as he goes. EX: For the word 'clap,' have him stop and blend the first two sounds 'c' 'l' ... 'cl' and then the next 'cl' 'a'... 'cla' and then add on the last sound 'cla'... 'p'... 'clap.'

frog

Variation of Presentation

Some children are simply unable to blend for a long period of time. This is especially true of young children. If this is the case with your child, try this variation before going on to the above presentation.

1. Show your child the first word. Say, "This is 'frog.'" Let's say all the sounds in 'frog.'
2. Use your finger to indicate each sound picture as your child says the segmented sounds "'f' 'r' 'o' 'g'."
3. Have him map the word onto a sheet of lined paper. Make sure he says each sound as he writes the corresponding sound picture.

Knowing what the word says and then blending it will help your child understand what blending is, and to hear the word happening as he blends it, by already knowing what the word is.

DIRECTED READING WITH ADJACENT CONSONANTS

For use with Directed Reading and Spelling Practice with Adjacent Consonants

aft	ask
act	and
elf	asp
elk	imp
elm	ink
alp	end

DIRECTED READING WITH ADJACENT CONSONANTS

For use with Directed Reading and Spelling Practice with Adjacent Consonants

lamp	golf
mask	desk
fast	hand
hump	milk
bend	tent
rust	help
pump	mint
bulb	soft

DIRECTED READING WITH ADJACENT CONSONANTS

For use with Directed Reading and Spelling Practice with Adjacent Consonants

frog	drip
plug	clam
flag	trip
twig	grab
swim	trap
stop	club
drum	grin
spot	twin

SPELLING PRACTICE WITH ADJACENT CONSONANTS

Readiness

Do this lesson with any child who has done fairly well at all the lessons in this chapter up to this lesson.

Goals

To give the child practice spelling words containing adjacent consonant sounds.

Materials

Lined paper and pencil or dry erase board and markers.

The word lists preceding this lesson plan.

Presentation

1. Explain that you're going to play a spelling game.
2. Give the child a piece of lined paper or use the dry erase board.
3. Call out one word at a time from your word list.
4. Explain that he should say the sounds as he writes the sound pictures.

Correcting Problems

The child doesn't say the sounds when spelling the words.

Do not allow him to spell silently. He may be spelling by letter names rather than sounds. Many children memorize whole words by making the letter names into a kind of song, "bee ar ay gee... 'brag.'" This undermines your efforts to help him learn to spell and read. Make him say each sound as he spells the words.

He leaves out sounds.

EX: 'brag' = bag.

Say, "You left out a sound. Cover the word that he has written and say, "Tell me all the sounds in 'brag.'" As the child says the sounds he will reveal his problem.

EX: He may say 'br' for the first sound as he writes **<b>**.

continued

Spelling Practice with Adjacent Consonants, continued

In this case, say, "'br' is two sounds. What's the first sound in 'br'?" Or, he may say 'b' 'a' 'g' are all the sounds in 'brag.' In this case say, "I'm going to say the word slowly so you can notice what sound is after the 'b' 'brrrrag'" (stretching out the sound as much as possible).

READING STORIES THAT CONTAIN ADJACENT CONSONANTS

Readiness

You should begin this lesson once your child has begun to read words containing adjacent consonant sounds with success. If you're working with an older child who might think the stories are silly, it is not necessary to do this lesson unless he wants to.

Goals

To practice reading adjacent consonants in stories.

Materials

The stories following this lesson plan.

Presentation

1. Explain to your child that you are going to read a story together.
2. Show him the story and ask him to read the words. Use your finger to redirect him and to correct problems as needed, just as you would if he were reading isolated words.
3. After each phrase or sentence say, "Yes, very good," then reread the phrase or sentence to him. This will assure that he follows the theme of the story despite any difficulty he has had in reading the words.
4. If your child doesn't want to read every sentence, you can take turns. You can read one sentence and she can read one sentence. When it's your turn, you should read slowly, modeling how you want her to say each sound and blend them into words.

Correcting Problems

All problems can be corrected in the same way as if he were reading isolated words. See the Directed Reading with Adjacent Consonants lesson plan on page 185.

STAN'S PLANT

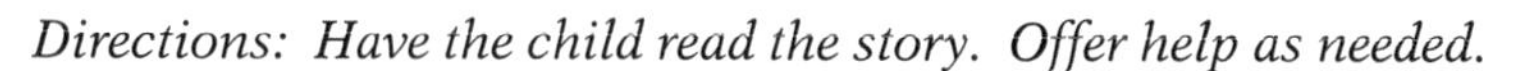

Directions: Have the child read the story. Offer help as needed.

Difficult words: 'a' 'to' 'his'

Stan did plant
a nut.

1

It did pop up
from its pot.

2

It did not stop.

3

His plant
got stu**ck**.
"It must
stop!"

4

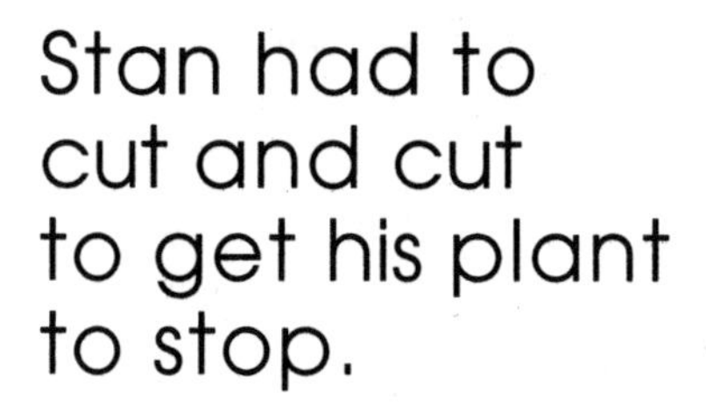

Stan had to
cut and cut
to get his plant
to stop.

5

It is a log.

6

And a desk.

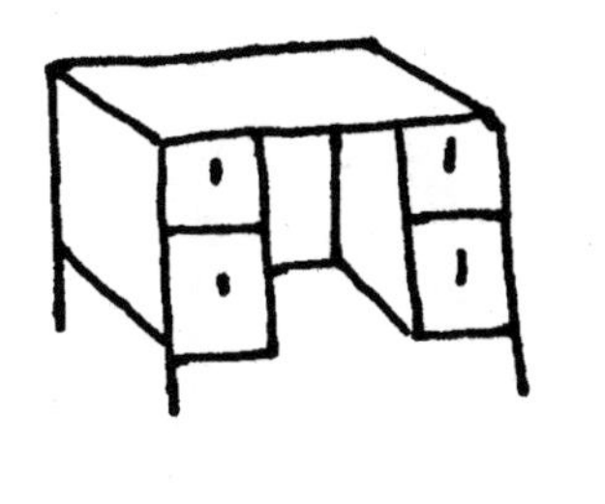

7

And a stump.

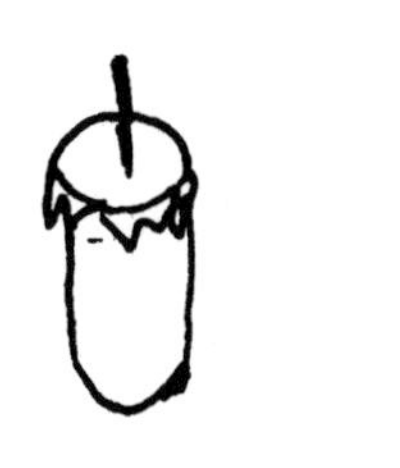

8

SKIP'S GIFT

Directions: Have the child read the story. Offer help as needed.

Difficult words: 'a' 'to' 'his'

Fred is sad.
His gift to Skip
is lost.
1

Skip is just a
kid. Skip will
be sad not to
get a gift.
2

In it is his gift.
4

Skip is glad to get his gift. It is a top.
5

"A gift is fun!"
6

Skip's gift will spin and spin.
7

The End
8

THE TRIP

Directions: Have the child read the story. Offer help as needed.

Difficult words: 'to' 'a' 'his'

Gle**nn** and Fran wi**ll** get a trip. Gle**nn** has a tent.

1

Gle**nn** and Fran will camp in a tent.

2

His tent is in his bag, and a cap

and a map.

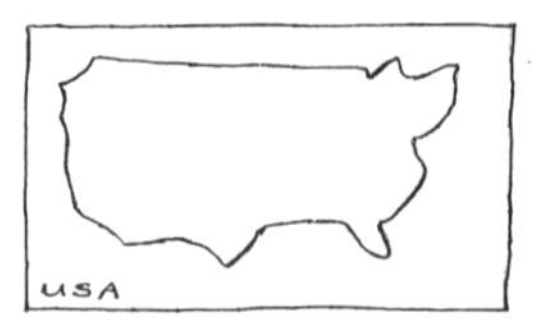

3

It is a fun trip to camp in a tent. It is up!

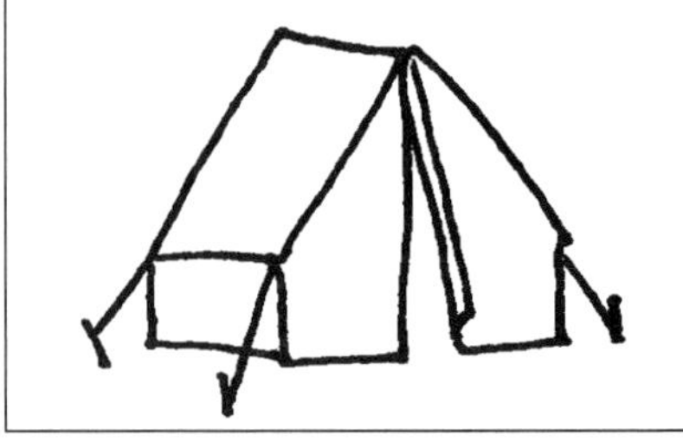

4

In it is a cot
and a frog!

5

Gle**nn** is mad.
Gle**nn** wi**ll** drop
it in a bag and
get it to a
pond to
get a
swim.

At camp is a
print. It is at
his tent.

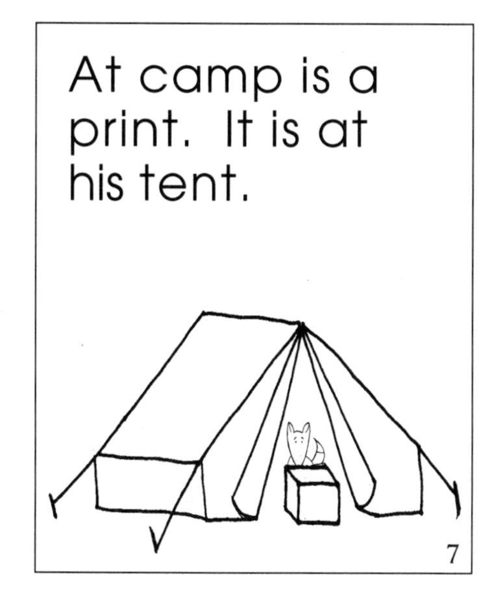

7

It is a fox

8

What's Next?

Now that you've finished the lessons in Chapter four it's time to move on to Chapter five. If your child is a new reader, first grade, sixth month, or younger, you should read the chapter and then, following the flying Sound Doggy  try a few of the first lessons to see how your child does. If he has a lot of trouble and doesn't respond to the error corrections, discontinue lessons in Chapter five for a few weeks and then try again. Continue to practice Chapter four lessons in the meantime.

If your child is older than first grade, sixth month, read Chapter five and then make your way through all the lesson plans and materials.

CHAPTER FIVE

TEACHING THE ADVANCED CODE

You and your child have come quite a long way. Let's look at our list of reading subskills from Chapter one, and see where you stand.

Subskills Necessary to Reading

- [x] Ability to scan text from left to right
- [x] Ability to match visual symbols to auditory sounds **<t>** = 't'
- [x] Ability to blend discrete sound units into words
- [x] Ability to segment sounds in words
- [ ] Ability to understand that sometimes two or more letters represent a sound (EX: sh i p)
- [ ] Ability to understand that most sounds can be represented in more than one way (EX: the sound 'a-e' can be spelled in several ways: train, play, paper, and more)
- [ ] Ability to understand that there is overlap in the code, that some components of the code can represent more than one sound (EX: **<o>** can spell 'o' as in hot, or 'oe' as in 'most')

By now your child should be scanning text from left to right, matching visual symbols to auditory sounds, blending discrete sounds into words, and segmenting sounds in words. He might still have occasional trouble blending all the sounds into a word, or including them all when he spells words, but overall he should be coming along nicely. Now that your child is able to decode words that contain sounds represented by one letter, it's time to address the goals of this chapter, the advanced code.

Goal #1. Ability to understand that sometimes two or more letters represent a sound (EX: sh i p)

Grasping the concept that two or more letters can represent a sound is very difficult for many children, and requires explicit instruction. As an accomplished adult reader, you take the advanced code for granted. It's a subconscious part of your inventory of reading skills. But parents mustn't assume that their new reader has this same inventory. Using a code that switches from a one symbol = one sound logic, to a two symbols = one sound logic, is not so very simple. By the middle of first grade, your child will begin to encounter numerous words containing sounds that are represented by two symbols. We call this *advanced code.* Don't make the assumption that a young child who is doing well at reading and spelling the basic code will make the cognitive leap to the advanced code level. He may not. By fourth grade approximately 60 percent of the written words your child is exposed to will contain sounds represented by advanced code. But according to the U.S. Department of Education test scores that we shared with you in Chapter one, 40 percent of American students fall below basic competency by the end of fourth grade. These numbers are not mitigated by I.Q., socioeconomic status, or any other factor you might be hoping will push your child to the fortunate side of the odds. In Chapter one, we told you of our survey of young children that proves that they can master the logic of the code. The more you rely on the concept of letters and groups of letters as pictures of sounds, the easier it will be for your child. Look at the left column that follows for a simple example of how children construct their art using multiple shapes. The right column shows how they can use that same logic to construct sound pictures using multiple letters.

Δ = triangle	**<a> = 'a' as in 'hat'**
❑ = square	**<i> = 'i' as in 'hit'**
but...	**but...**
Δ❑ = house	**<ai> = 'a-e' as in 'rain'**
...no relation to triangle or square	**...no relationship to 'a' or 'i'**

As our example depicts, children combine symbols to build objects in their artwork. They have no trouble with this logic whatsoever. So, as their mentors, we must give them opportunities to see that the same logic applies to the written code for their language. The lessons in this chapter accomplish that goal carefully.

Goal # 2. Ability to understand that most sounds can be represented in more than one way (EX: The sound 'a-e' can be spelled in several ways...train, play, paper, and more)

Unfortunately, the English written code was not created in a vacuum. Over several hundred years, from the late sixth century until about 1500, the code evolved in remote locations of Great Britain. Great Britain is a country that had many cultural influences during that period of history, so we see French and Latin influences, Germanic influences, and a great deal of creativity. This is how we ended up with so many ways to spell a given sound. The **<eigh>** spelling of the sound 'a-e', for instance, has a Germanic origin, while the **<ay>** spelling of the same sound comes from our French forefathers.

Although some older children appreciate knowing how the code got so confusing, it isn't necessary that you tell your child about the history of our language. Learning the various spellings or sound pictures for the various sounds requires no background, but does require lots and lots of repetition. In addition to the mapping and word analysis lessons contained in this chapter, your child needs to be reading every day, with you in attendance and ready to offer code support as needed. We're not saying that this will be easy for your child to understand, or that he will like the idea that he has to memorize a bunch of sound pictures. What we are saying is that he *can* do it.

Some children actually get kind of irritable when they begin to learn the advanced code. At present I have seven-year-old Lucy in reading therapy. Lucy is a very bright little girl who was held back to repeat first grade last year because of reading failure. At the point in her therapy when we began working on advanced code, she expressed deep disgust at the nature of the advanced code. We were working on the sound 'o-e', and all the ways to represent it, when she looked me right square in the eyes and said, "This is so stupid! Why are some sounds spelled with one letter and some with two letters? How come there are so many ways to spell each sound?" We get this kind of irritability a lot at the point of discovery. Young children tend to think we at Read America are somehow responsible for this lack of consistency. I told Lucy that the English written code is an ancient one, that it was invented a long time ago and that I personally had nothing to do with it. I explained that my job was to teach her how it works. She was happy with that, especially when she began to see that our system for organizing the information works quite well.

Giving the child new information is only one job of education. Giving him a plan for organizing that information is just as important. Without that, he cannot possibly understand and retain the new information. The word list on the left below, shows twenty-eight words that contain the sound 'o-e'. The picture on the right shows how your child can organize these 'o-e' words under the various 'o-e' sound pictures. By using this seemingly simple procedure, your child will come to learn all the sound pictures for all the sounds, and that although there is variation, it is predictable.

note	so
show	glow
tone	toe
host	coal
goat	stroke
most	crow
roast	loaf
poke	toast
throw	home
coast	grow
pole	boat
know	no
foe	boast
cone	mold

oa	oe
boat	note
toast	cone
goat	tone
roast	tote
float	hope
groan	
coat	

ow	o
show	hold
glow	bold
grow	most
know	host
throw	no
snow	mold

As the Mapping and Sorting lesson plan explains, your child will say each sound as he writes the words in the various categories. This will give him continued practice at segmenting, and it will encourage him to notice the various sound pictures each time he writes them in a word.

Goal #3. Ability to understand that there is overlap in the code, that some components of the code can represent more than one sound (EX: **<o>** can spell 'o' as in 'hot,' or 'oe' as in 'most')

With the historical influences mentioned above, it is no wonder that the resulting English written code contains a great deal of overlap. Children are capable of understanding that there is overlap in the code, as long as they are taught that it's predictable and not just chaos at work. The following word list on the left shows words that contain the sound picture **<ow>** which can represent the sound 'o-e' as in 'show,' or 'ow' as in 'now.' By having your child read these words and decide if they are 'o-e' or 'ow' words, as we do in the Sound Sorting lesson you are carefully teaching him about the overlap in the code.

sh **ow**
c **ow**
h **ow**
g r **ow**
th r **ow**
t **ow**
f l **ow**
n **ow**
f r **ow** n
c l **ow** n
c r **ow**
b r **ow** n

the sound 'oe'	the sound 'ow'
know	brown
show	town
grow	clown
glow	frown
throw	down

In addition to understanding it, children need a strategy for managing the overlap. We've already demonstrated that children don't manage rules very well. It's important to understand that the rules of typical phonics programs are inaccurate. So, the strategy we teach is to simply try the possibilities. This requires, of course, that your child should *know* the possibilities. The first step is to know what sounds all the symbols can represent. The second step is to learn to try them when you encounter a word you don't know. The lesson plans at the back of this chapter explain the steps in detail.

With the numerous challenges of the advanced code level, it becomes more important than ever to offer clear instruction and example to your young reader. This story of nine-year-old Daniel demonstrates how important it is to offer clarity to your child as he approaches the advanced code. Daniel's mother contacted our clinic in the fall of 1992. At the intake appointment she expressed her frustration. Daniel was a bright child with an I.Q. of 129. As a kindergartner, he had taught himself to read. "It just happened," his mother explained. "He could read all his little books by first grade. He just never got any better at it when the words got longer." Daniel began having trouble in second grade, and by third grade he had been placed in a learning disabilities (L.D.) classroom. Daniel's mother had just attended his annual school staffing, intended to report Daniel's standardized test scores to all parties working with him. A standardized score is a score that has been statistically adjusted so that it can be compared to other standardized test scores. Standard scores are considered to be within the normal range from 95 to 105.

Daniel's classroom teacher, the school L.D. teacher, the guidance counselor, and Daniel's parents were present. The staffing had revealed that Daniel's reading scores had not improved in the twelve months since he was last tested, despite the fact that during that period he had been included in an L.D. pull-out class where he received special clinical reading instruction in a small group format for fifty minutes each day. The L.D. class that Daniel attended was part of a federal program. Each school in Daniel's school district received an allotment of federal funds to pay for the teacher and materials necessary to run the program. Daniel qualified for this program because his I.Q. (standard score 129) was significantly higher than his reading performance score (standard score 71). Standard scores are considered within the normal range from 95 to 105, so Daniel's I.Q. was considerably above normal, and his reading score was seriously low. This standard score was derived from the standardized Woodcock Reading Mastery Test, which revealed that at the start of fourth grade, Daniel was reading at a second grade, first month level. The following are some examples of his errors on the Woodcock word identification subtest:

watch	white	**sleep**	sheep
find	found	**early**	easy
heavy	hurry	**already**	really
expert	export	**work**	wreck

We did a test to determine Daniel's code knowledge. Daniel scored correctly on 29 of 50 sound pictures, which placed his code knowledge at 58 percent. His ability to blend sounds into words was 14 of 15 trials (within the normal range). His ability to segment sounds in words was also within the normal range. His only problems were that he didn't know the code, and he failed to understand that he was supposed to decode the sound pictures in words. Daniel's only strategy was to look at the whole word as a unit and try to match its attributes to a prototype in his visual memory. Daniel was so accustomed to reading with low success that he did not even attempt to correct himself when his reading was obviously wrong, as in this example read at one early clinical session:

> Leroy got his car keys and
> walked out to the garage.

which Daniel read as, "Larry got his care keys and went out to his garbage."

Daniel attended twelve sessions of Phono-Graphix training at Read America during which time his mother conducted twelve at-home sessions to supplement therapy. At his final testing in January of 1993 (three months after therapy commenced) he scored at fourth grade, second month, on the Woodcock word identification subtest. On a recent longitudinal survey, Daniel's mother reported that he is now in a full-time gifted class, and getting As and Bs.

Daniel's is an extreme example of doing nothing to teach your child to read. As Daniel's mother confessed, he appeared to have taught himself to read, so she did nothing to help him along. Almost as detrimental as doing nothing to teach your child to read is doing the wrong things. The following story of eight-year-old Sandy shows how erroneous rules and misleading language can confuse the young reader.

Sandy's grandparents presented her for testing at the Read America clinic in the spring of 1993 following a meeting with her second-grade teacher. Sandy's teacher had advised that she be retained for another year in second grade due to poor reading. She had also referred Sandy to the school psychologist for diagnostic testing, and strongly suggested that Ritalin might help Sandy to "pay attention." Sandy's grandparents were opposed to holding her back and were adamantly against the use of Ritalin or any other drug to control Sandy's attention. We tested Sandy in May of 1993. Her code knowledge was 48 percent, her blending was perfect, and her segmenting was 61 correct out of 63 trials (in the high normal range). Her Woodcock word identification score was first grade, third month. Sandy's reading was like that of a computer-generated voice. When she attempted to read words, she made a sound for each letter of the word, regardless of whether or not certain letters worked together to spell one sound. So 'ship' was read as 's' 'h' 'i' 'p'➡ "s...hip," and 'train' was read as 't' 'r' 'a' 'i''n' ➡ "tra..in." Yet on the code knowledge test she scored correctly on the sound pictures **<ai>**, **<oa>**, and **<ee>**. Some of her errors included reading **<oy>** as 'o-e', **<au>** as 'ae', and **<ou>** as 'o-e'. Clearly, the limited code knowledge she had was not being used when she actually attempted to read a word. Also clear to us was the fact that someone had taught her the "two vowels walking" rule. This is an old phonics rule that says, "When two vowels go walking, the first one does the talking," which the child is supposed to ascertain means that the first vowel will say its long sound. This explains why Sandy knew the sound pictures **<ai>** as in 'rain,' **<oa>** as in 'boat,' and **<ee>** as in 'green,' but not **<oy>** as in 'joy,' **<au>** as in 'fault,' or **<ou>** as in 'loud,' which are among the 60 percent of the sound pictures which do not follow this rule.

When we began therapy with Sandy it became apparent that she had a lot of confusion about the nature of sound pictures. She kept proclaiming letters to be "silent." "Oh, I get it," she said early on in the first session, the "the 'double-you' is silent!" referring to the sound picture **<ow>** in the word 'down.' At the next session she announced that the **<o>** in 'most' said 'oe' because it was "long." Much time was spent in helping her to see that the vowels are all about the same length and that, indeed, all the letters are silent, and that it is we (the readers) who do the talking. The most misleading language I've heard regarding the advanced code is that of "silent letters." In Sandy's case it required holding the page to my ear and showing her that all the letters are silent. In fact, if letters spoke we wouldn't need to learn to read at all. We would need only to listen to their stories.

Another, quite comical example of a child confusing the issue of silence occurred just about a week ago. Richie, who is amost seven years old, has recently moved to our clinic from another clinic here in Orlando which uses a regimented phonics program. It has been clear in his first three sessions that he has been heavily indoctrinated with phonics rules, none of which has helped him read any better according to his father. Recently, we observed him working with his therapist, reading words containing adjacent consonant sounds. When presented with the word 'plan' he read it as 'plant.' His therapist repeated the word slowly as she ran her pencil point along under the word and accentuated the 't' he had read at the end. When she reached the end of the word she asked, "Where's the 't'?" He stared for a moment at the word 'plan' in front of him and then responded with cool confidence, "It's silent." Clearly, Richie was confusing the concept of silence with the concept of invisibility.

As you proceed through the lesson plans and word lists to teach your child the advanced code, we recommend that you present one sound per week. After the initial presentation you should do the lesson at least two more times during the week. As with the other chapters, do not allow your child to do the lesson alone. You must be present to supervise and make sure he is saying the sounds aloud, not using letter names, and not misreading words. Each of the lesson plans is followed by word lists you will use to do the lessons, or refers you to the page where you can find the word lists you need. Please take the time to read each lesson plan through and practice it carefully before doing it with your child.

If you're working with a new reader of first grade, sixth month, or younger, follow the flying Sound Doggy, as he appears on the lesson plans and in the boxes on the word lists.

If you're working with a child older than first grade, sixth month, you should do all of the lessons, having your child work with all of the words (including the Sound Doggy words).

The following sound picture charts are not necessary for instructional use, but are presented here as a quick visual aid. Each box contains a sound. On the left is the sound picture and on the right is a sample word. Keep in mind, as you look these over, that we live in a big country. Pronunciation of words and sounds varies considerably from region to region of the country. If you find that some of the words on the chart don't match your pronunciation of them, don't worry about it. Children approximate language quite well. Your child will likely not notice that there is a slight discrepancy. If he does, simply explain that some people say the sound as it is presented in the chart. Also, please notice that many of the sounds have very rare spellings. These rare spellings are presented last in each box. They are there for your reference and needn't be presented to children. They are not included in the word lists following the Mapping and Sorting lesson plan. Poster-size charts are available from Read America, Inc.

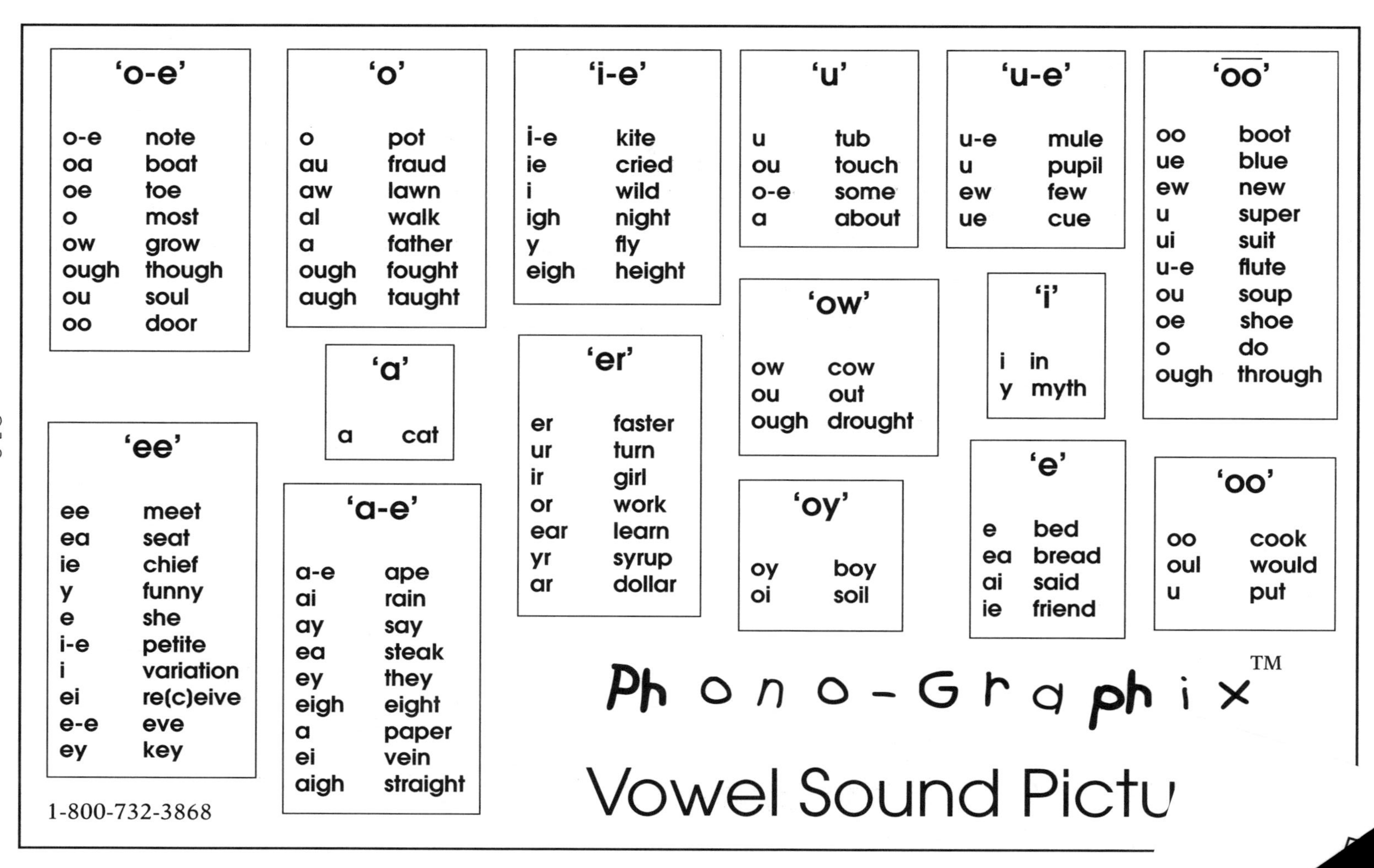
Phono-Graphix™
Vowel Sound Pictu
'o-e'
o-e note
oa boat
oe toe
o most
ow grow
ough though
ou soul
oo door
'o'
o pot
au fraud
aw lawn
al walk
a father
ough fought
augh taught
'i-e'
i-e kite
ie cried
i wild
igh night
y fly
eigh height
'u'
u tub
ou touch
o-e some
a about
'u-e'
u-e mule
u pupil
ew few
ue cue
'oo'
oo boot
ue blue
ew new
u super
ui suit
u-e flute
ou soup
oe shoe
o do
ough through
'a'
a cat
'er'
er faster
ur turn
ir girl
or work
ear learn
yr syrup
ar dollar
'ow'
ow cow
ou out
ough drought
'i'
i in
y myth
'ee'
ee meet
ea seat
ie chief
y funny
e she
i-e petite
i variation
ei re(c)eive
e-e eve
ey key
'a-e'
a-e ape
ai rain
ay say
ea steak
ey they
eigh eight
a paper
ei vein
aigh straight
'oy'
oy boy
oi soil
'e'
e bed
ea bread
ai said
ie friend
'oo'
oo cook
oul would
u put
1-800-732-3868

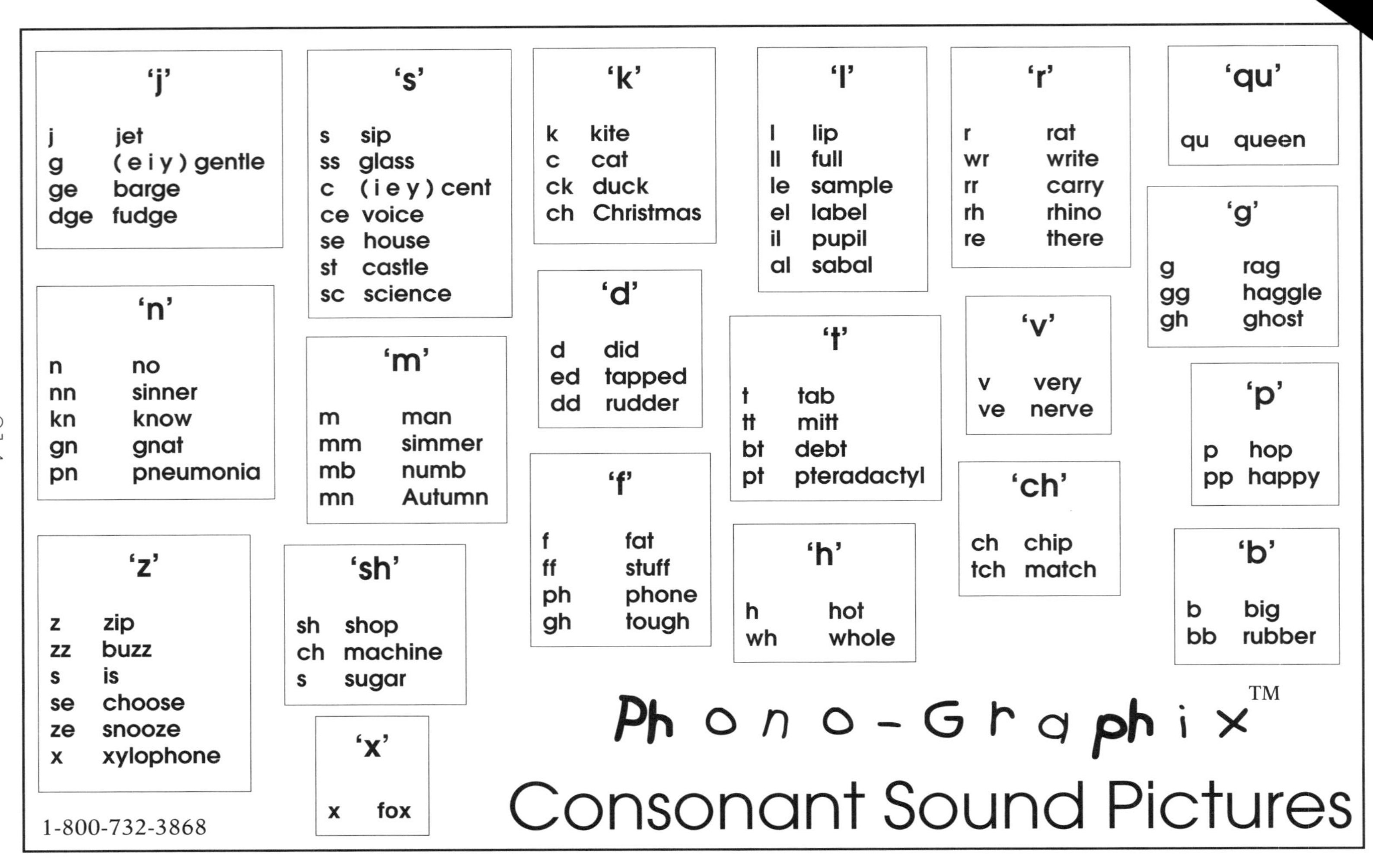
'j'
j jet
g (e i y) gentle
ge barge
dge fudge
's'
s sip
ss glass
c (i e y) cent
ce voice
se house
st castle
sc science
'k'
k kite
c cat
ck duck
ch Christmas
'l'
l lip
ll full
le sample
el label
il pupil
al sabal
'r'
r rat
wr write
rr carry
rh rhino
re there
'qu'
qu queen
'n'
n no
nn sinner
kn know
gn gnat
pn pneumonia
'm'
m man
mm simmer
mb numb
mn Autumn
'd'
d did
ed tapped
dd rudder
't'
t tab
tt mitt
bt debt
pt pteradactyl
'v'
v very
ve nerve
'g'
g rag
gg haggle
gh ghost
'p'
p hop
pp happy
'z'
z zip
zz buzz
s is
se choose
ze snooze
x xylophone
'sh'
sh shop
ch machine
s sugar
'f'
f fat
ff stuff
ph phone
gh tough
'h'
h hot
wh whole
'ch'
ch chip
tch match
'b'
b big
bb rubber
'x'
x fox
Phono-Graphix™
Consonant Sound Pictures
1-800-732-3868

WORD BUILDING WITH ADVANCED CODE

Readiness

Do this lesson with any child. If your child is younger than first grade, sixth month, try this lesson and see how he does. If he has a lot of trouble and doesn't respond to the error correction procedures, discontinue the lessons in this chapter for about two months and then try again.

Goals

To help your child make the connection that sound pictures can be constructed with more than one letter, and to offer him practice at mapping words with two-letter sound pictures.

Materials

The word building materials on the next four pages.

Presentation

The following lesson is offered with the word 'ship' as an example.

1. Draw a line for each sound along the bottom of your dry erase board. Being careful not to reveal the word on the envelope, lay out the sound pictures from the envelope marked 'ship.' Say, "What's the first sound you hear in 'ship'?" Run your finger along the three lines as you slowly say 'ship.' Do not segment the sounds in the word, but say the word very slowly.
2. After he tells you what sound he hears first say, "That's right, 'sh' is the first sound in 'ship.'" Show him the sound picture **<sh>** and say, "This is 'sh'." Ask him to say the sound and place it on the first line. Once he has placed the first sound picture say, "Good, what's the next sound you hear in 'ship'?" Once again, you should run your finger along over the lines as you slowly say, 'ship.' Make certain that he says each sound as he locates the corresponding sound picture and places it in sequence.
3. After all sound picture cards have been placed, have him say each sound as you point to its sound picture in sequence. Once all the sound pictures have

continued

Word Building with Advanced Code, continued

been placed, have him map the word on a piece of lined paper. When mapping he should say one sound at a time *as* he writes the sound picture for that sound. Mapping gets a little tricky when you are saying one sound and writing two letters. As always, mapping should be clear, concise and completely segmented.

Correcting Problems

Child sounds a two-letter sound picture as if it were two separate sound pictures.

EX: <**sh**> = 's' 'h'.

Point to the sound picture and say the sound. EX: 'sh'.

Child forgets the sound or uses the wrong sound for a sound picture.

Point to the sound picture and say the sound. EX: 'sh'.

WORD BUILDING WITH ADVANCED CODE

For use with the lesson Word Building with Advanced Code.

ship

shot

dish

shop

WORD BUILDING WITH ADVANCED CODE

For use with the lesson Word Building with Advanced Code.

bath

moth

that

thug

WORD BUILDING WITH ADVANCED CODE

For use with the lesson Word Building with Advanced Code.

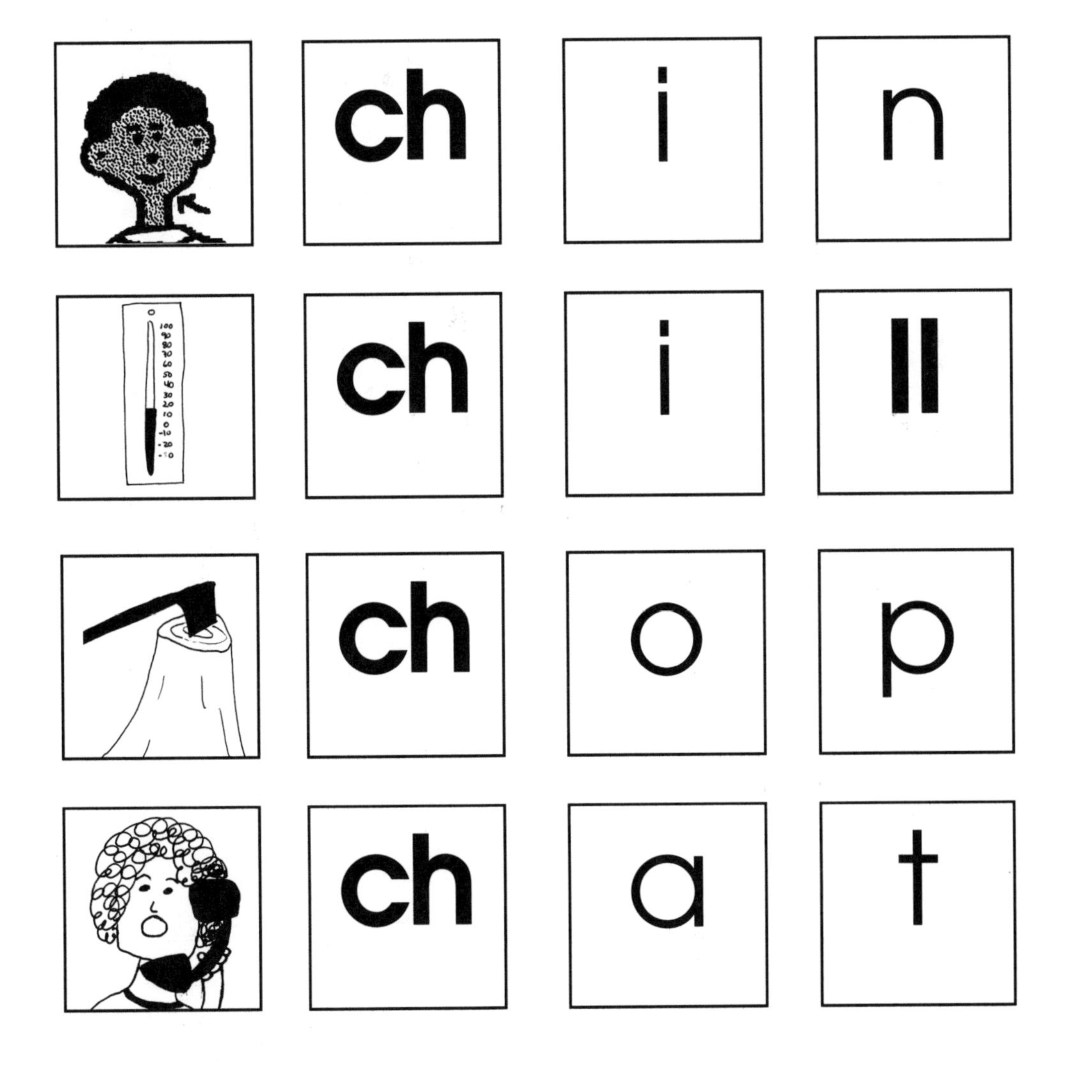

chin

chill

chop

chat

WORD BUILDING WITH ADVANCED CODE

For use with the lesson Word Building with Advanced Code.

sock

lock

tick

lick

PRACTICING COMMON CONSONANT SOUND PICTURES

Readiness

Once your child has completed the lesson Word Building with Advanced Code, he should be ready to begin learning the rest of the advanced code without having to word build. If your child is younger than first grade, sixth month, try this lesson and see how he does. If he has a lot of trouble and doesn't respond to the error correction procedures, discontinue the lessons in this chapter for about two months and then try again.

Goals

To familiarize your child with commonly seen consonant sound pictures represented with two letters. Being familiar with these will allow him to begin to read and spell using these commonly seen sound pictures.

Materials

The common sound pictures lists that follow this lesson.

Presentation

1. Explain to your child that the sound 'sh' is shown as **<sh>**.
2. Invite him to 'map' the list of **<sh>** words on the next page. To map, he should say each sound as he writes the corresponding sound picture. So, he would write **<sh>**, as he says the sound 'sh', and **<i>** as he says 'i', and **<p>** as he says 'p'.
3. Continue on with the **<ch>** and **<th>** words in the same way.

Correcting Problems

He tries to sound out each letter.

EX: 's' 'h' 'i' 'p'

Remind him that, as you have already said, **<sh>** (indicating the sound picture with your pencil point) is a picture of one sound 'sh'.

The Sound Picture <sh>

	shop	di**sh**
	shot	**sh**e**ll**
ship	wi**sh**	**sh**ut
shag	swi**sh**	**sh**in

The Sound Picture <th>

	this	**th**em
thug	wi**th**	ba**th**
that	**th**en	mo**th**

The Sound Picture <ch>

	chip	**ch**in
chop	**ch**ug	**ch**imp
mu**ch**	**ch**ap	**ch**i**ll**

The Sound Picture <ck>

	tu**ck**	li**ck**
	sa**ck**	Ri**ck**
du**ck**	**st**i**ck**	do**ck**
si**ck**	ti**ck**	**Ch**u**ck**

After practicing ***<ck>*** *have your child read Jack Rat Ran Past on page 258, This Ship on page 260, and The Stick on page 261.*

MAPPING AND SORTING

This lesson plan is explained using the sound 'o-e', as that is the first sound to introduce to your child. All other sounds will be introduced in the same manner. Use the word lists following this lesson plan in the order they occur.

Readiness

Do this lesson with your child after you have completed the lesson Practicing Common Consonant Sound Pictures. If your child is younger than first grade, sixth month, try this lesson and see how he does. If he has a lot of trouble and doesn't respond to the error correction procedures, discontinue this lesson for about two months and then try again. In the meantime keep practicing the sound pictures **<sh>**, **<th>**, **<ch>**, and **<ck>** in the last lesson and the lessons in Chapter four.

Goals

To assist your child in understanding the sound picture nature of written language, so that he can begin to organize the written code.

To expose him to the specific sound pictures of the written language.

To cause him to understand that some sounds are represented by one symbol and that other sounds are represented by two or more symbols; and to cause the child to perceive two or more letters as a unit rather than as discrete letters working together under a rule.

To cause him to understand that there is more than one way to represent most sounds.

To cause him to segment sounds in words as he maps the words, establishing a left to right, symbol to sound response to reading and a left to right sound to symbol response to spelling.

Materials

The word lists on pages 231 through 244.

For new readers use the word in the box only. For older children use all of the words.

continued

Mapping and Sorting, continued

Presentation

1. Say to your child, "One of the things that really good readers know is that written words are made up of pictures of sounds. So, let's take the word 'cat.' If we want to show that word on paper we can show it like this (draw a cat face). This is a picture of a cat. Or, we can show it with sound pictures. First we need to know what the sounds are in 'cat.' What's the first sound?" He should say 'c'. Say, "Good, this is a picture of the sound 'c'. It's the code for that sound. All the people who can read agree that when they see this picture they say the sound 'c'. What's the next sound in cat?" He should say 'a'. Say, "Good, this is a picture of the sound 'a'. It's the code for that sound. All the people who can read agreed that whenever they see this picture they'll say 'a'." Continue with the sound 't'. "So what written words are is really nothing more than just pictures of sounds. Right now, you know most of the sound pictures really well, but you don't know them all, so what we're going to work on is some of the really hard ones. The hard ones are mostly long ones too, like **<oa>** (write the sound picture **<oa>** on the white board). Lots of people think **<oa>** is two sound pictures, (indicate **<o>**) 'o' and (indicate **<a>**) 'a'. But they aren't; <oa> is a picture, a code for the sound 'o-e'. Just like this (draw a picture of a balloon on a string) can be a balloon. Or, if you add this (draw petals on it) it can be a flower. This (make **<o>**) is a picture of 'o', and this (add **<a>**) is a picture of 'o-e'."

2. Then, show your child the word list in your book and say, "We're going to discover some of the other ways to show the sound 'o-e'." Get out a piece of lined paper. Referring to the 'oe' word list, make columns with headings of all the ways to spell the target sound. Your piece of paper should look like this.

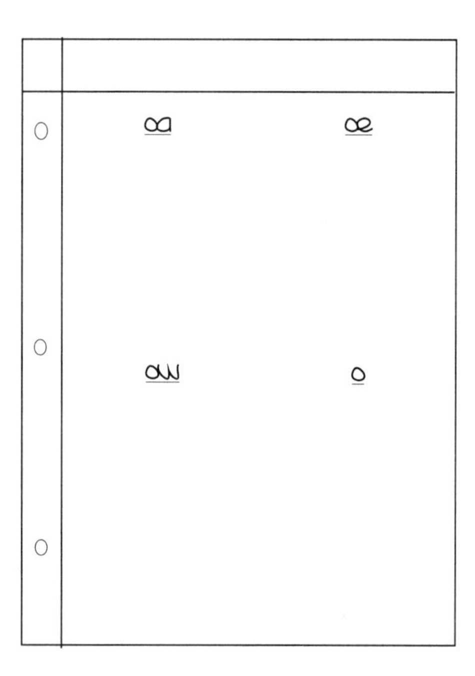

Mapping and Sorting, continued

3. Show your child the 'oe' word list on page 231 and ask him to read the first word. Then tell him to, "Say each sound as you write the picture for that sound" (this is what we call mapping). Do not allow him to map sounds together. EX: 'blend'...'bl' 'e' 'n' 'd', 'b' 'l' 'en' 'd', etc. Do not allow your child to map with letter names. Do not allow him to map silently as he may not be "thinking" the sound, or he may be "thinking" the letter names. Do not allow him to map in cursive. Sound pictures should have beginnings and endings and not be run together as in cursive writing. When you get to a word that has the <o-e> spelling of the sound 'o-e' say, "This sound picture is really odd. It's separated. See, it should look like this (use a piece of paper to illustrate):

n **oe** t

But instead, somebody decided that this part of it (indicate the **<e>**) should be at the end of the word, even though the sound happens here (indicate the **<o>**). As he maps this first **<o-e>** word, say the sounds aloud to model for him that there is no additional sound when he writes the **<e>**. Do not refer to the **<e>** as "silent." Remember, it works with the **<o>** to represent the sound 'oe'. When you're done, your page should look something like this.

Note: After your child has mapped all of the words on the list, point out that the sound picture **<o>** *can represent either the sound 'o-e' as in 'most' and 'host,' or the sound 'o' as in 'hot' and 'not.'*

oa	oe
boat	note
toast	cone
goat	tone
roast	tote
float	hope
groan	
coat	

ow	o
show	hold
glow	bold
grow	most
know	host
throw	no
snow	mold

continued

Mapping and Sorting, continued

Correcting Problems

Your child won't map aloud after having been prompted several times.

Try encouraging him to say the sounds. Some children are very hesitant about saying the sounds. If he really won't, you should say each sound aloud as he writes its sound picture. This serves your purpose in linking the sounds to the symbols and will cause echoic interference if he is silently using letter names when mapping.

He is having difficulty decoding the words. He is unable to blend all the sounds in the correct order or she is adding or deleting sounds.

He needs additional blend work. Continue doing lessons in Chapter four as you progress through Chapter five. In the interim you can have him blend the word as he moves through it.

EX: 't' 'r'...'tr' 'ai'...'trai' 'n'...'train'

This will require you to stop after each new sound and say, "What does that say so far?"

He reads sound pictures incorrectly. EX: train = tran

Simply say the correct sound in isolation as you point to the sound picture with your pencil point.

EX: he reads 'tran,' you say 'a-e'

She guesses at words. EX: float = flag

Simply show him, sound picture by sound picture, what he's done. Point to each sound picture in the actual word as you say the sounds in the word she guessed, "If this were flag it would show 'f' 'l' 'a' 'g'." Take time to accentuate the 'a' sound as you point to the **<oa>** sound picture so that he notices what he's done wrong.

NOTE: Word lists that contain words with sound pictures that have not yet been introduced carry a warning in italics to mention this to your child, for example, the ***<kn>*** *spelling for the sound 'n' on the 'o-e' word list. Simply say, "This is something I haven't shown you yet. This (indicate the* ***<kn>****) is another sound picture for the sound 'n'."*

Sound 'oe' Word List

*Explain about the **<kn>** spelling for the sound 'n' when you get to the word 'kno*

	t**oe**
	cr**ow**
note	l**oa**f
sh **ow**	gr**ow**
host	b**oa**t
g**oa**t	no
most	cold
cone	home
so	go

tone	stroke
r**oa**st	t**oa**st
poke	d**ough**
thr**ow**	b**oa**st
c**oa**st	mold
pole	f**oa**l
kn **ow**	**th**r**oa**t
f**oe**	fl**oa**t
gl**ow**	scold
c**oa**l	**th** **ough**

After completing the sound 'oe', go to the Vowel + e lesson plan on page 245. After mapping and sorting 'oe', have your child read The Coach on page 262.

Sound 'ow' Word List

	owl
	c**ow**
n**ow**	t**ow**n
sh **ou**t	**ou**t
p**ou**t	l**ou**d

h**ou** **se**	r**ou**nd
m**ou** **se**	fr**ow**n
g**ow**n	gr**ou**nd
pr**ou**d	f**ou**nd
h**ow**l	br**ow**n
c**ou**nt	n**ou**n

*After you've completed the sounds 'oe' and 'ow', do the Sound Sorting lesson on page 247 using the sound picture **<ow>**.*

Also do the Word Analysis lesson on page 251.

After completing the sound 'ow', have your child read The Cloud on page 266.

The Sound 'er' Word List

	h **er**
	sh ir t
g **ir** l	c **ur** l
h **ur** t	b **ur** n
d **ir** t	f **er** n
b **ur** p	s **ir**
b **ir** d	f **ur**
j **er** k	s **ir**
t **ur** n	h **er** d
s **ur** f	l **ur** k

c **ur** b	w **or** l d
w **or** m	w i n t **er**
f a s t **er**	h **ear** d
w **or se**	l **ear** n
f **ir** m	w **or** k
s k **ir** t	f l **ir** t
t **er** m	**ch ur** n
e n t **er**	s t **ir**
ear n	f **ir** s t
c o **ll ar**	l a n t **er** n
h o **ll er**	d o **ll ar**

After completing 'er', have your child read The Hurt Girl on page 267.

The Sound 'r' Word List

r a t	**wr** e n **ch**	**wr** e **ck**	r i d **e**
wr i t **e**	**wr** a p	t r a p	c r o p
th e **re**	r i s k	a **re**	g r a b

After completing the sound 'r', do the Word Analysis lesson on page 251 using the sounds 'r' and 'er'.

The Sound 'ee' Word List

	s**ee**	gr**ie**f	sw**ee**t
	b**ee**p	br**eeze**	**kn ee**
east	me**ss**y	f**ie**ld	l**ea ve**
eat	f**ee**l	lu**ck**y	pr**ie**st
l**ea**p	su**nn**y	**sh ie**ld	cr**ea**m
f**ee**t	t**ea**m	indian	st**ea**m
he	n**ee**d	k**ey**	tr**ea**t
m**ee**t	r**ea**d	tr**ee**	str**ee**t
she	we	fu**nn**y	pl**ea se**
s**ee**m	**ch ie**f	st**ea**l	pe**nn**y
ha**pp**y	**sh ee**t	br**ie**f	va**ll ey**
b**ea**n	h**ea**t	fr**ee ze**	dr**ea**m
si**ll**y	me	monk**ey**	r**ea**l
		s**ea**	sn**ee ze**

After completing 'ee', have your child read The Jeep on page 268.

m**ay**
at**e**
r**a**k**e**
m**a**k**e**
d**ay**
s**ay**
t**ai**l
p**ai**n
g**a**t**e**
r**ay**
n**ai**l
t**a**p**e**
aim
m**ai**n
r**ai**n
b**ai**t
l**a**k**e**
s**a**l**e**
l**a**t**e**
s**ai**l

tr**ay**
p**ai**l
c**a**k**e**
br**ai**n
w**eigh**
w**ai**st
w**eigh**t
tab**le**
sl**eigh**
gr**ey**
sn**ai**l
eight

th **ey**
stab**le**
st**ea**k
sn**a**k**e**
pr**ey**
pr**ay**
str**ay**
cl**ay**
pl**ay**
st**ai**r
fl**a**k**e**
pap**er**

After completing the sound 'a-e', do the Word Analysis lesson on page 251 with the sounds 'a-e' and 'ee', and have your child read Jane and Blain on page 269.

The Sound ‘oo’ Word List

	sp**oo**n	br**ui se**	**kn ew**
	pr**u**n**e**	r**u**d**e**	can**oe**
fl**ew**	s**ou**p	gl**ue**	sn**oo ze**
cr**ew**	to	r**oo**st	cr**u**d**e**
n**ew**	cr**ui se**	do	l**oo se**
st**ew**	br**u**t**e**	gr**ou**p	tr**oo**p
tr**ue**	**sh oo**t	s**ui**t	m**oo se**
bl**ue**	sup**er**	**sh oe**	sc**oo**p
r**oo**t	tod**ay**	**ch oo se**	t**u**n**e**
s**oo**n	fl**u**t**e**	l**oo**t	h**oo**t

After completing ‘oo’, have your child read The New Blue Boot on page 270.

The Sound ‘oo’ Word List

	l**oo**k	t**oo**k
	sh ook	c**oul**d
c**oo**k	bu**sh**	h**oo**k
w**oo**d	pu**dd**i**ng**	**sh oul**d
put	cr**oo**k	w**oul**d

After completing the sound 'oo', do the Word Analysis lesson on page 251 with the sounds 'oo' as in book and 'oo' as in boot.

Also do Sound Sorting on page 247 with the sound picture **<oo>**.

After completing 'oo', have your child read The Crook on page 271.

The Sound 'u' Word List

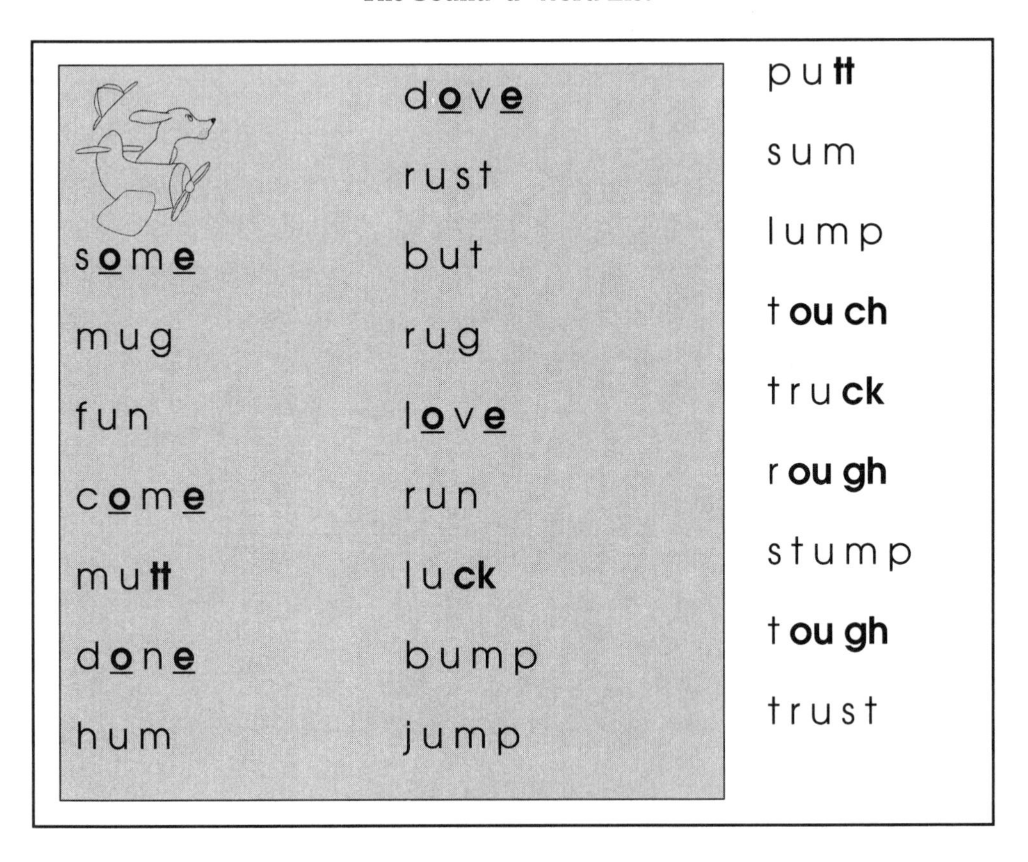

some
mug
fun
come
mu**tt**
done
hum

dove
rust
but
rug
love
run
lu**ck**
bump
jump

pu**tt**
sum
lump
t**ou** **ch**
tru**ck**
r **ou** **gh**
stump
t **ou** **gh**
trust

After completing the sound 'u', do Sound Sorting on page 247 with the sound picture **<ou>**.

Also do Word Analysis on page 251 with the sounds 'u', 'ow', and 'oo'.

After completing 'u', have your child read Come Home on page 272.

The Sound 'e' Word List

shed
s**ai**d
bet
pet
net
men
led
l**ea**d
set

r**ea**d
Fred
red
br**ea**d
met
tent
h**ea**d
ten
te**ll**
ne**ck**
dent

sw**ea**t
dr**ea**d
tr**ea**d
thr**ea**d
tend
f**ou**nt**ai**n
spr**ea**d
m**ea**nt
l**ea**pt
capt**ai**n
ag**ai**n

After completing this lesson, do the Word Analysis lesson on page 251 using the sounds 'a-e', 'e', and 'ee'.

Also do the Sound Sorting lesson on page 247 using the sound picture ***<ea>****.*

After completing 'e', have your child read Bread on page 273.

	mild	c r**ie**s
	I	**wh**y
shy	l**ie**	mind
fly	fry	s**igh**
h**igh**	k**i**t**e**	str**i**p**e**
p**i**p**e**	cry	p**ie**s
n**igh**t	p**i**n**e**	**wh i**t**e**
wild	d**ie**	tw**i**n**e**
p**ie**	r**igh**t	l**ie**s
child	my	t**ie**s
t**igh**t	t**ie**	hind
l**igh**t	**sky**	spy
		pry

*After completing this sound, do the Sound Sorting lesson on page 247 using the sound picture **<ie>**.*

Also do the Word Analysis lesson on page 251 using the sounds 'i-e' and 'ee'.

After completing 'i-e', have your child read Spike on page 274.

The Sound 's' Word List

Explain what ***<oi>*** *represents in 'voice' and 'choice.'*

v **oi ce**	s i t	c e n t	m **ou se**
l e **ss**	m **er** c y	h **ou se**	**ch oi ce**
s a t	c i t y	s a n d	s a d
s i **ll** y	s i **ck**	s o f t	s i p

The Sound 'z' Word List

Explain what 'wh' represents in the word 'whose.'

i s	s n **oo ze**	**ch oo se**
z i **pp er**	l o **se**	**wh** i z
f u **zz**	**wh** o **se**	b u **zz ar** d
h i s	**z i p**	x y l o **ph** **o** n **e**

After completing 'z', do Sound Sorting with the sound picture ***<se>***.

Also do Word Analysis on page 251 using the sounds 's' and 'z'.

The Sound 'l' Word List

l i f t	p u p **il**	h o s p i t **al**
d o **ll**	w e **ll**	l o f t
l a b **el**	l a m p	a **pp le**
s a b **al**	s i m p **le**	l i **tt le**

The Sound 'o' Word List

sto**ck**	fa**th** **er**	swat
w**al**l	d**aw**n	cl**aw**
knot	br**ough**t	s**ough**t
star	got	t**al**k
f**au**lt	**ough**t	want
pot	t**al**l	b**ough**t
l**aw**n	r**aw**	car
w**al**k	b**al**l	wat**er**
fr**au**d	f**aw**n	j**aw**
th **ough**t	**ch** **al**k	l**aw**
s**aw**	h**au**l	P**au**l
f**ough**t	y**aw**n	con

The Sound 'k' Word List

so**ck**	kept	**Ch**ri**st**mas
can	c**a**p**e**	cat
clo**ck**	bri**ck**	**ch**i**ck**en
chlor**i**n**e**	k**ee**p	sti**ck**
k**i**t**e**	blo**ck**	co**ff** **ee**

The Sound 'oy' Word List

b **oy**	**oi** n k	r **oy al**
t **oy**	s p **oi** l	s **oi** l
j **oy**	c **oi** l	b **oi** l
	oi l	a h **oy**
	f **oi** l	T r **oy**
	t **oi** l	l **oy al**

The Sound 'd' Word List

l **oo** k **ed**	l a **dd er**	h e l d
d a d	b i d	p l a n t e d
s l i **pp ed**	kn i **tt** e d	o p e n **ed**
d **ir** t	m i **dd le**	t a s t e d
p a **ck ed**	s t r a n d e d	d r i p
h e l p **ed**	f i **dd le**	k i **dd** i **ng**
d o g	d a m p	f i **tt** e d
	d **ow** n	l a n d e d
	t r a **ck ed**	h a n d e d

The Sound 'j' Word List

jump	bri**dge**	gent**le**
jung**le**	bar**ge**	gym
ju**dge**	lar**ge**	gin
jam	nu**dge**	bu**dge**
fu**dge**	j**ui** **ce**	Ja**ck**

The Sound 'v' Word List

vine	n**er** **ve**	c**ur** **ve**
va**ll** **ey**	s**er** **ve**	ha**ve**
vap**or**	visit	l**ea** **ve**

The Sound 'i' Word List

mi**tt**	did	bit
hit	tib	in
sit	rift	sip
tip	bib	it
crypt	pit	crisp
his	cylind**er**	pip

The Sound ‘g’ Word List

gh e **tt** o	g o **sh**	h a **gg** **le**
g e t	g **a** t **e**	w a **gg** **ed**
gh o s t	g a m b **le**	l o g

After completing this lesson, do Sound Sorting on page 247 using the sound picture ***<g>****.*

The Sound ‘m’ Word List

m o m	n u **mb**	**au** t u **mn**
b u m p	s **o** m **e**	s u **mm** **er**
m a p	d u **mb**	l u m p

The Sound ‘u-e’ Word List

c **u** t **e**	c **ue**	p **ew** t **er**
p u p **il**	p **ew**	f **ew**
f **ew**	h **ue**	**u** s **e**
c **u** b **e**	f **ue** l	m **u** l **e**

After you present this sound, do Sound Sorting on page 247 using the sound picture ***<ew>****.*

The Sound 'f' Word List

gra**ph**	fun	**ph**onics
ph<u>**o**</u>n<u>**e**</u>	f<u>**a**</u>k<u>**e**</u>	f<u>**i**</u>v<u>**e**</u>
fat	t**ou** **gh**	fib
pu**ff**	fin	fact
Phil	en**ou** **gh**	fancy

The Sound 'n' Word List

no	**kn** **ow**	si**nn** **er**
gnat	fu**nn**y	**gn**<u>**o**</u>m<u>**e**</u>
di**nn** **er**	**kn** **ew**	wi**nn** **er**
sn**ow**	**kn**ot	**not**

The Sound 'w' Word List

when	**wh**y	**wh**en
wi**sh**	w<u>**a**</u>st<u>**e**</u>	**wh**ip
what	w**ai**t	**wh**isk**er**
want	wint**er**	we

VOWEL + e

Readiness

Do this lesson with any child. If your child is younger than first grade, sixth month, try this lesson and see how he does. If he has a lot of trouble and doesn't respond to the error correction procedures, discontinue this lesson for about two months and then try again. In the meantime, keep practicing the sound pictures **<sh>**, **<th>**, **<ch>**, and **<ck>** in the last lesson, and continue on to the other sounds following the Mapping and Sorting lesson.

Goals

To help your child understand that the **<e>** works with the earlier vowel to represent one sound.

To give him practice at reading vowel + e words.

Materials

The vowel + e word list on the next page.

Presentation

1. Have him read each word.
2. As necessary, remind him what the **<e>** means, telling him that it works with the other vowel as part of the same sound picture. Remind him that sound pictures with **<e>** are the only ones that get separated like this.

Correcting Problems

He reads 'note' as 'not.'

Indicate **<e>** with your pencil point and then point back to **<o>** and say the sound 'oe'.

Note: Use the word list on the following page for practice. The words on the left side of the list are coded to help him remember that the **<e>** *and the other underlined letter are one sound picture. The words on the right side of the list are uncoded to give him practice reading uncoded words.*

VOWEL + e WORD LIST

Read across the columns from left to right (con...cone).

con	→	c**o**n**e**	can	→	cane
fat	→	f**a**t**e**	win	→	wine
cub	→	c**u**b**e**	rob	→	robe
cod	→	c**o**d**e**	mad	→	made
mop	→	m**o**p**e**	hat	→	hate
man	→	m**a**n**e**	hid	→	hide
pin	→	p**i**n**e**	cut	→	cute
mut	→	m**u**t**e**	rid	→	ride
rat	→	r**a**t**e**	kit	→	kite
rip	→	r**i**p**e**	rod	→	rode
Tim	→	t**i**m**e**	dim	→	dime
tot	→	t**o**t**e**	fin	→	fine

SOUND SORTING

This lesson plan is explained using the sound picture **<ow>**. *All other sound pictures where code overlap occurs will be introduced in the same manner.*

Readiness

This lesson is for children older than first grade, sixth month who have completed the lesson Mapping and Sorting, for the sounds, 'o-e' and 'ow'. Do not do this lesson with a child younger than first grade, sixth month.

Goals

To assist your child in understanding that some sound pictures can represent two or more sounds.

To offer him a strategy for managing the overlap in the code.

Materials

The sound sorting word lists following this lesson plan.

Presentation

1. Point out that the sound picture **<ow>** can represent the sound 'oe' as in the word 'show,' or 'ow' as in the word 'now.' Create a piece of paper that has two columns and the headings 'ow' and 'oe'. Have him read each of the words on the **<ow>** sound sorting list, trying both sounds for the sound picture **<ow>**. Have him decide if each goes onto your 'o-e' list or your 'ow' list. Your paper should look like this.

the sound 'oe'	**the sound 'ow'**
know	brown
show	town
grow	clown
glow	frown
throw	down

continued

Sound Sorting, continued

2. If a word can be a real word (though misspelled) either way (EX: 'town'), simply explain to the child that if he saw it in a sentence it would only make sense one way.

EX: 👍 I want to go to town. 👎 I want to go to tone.

Use the following sound sorting word lists for this lesson plan. Follow the directions on the Mapping and Sorting word lists for instruction on when to introduce each overlap sound picture.

<ow> Sound Sorting ‘o-e’ as in ‘tow’ or ‘ow’ as in ‘now’

sh ow	**th** r **ow**	f r **ow** n
c **ow**	t **ow**	c l **ow** n
h **ow**	f l **ow**	c r **ow**
g r **ow**	n **ow**	b r **ow** n

<ea> Sound Sorting ‘ee’ as in ‘bean,’ ‘a-e’ as in ‘bear,’ or ‘e’ as in ‘bread’

b **ea** r	b **ea ch**	t r **ea** d
ea ch	**th** r **ea** d	c l **ea** n
s t **ea** k	b **ea** n	m **ea** n
b r **ea** d	d **ea** d	t **ea** m
m **ea** t	b r **ea** k	g r **ea** t

<oo> Sound Sorting ‘oo’ as in ‘soon’ or ‘oo’ as in ‘cook’

f **oo** t	l **oo** k	n **oo** n
t **oo** k	b **oo** m	r **oo** m
w **oo** d	s p **oo** n	**sh oo** k
m **oo** n	c **oo** k	f **oo** d

<ou> Sound Sorting 'ow' as in 'pout,' 'oo' as in 'group,' or 'u' as in 'touch'

g r **ou** p	s **ou** p	r **ou** n d
h **ou se**	p **ou** t	t **ou gh**
t **ou ch**	r **ou gh**	g r **ou ch**
f **ou** n d	l **ou** d	s **ou** n d

<ie> Sound Sorting 'ie' as in 'tie' or 'ee' as in 'chief'

p **ie** s	l **ie**	t r **ie** d
ch ie f	g r **ie** f	**sh ie** l d
d **ie**	f **ie** l d	s p **ie** d

<se> Sound Sorting 's' as in 'mouse' or 'z' as in 'choose'

h **ou se**	p l **ea se**	b l **ou se**
m **ou se**	**ch oo se**	**ea se**

<ew> Sound Sorting 'oo' as in 'new' or 'u-e' as in 'few'

n **ew**	c r **ew**	s t **ew**
f **ew**	**kn ew**	f l **ew**

WORD ANALYSIS

Readiness

This lesson is appropriate for children older than first grade, sixth month, who have done the corresponding Mapping and Sorting lesson.

Goals

To cause your child to analyze the sound pictures in each word as an intervention to a global strategy.

To cause him to notice the various ways that the sounds are spelled. EX: **<ai>** represents the sound 'a-e' in the word 'train.'

Materials

Use the dry erase board for this lesson.

Words from the Mapping and Sorting word lists on pages 231 through 244.

Presentation

1. Cover the words so your child can't see what is bolded. Write one word at a time on the dry erase board.
2. With his own marker, he should say each sound as he underlines the sound picture for the sound.

Correcting Problems

He underlines two letters that do not represent one sound (for example, two consonant blend sounds).

Simply say, "'st' is two sounds. What's the first sound in 'st'?"

He reads the word correctly, but fails to underline two letters that represent one sound.

Say, "You missed one. What's the first sound... second sound. . ." etc., until he notices that one of the sounds is represented by more than one letter.

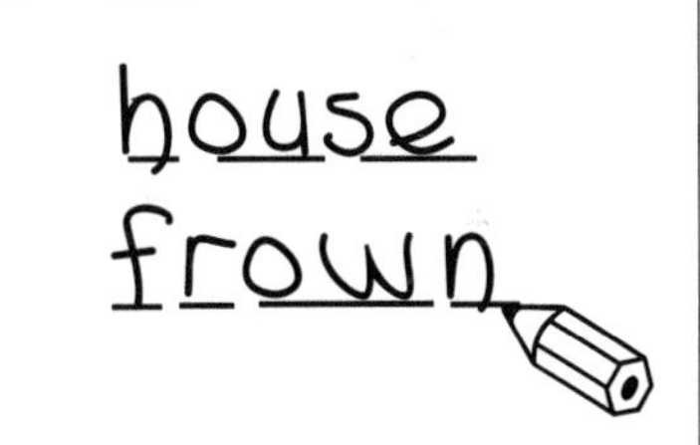

continued

Word Analysis, continued

He is unable to read the word at all.

Say, "What letters do you think might work together? You've seen them before." When he finds them and underlines them say, "What sound can that represent?" If he is uncertain, tell him. If he is still unable to read the word after you have done the above, direct him through the word, indicating each sound picture as you say the sound.

EX: choose. "This **<ch>** is 'ch', this **<oo>** is 'oo', and this **<se>** is 'z'.

SCRATCH SHEET SPELLING

Readiness

This lesson is appropriate for children older than first grade, sixth month, once the corresponding Mapping and Sorting lesson has been presented.

Goals

To establish a spelling strategy for managing the variation in the code.

Materials

Mapping and sorting word lists.

Presentation

1. Choose a sound to practice spelling. EX: 'o-e'
2. Discuss any missing spelling variations and add them to the list. You can reference your Sound Picture Charts on pages 213 and 214 to check.
3. Using the words on the corresponding word list following the Mapping and Sorting lesson plan, choose a word and ask him to try spelling it with any of the spelling variations he thinks might be the accepted spelling for the word.
4. After he has tried some of the spelling variations, ask him which he thinks is the correct spelling. If he is wrong, tell him which is right. Have him circle the correct spelling of each word.

We use the term "accepted" as it helps to encourage the child to understand that the written system of language is an agreed-upon code.

Correcting Problems

He has tried all the variations except the accepted one.

Tell him you would like him to try all the variations.

NOTE: Remember, there are no incorrect answers if a word is spelled with a sound picture that can spell the target sound. Simply say, "Yes, that does spell train, (trayn) but it is not the accepted way to spell it."

STUDYING FOR SPELLING TESTS

Readiness

You should use this lesson to help your child study for his weekly spelling tests.

Goals

To offer your child practice at using good spelling strategies for his spelling tests and for spelling words in text.

Materials

Your child's spelling words.

Several pieces of lined paper.

Something to write with.

Presentation

Do steps 1, 2, 3 each night for three nights before your child's spelling test.

On the third night add step 4.

1. Give your child a piece of lined paper. On another piece of paper, write your child's spelling words in a column in nice, big, bold print. Skip a line or two between each word. Lay this piece of paper to the left (right if your child is left-handed) of your child's piece of paper.
2. Have him read the first word. Now have him map the first word onto his paper. When he maps he should be saying each sound aloud while he writes the sound picture that represents that sound. Continue on to the next word.
3. When he has completed each word, have him repeat the process two more times.
4. On the third night, after he has completed steps 1, 2, 3, give him a practice spelling test without seeing the words. Be sure to enunciate the words very clearly.

continued

Studying for Spelling Tests, continued

Solving Problems

Your child won't map aloud after having been prompted several times.

Try encouraging him to say the sounds. If he won't say them, you should say each sound aloud as he writes its sound picture. This serves your purpose in linking the sounds to the symbols and will cause echoic interference if he is silently using letter names when mapping.

He is having trouble reading the words.

He needs continued lessons in this chapter. If he is omitting sounds he may also need continued work in Chapter four.

In step 4, he is having trouble remembering the sound pictures that are represented with more than one letter.

EX: He spells 'train' trane or tran.

Repeat step 2. Encourage him to notice the sound pictures that are represented with two or more letters. Ask him to make a picture of them in his mind. Do not use letter names when you do this. Simply indicate the sound pictures with a pencil point or your finger.

READING CODED TEXT

Readiness

See Materials section below.

Goals

To assist your child in reading advanced text.

To make the phono-graphic nature of the English written language explicit to your child.

To direct your child's attention to the various sound pictures.

To cause your child to notice the orthographical tendencies of the English language.

Materials

New readers (younger than first grade, sixth month).

The coded stories on pages 258 through 274. These should be read after the sound mapping and sorting lesson for that particular sound.

Older children.

The coded stories on pages 275 through 285. These should be started once the older child has done several of the mapping and sorting word lists with fairly consistent success.

Presentation

1. Invite your child to read an age-appropriate story.
2. After your child has read the story, go back and point to some of the sound pictures, asking him what sound each one represents.

Correcting Problems

Your child encounters a sound picture he doesn't know or has forgotten.

When a given sound picture is new to your child, it's alright to tell him the sound. Do not tell him the entire word. Just indicate the sound picture and tell him the sound. As your child becomes more adept at recognizing the sound pictures, allow him additional time to analyze the word before you supply a sound.

Reading Coded Text, continued

Just **th**en a big br**ow**n
dog c**a**m**e** l**ea**pi**ng** up.

Your child misreads a sound picture in a word. EX: He reads the **<ea>** *in 'pear' as 'ee'.*

If a sound picture could represent more than one sound (EX: **<ee>**), say "That (indicating the sound picture **<ea>**) can be 'ee', but it isn't in this word. In this word it's 'a-e'."

JACK RAT RAN PAST

Directions: Have the child read the story. Offer help as needed.

This story focuses on the sound picture ***<ck>***.

Ja**ck** Rat ran fast. Ja**ck** ran past a fat cat.

1

And past a bla**ck** bat.

2

Ja**ck** ran past a bad dog.

3

And past a mad hog.

4

Ja**ck** Rat sat.

5

A fat cat ran past. A bla**ck** bat ran past. A bad dog ran past. A mad hog ran past.

6

Ja**ck** rat went ba**ck**. Fat cat went ba**ck**. A bla**ck** bat went ba**ck**. A bad dog went ba**ck**. A mad hog went ba**ck**.

7

The End

8

THIS SHIP

Directions: Have the child read the story. Offer help as needed.

This story focuses on the sound pictures ***<sh>***, ***<th>***, ***<ch>***, ***<ck>***.

This **sh**ip got a ba**sh**.

1

It went swi**sh** and hit a ro**ck**.

2

Then it did not **ch**ug mu**ch**.

3

A **ch**ap wi**th** a sa**ck** got on and got **th**e **sh**ip in **th**e **sh**op.

4

THE STICK

Directions: Have the child read the story. Offer help as needed.

This story focuses on the sound pictures **<ck>** *and* **<ch>**.

The **ch**i**ck** got a sti**ck**. It is not his sti**ck**. It is **Ch**u**ck**'s sti**ck**.

1

Let's get **th**e sti**ck** ba**ck**. Get on ba**ck** **Ch**u**ck**. **Ch**u**ck** got on ba**ck**.

2

Ri**ck** and **Ch**u**ck** went fast.

3

The **ch**i**ck** felt si**ck**. **Ch**u**ck** and Ri**ck** got **th**e sti**ck**.

4

THE COACH

*Directions: Have the child read the story. Offer help as needed. This story focuses on the sound 'o-e' represented by the sound pictures **<o-e>**, **<ow>**, and **<o>**.*

The c**oa ch** is

J**oe** did a
job wi**th** his
hit.
2

J**oe** wi**ll** get
a c**o**n**e** as
a gift for
the big hit.
3

C**oa ch** wi**ll**
get a fl**oa**t.

The cone will
melt fast.
5

The float will
go slow.
6

7

The End
8

JAKE AND KATE

Directions: Have the child read the story. Offer help as needed.
This story focuses on vowel + e.

Kate got a ride on a bike.
1

It is Jake.
2

Take a rake Kate. Make a pile.
3

It got late. The sun did hide.
4

It is time to
get a bite.
12 1 2 3 4 5 6 7 8 9 10 11
5

Jake and Kate
did bake a
cake.
6

It is time to
get home
Kate.
7

The End
8

THE CLOUD

Directions: Have the child read the story. Offer help as needed. This story focuses on the sound 'ow' represented by the sound pictures **<ou>** *and* **<ow>**. *Difficult word 'house' contains the sound picture* **<se>**.

The cloud is big.

1

It will get the cow's house wet.

2

The cow will frown and pout.

3

Then the sun will get out and the cow will jump and shout.

4

THE HURT GIRL

Directions: Have the child read the story. Offer help as needed. This story focuses on the sound 'er' represented by the sound pictures ***<ir>***, ***<ur>***, *and* ***<ear>***.

The girl got hurt.
1

A bird hurt her leg.
2

Bad, bad bird!
3

The girl can learn not to mess with a bird that can hurt.
4

THE JEEP

Directions: Have the child read the story. Offer help as needed. This story focuses on the sound 'ee' represented by the sound pictures ***<ee>****,* ***<y>****, and* ***<ea>****. It also contains the vowel + e words 'came,' 'scared,' and 'named.'*

The jeep came
from a peak.
1

It went beep
beep. And
scared a
bunny named
Teak.
2

To get a bit
of grass and
go to sleep.
4

JANE AND BLAIN

Directions: Have the child read the story. Offer help as needed. This story focuses on the sound 'a-e' represented by the sound pictures ***<a-e>****,* ***<ai>****,* ***<ay>****, and* ***<ey>****.*

Then they will
take a break
and get cake.
2

Then it will be
late.
3

It is a long
day to paint
a gate!
4

NEW BLUE BOOT

Directions: Have the child read the story. Offer help as needed. This story focuses on the sound 'oo' represented by the sound pictures **<oo>**, **<ou>**, *and* **<ew>**. *Difficult words: The word 'two' is one of 54 words in the English language that are spelled with a combination seen nowhere else in the English writing code.*

Sue and you found a boot. It is not a green boot.

1

It is not a brown boot. It is not a red boot. It is a blue boot. It is not too big. It is not too old.

2

It is a new blue boot that fits Sue.

3

"I like the new blue boot," said Sue. "I wish I had *two*."

4

THE CROOK

Directions: Have the child read the story. Offer help as needed. This story focuses on the sound 'oo' (as in 'crook'), represented with the sound pictures **<oo>**, **<u>**, *and* **<oul>**.

"Look! In the bush is a crook."
1

"We should get a cop." We would if we could, but we shook.
2

"Look! The crook put the wood in the box. He took the wood."

3

"Look! It is a cop with the crook." Good!
4

COME HOME

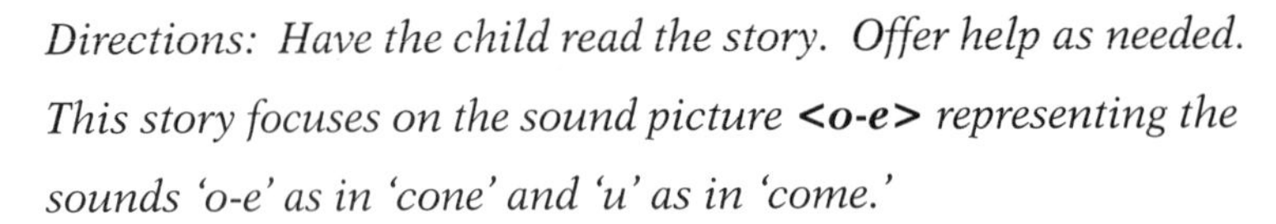

Directions: Have the child read the story. Offer help as needed. This story focuses on the sound picture ***<o-e>*** *representing the sounds 'o-e' as in 'cone' and 'u' as in 'come.'*

Come! Come and get some. It is a cone at home.

1

Come and get a cone. Come and get some cone at home.

2

I had some.

3

I had none. And the cone is done.

4

BREAD

Directions: Have the child read the story. Offer help as needed. This story focuses on the sound 'e' represented by the sound pictures ***<e>****,* ***<ea>****, and* ***<ai>****. The difficult word 'again' is a two-syllable word.*

"Br**ea**d is not for a b**ir**d," s**ai**d Fred. Br**ea**d is for men.

1

The b**ir**d did pe**ck** at Fred's h**ea**d to get **th**e br**ea**d.

2

A g**ai**n Fred s**ai**d, "**Th**is br**ea**d is for men." And **th**en **th**e b**ir**d r**ea**d **th**e bag.

3

"Br**ea**d is for men," it s**ai**d.

4

SPIKE

Directions: Have the child read the story. Offer help as needed. This story focuses on the sound 'i-e', represented by the sound pictures ***<i-e>***, ***<y>***, *and* ***<igh>***.

It is a hive.
Spike has a
hive in sight.

What a fright!
It can fly!
2

Five can fly!
Nine can fly!
3

Spike has to
hide.
4

Cowboys

A long time ago there were lots and lots of cowboys. Now there are not as many cowboys, but we still need some.

A cowboy's job is to take care of cattle. A cowboy's biggest helper is his horse. Together a cowboy and his horse can look after hundreds of cows.

Each morning the cowboys saddle up the horses and go out on the range. Then they round up the cattle. When baby cows are born, the cowboys brand them. They put a mark on them so that everybody will know who they belong to.

Deserts

Deserts are very dry and very hot places. It rains very little in the desert. The mountains around the desert stop the rain clouds from getting over the desert. Sometimes it won't rain for a whole year. With very little rain, there are not many plants in the desert. Mostly there is sand and rocks. Strong winds blow the sand into hills called sand dunes.

The small animals that live in the desert dig little holes into the ground. These are called burrows. In the burrows, the desert animals can stay cool and safe from the hot desert sun.

Large desert animals protect themselves from the sun by sleeping under big rocks during the heat of the day. Camels carry water with them in humps on their backs.

Helen Keller

Helen Keller was born a long time ago. She lived in a big house with a long porch. She was a normal baby. But when she was eighteen months old she became very sick. She did not die, but she became deaf and blind.

When Helen was a child she got a teacher named *Anne* Sullivan. She taught Helen to speak and to do things that most blind and deaf *people* could not do at that time in history.

Helen spent the rest *of* her life giving speeches to inspire the handicapped to learn and do as much as they can.

Whales

Whales are the largest animals on the earth. They live in the sea, but they are not fish. Some whales can dive deep in the water.

The sperm whale can dive *two* miles deep. Sperm whales eat fish and squid.

Whales have families just like we do. A whale spends its whole life with its family.

Most animals that live in the sea hatch their babies from eggs. Whales are mammals. All mammals have live babies. They do not hatch their babies from eggs.

Wind

It is invisible, but we can see how it moves leaves and other things in our world. It moves sailboats across lakes and seas. It causes flags to unfurl. It pushes clouds across the sky. It is wind!

Wind is the movement *of* air. Air is all around the earth. Air movement is caused by warm air rising and cool air falling.

Prevailing winds are strong winds that always come from the same direction. Prevailing winds cause the formation *of* mountains and valleys.

Some winds have particular names. A gale is a strong wind that can blow tiles off roofs. A tornado is a very strong wind that whirls around in a cone shape. A tornado can lift cars and destroy homes. Hurricanes and typhoons are large wind storms that move in from the sea.

Rocks

Rocks are made *of* minerals. A mineral is a chemical that is not an animal or a plant. It is not a living thing.

Some rocks are very common and not valuable, like salt. Others are very hard and not easy to find, like sapphires and rubies. They are very expensive.

Rocks are used to make walls and tiles and other things. Some rocks are melted to make metal. Jewelry is made *of* rocks. The metal is gold or silver and the gem is a stone.

The world's oldest rocks were formed millions *of* years before we were born. They were made from liquid magma which cooled and hardened. Some rocks were formed on the surface *of* our planet, when volcanoes erupted and the magma flowed from the earth. Other rocks formed deep beneath the earth.

Electricity

Natural electricity is caused by *two* clouds rubbing against each other. We make electricity in power plants to give us energy to operate machines.

The things that make electricity have power to run machines are called atoms. Everything in our world is made *of* atoms. Inside atoms are millions *of* tiny electrons. The electrons in electricity are moving from atom to atom. This causes tremendous power. It causes enough power to run your television, your refrigerator, and your computer.

An Englishman named Swann and an American named Edison invented light bulbs. Now we can use electricity to light our homes and offices.

You should be very careful around electricity. It is powerful and can harm you.

Hawks

Hawks have sharp beaks and talons. They have strong feet for catching small animals. Hawks are birds *of* prey.

Hawks fly and hunt in the daytime. Hawks are among the highest flying birds. Hawks perch on high branches and towers and search the ground for prey below them.

When a hawk has found its prey, it dives from its perch very quickly. The duck hawk is among the fastest diving hawks. It can dive at a speed *of* 175 miles per *hour*. It can also catch its prey in mid-air.

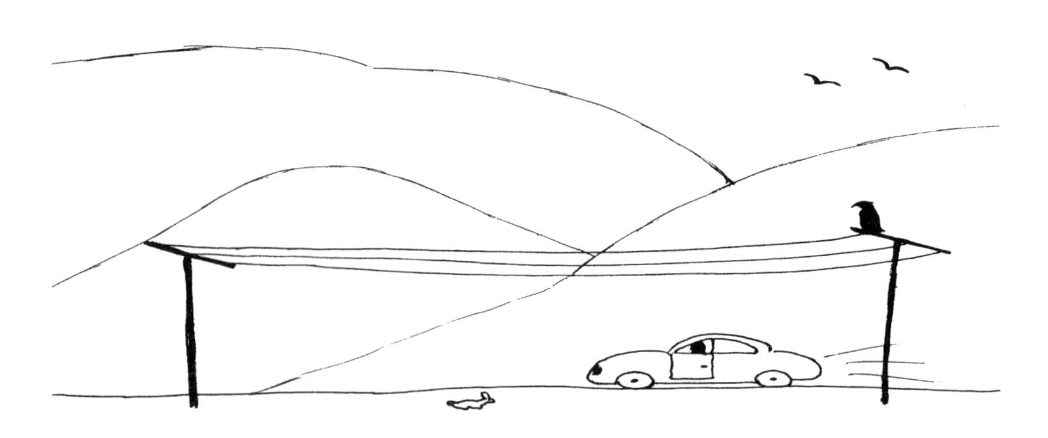

Another very fast flying hawk is the falcon. Falcons have long pointed wings and narrow tails. The kestrel is a kind *of* falcon. It is smaller than most hawks. It is about the size *of* a robin.

The largest hawks are called eagles. There are different kinds *of* eagles on every continent in the world. In America there are bald eagles. They are not really bald, but have white feathers on their heads that make them appear bald from far away. The bald eagle usually lives near the sea. It is used as the national symbol *of* our country.

Martin Luther King, *Jr.*

Martin Luther King, *Jr.* had but *one* cause. He wanted to help blacks to have a better life. When Martin was a boy blacks did not have such a good life. Blacks found it difficult to go to good schools and to get a good job. In some states blacks were not even allowed to vote.

When he grew up, Martin Luther King became a minister. He preached to blacks to expect more from life. He preached to whites to give blacks a chance to have a better life. Martin Luther King believed there should be a peaceful movement toward equal rights for blacks. He organized many peaceful rallies, speeches, and marches. This became known as the civil rights movement.

After twenty years *of* work to help blacks, Martin Luther King was murdered on April third, 1968. His death was mourned throughout the world. He is an American hero.

SOUND SEARCH

Readiness

Do this lesson after you've completed the lesson plan Reading Coded Text and have read the stories on pages 275–285 for older children.

Goals

To help your child make the transition to uncoded text.

To help your child notice the various sound pictures that represent the target sound in each story.

Materials

The stories on pages 287 through 291, following this lesson plan.

A piece of notebook paper.

Presentation

This lesson is written for the story Shirl's Curls. The lesson is the same for the other sound search stories, but the target sound is different.

1. Show your child the story and tell him the story has lots of 'er' words in it. Ask him to listen for these as he reads the story.
2. As he reads the story and finds 'er' words, have him list them on a piece of notebook paper.
3. When he has found them all, have him go back and write the sound picture for the target sound next to each word.

Shirl's Curls	
Shirl	ir
curls	ur
Thursday	ur
Burt	ur
barber	er
Shirl's	ir
work	or
ever	er
dirt	ir
worm	or
learn	ear
shirt	ir

Shirl's Curls

The Sound 'er'

I once knew a girl named Shirl, who really had so many curls. On Thursday each week she went to see Burt the barber, who gave Shirl's hair the works.

"Now whatever you do," said Burt, "don't roll around in the dirt. Your curls will fall, and you might get a bite from a worm."

On Saturday Shirl went to the park. She fell from the swing to the dirt. She rolled all around, got some dirt on her shirt, and messed up her pretty soft curls.

On Thursday she went back to Burt, who said, "Shirl will you ever learn? Stay out of the dirt, keep it off your shirt, and don't mess up these pretty brown curls."

Peter the Eager Eagle

The Sound 'ee'

A long time ago in another land there was an eagle named Peter. Peter was in a great rush to grow up.

His mom said, "Peter, you're much too eager."

His dad said, "Peter, you shouldn't be in such a fierce fever to flee the nest."

"My life is so meager," said Peter. "I want to go east, and live in a tepee and drink tea and eat crumpets with the Queen of Egypt."

"You're just a chick," said his grammy. "You need to stay home with your family."

But Peter was really so eager. At the age of thirteen he jumped in a jeep and headed due east without heed.

Things really weren't ideal. But Peter still had his old zeal. He got a degree from Eton, and a job counting sheep on a farm in Egypt.

"I might not be a great hero," said Peter. "But I'm as happy as a pea in a pod. I sleep in a field of daisies, in a green tepee, count lots of sheep, and on Sundays have tea with the Queen."

Lou the Moose

The Sound 'oo'

There was once a moose named Lou. Lou was young and quite new. He loved to go to the zoo. He ate cotton candy and bought balloons and sat up top with a goose. Now Lou never knew it 'til June, that next year he was off to school.

"I can't go to school," said Lou. "I have to spend time at the zoo. I have no time for scissors and glue, to do that would make me quite blue."

"But school is super," said Mom. "You'll like it. It's really cool. You'll soon be part of the group. You'll learn to read and to count and to spell, and maybe they'll teach you the flute."

Oscar the Otter

The Sound 'o'

Oscar the otter sought a pot of rock salt. "I need that salt," said Oscar, "for a project in the Bronx. What shall I do? Where shall I look?"

Oscar's mom hadn't a thought where to get rock salt. And his father didn't know either.

Now Oscar's teacher, Miss Hart, was really awfully smart. She always taught Oscar to never give up. "You need that salt for your project in the Bronx. It's not your fault that salt is hard to spot."

So Oscar walked down to the park and caught a cab to the dock. He soon saw a sign written in chalk that said, "Rock Salt Only 1 Dollar." He bought a lot of the stuff. You never can have quite enough. And I've heard he's still busy today with his rock salt project in the Bronx.

CHAPTER SIX

MULTISYLLABLE MANAGEMENT

Congratulations! You've made your way through the most difficult level of reading instruction—the advanced code. By now your child:

- Understands that sometimes two or more letters represent a sound (EX: sh i p)
- Understands that most sounds can be represented in more than one way (EX: the sound 'a-e' can be spelled in several ways, train, play, paper, and more)
- Understands that there is overlap in the code, that some components of the code can represent more than one sound
  (EX: **<o>** can spell 'o' as in 'hot,' or 'oe' as in 'most')

Many parents and reading methods stop here, never offering the child Directed instruction or guided experience in the management of multisyllable words. This is a big mistake. Most new readers need some help to bridge the gap between words that can be said in one gulp, and words that require two or more. Let's look at why that is.

Multisyllable words really are more than a mouthful. They are quantitatively different from most single-syllable words in that they are longer and they contain more sounds. They are qualitatively different because the large number of sounds they contain cannot be articulated in one continuous flow. This forces us to stop the natural flow of blended sounds, and to start again with another set of blended sounds. Each set of blended sounds contains a vowel sound. Sometimes a syllable is just a vowel sound with no consonants. If children are not told about this phenomenon and given a strategy for managing it, they will attempt to push all the sounds into one neat little blended unit. This simply doesn't work. Something must get squeezed out. Usually this something is a vowel sound, like in the commonly misread word 'polish.' Typically we hear this:

'p' 'o' 'l' 'i' 'sh' plish

This kind of error is the norm with children who have had no instruction at the multisyllable level of reading and spelling. Typically these children get to about a fourth-grade reading level, and then start having trouble. If we teach children about multisyllable words, and offer them a strategy for managing them, they will have much greater success.

Some instructional methods teach children about multisyllable words, but they actually start at the syllable level and never teach the child to break down words by sounds (segmenting). The rationale that developers of these methods offer is that children can not easily perceive sound units. These methods recognize that whole words are too long, so they teach children to process in syllables, without having taught them about the sound units within syllables. The problems with this assumption are numerous. The most obvious problem is inherent in the nature of the written language. Our written language is not a syllabary like many of the oriental languages, in which each symbol represents a syllable. The Chinese symbol for instance, represents the syllable 'tang.' In Chinese, each symbol represents a syllable. English, on the other hand, is a sound symbol code, in which it is the various sounds that are represented by symbols. Syllables are the natural result of sounds being blended together. It is the sounds that are the raw material of written words, not the syllables. Methods that ignore this fact are not based on the true nature of our language. Teachers of English reading do not have the luxury of saying, "It's difficult, so we won't do it." They must develop instructional methods based on the realities of our written language.

Another problem with this assumption is that it is wrong. It is not necessarily difficult to teach children to process by sounds. It is as easy as your method allows it to be. By the time you reach this chapter, your child has been successfully segmenting sounds in words for some time now. If we had instructed you to skip that skill because it is difficult, your child would be having considerably more trouble than she is. She would not, for instance, be able to consistently detect subtle differences in words like 'cat' and 'cot.' By the time she reached this chapter, she would be making errors like this one which was read to me by a third-grade client who came to us from a school that uses a popular phonics reading program. The passage read:

You'll be sorry you stuck your nose in my business.

She read the passage as:

"You'll be sorry you stuck your nose in my 'busses.'"

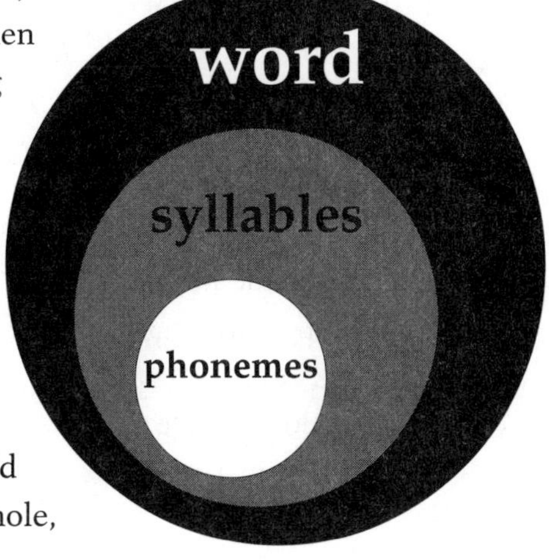

If we understand the nature of the written language, we will teach children in ways that support that nature, rather than undermining it. If we look at words as units of meaning that contain subunits which have no meaning, but are merely building blocks, we will be off to a good start. However, when children are reading, they are not starting from the meaning and moving down to the parts. As we explained in Chapter one, it is too difficult to recognize most words on sight. So when children read, they are building up from the sounds to the syllables and finally to the meaning, the word. So, we must use methods which teach children to build words from the smallest parts to the whole, from the phoneme to the syllable to the word. This is only logical. If we were to build anything, a house for instance, we would start with the raw materials. Cabinets don't grow on trees, or carpeting, or windows. They are constructed of raw materials, like sand, rubber, and wood.

The above model of words is best illustrated with an actual word. If the child encounters the word whisker,

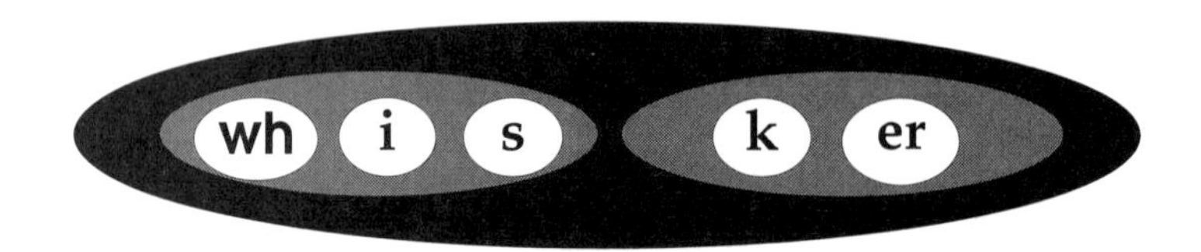

she does not necessarily recognize it on sight. Remember, as we mentioned in Chapter one, the average number of words that anyone can recall on sight is about two to five thousand. She must assess the word, one sound picture at a time. Her ability to do so is dependent upon her knowledge of the written sound picture code, and upon her ability to blend sounds into syllables, and syllables into words. Let's look at the goals for this level so that you'll be prepared to help her toward successful management of multisyllable words.

Goal #1. To understand that sometimes words have "chunks" of blended sounds

We use the word "chunk" to describe syllable units to new readers. This works better for two reasons.

1. The word "chunk" is more descriptive to a child than the word "syllable."
2. She won't confuse what we teach her about chunks with what she learns at school about syllables.

These chunks can make reading very difficult. A syllable chunk is linguistically the same as a single-syllable word, except that it lacks meaning. When we say "the dog ran," it sounds no different in its pauses and inflections than a multisyllable word. It is said that love is an illusion. Linguistically it is very similar to an illusion. The commonly spoken term of endearment, "I love you" sounds very much like the word 'illusion.' The pauses between the words 'I love you' are no longer than the pauses between the syllables 'ill' 'u' 'sion'. The second word 'love' is more stressed (higher) in 'I love you,'

'I love you'

and the second syllable 'u' is more stressed in 'illusion.'

'ill' 'u' 'sion'

They are indeed very similar. So why is it so much easier to read 'I love you' than it is to read 'illusion'? There are two reasons. The words 'I love you' are written with a space between them. This cues the reader to pause and chunk what she has so far. When reading 'illusion' the reader has no visual cues about the chunk. She must determine on her own when she has a mouthful of sounds. If 'I love you' were written like a multisyllable word, it would be harder to read than when the words are separated.

'Iloveyou'

But you already knew what that said. Let's come up with something less obvious. Try this phrase:

readingwordsthathavebeenruntogetherisnotaseasyasyouthinkitis

You can see that learning to tell when you've got a mouthful (a syllable chunk), and keeping track of where you are in the word at that particular time, is a very useful skill.

Another reason that 'I love you' is easier to read than 'illusion' is that the reader is assisted, much sooner in her efforts, by meaning. Her natural anxiety to seek meaning is assuaged in three short bursts.

'I'... me, myself
'love'... hugs and kisses
'you'... somebody else, not me

Goal #2. To understand that the chunks of sounds in words are determined by linguistics not orthography

Like any other word, there are two things that children do with multisyllable words. They read them, which we think of as breaking them down, and they spell them, which we think of as building them up. We teach children to build words and break words down according to the chunks of sounds, not according to orthographically driven dictionary syllables. If you open your dictionary to the word 'pillow' you'll see something like this:

pil · low

This orthographic split of the word 'pillow' is not linguistically accurate. The **<ll>** in this word is a sound picture, a single picture of one sound. A sound cannot be split. It is, by definition, the smallest audible unit. Yet, every word in your dictionary that contains double consonants is split between the two like consonants. We don't say the sound 'l' twice in the middle of the word 'pillow,' so why do we see it appearing in both syllables? When a child attempts to spell pillow, she hears either 'pi' 'llow' or 'pill' 'ow'. She does not hear 'pil' 'low'.

In pointing this out to parents and in teaching children to think about syllables linguistically we're not picking a fight with Mr. Webster. We're simply trying to help children to break down and build up words as easily as possible. Remember, we call syllable units chunks because they are different from what a child is likely to learn at school about syllables. Using this term allows children to learn about processing words by chunks, without confusing what we teach with what their teacher teaches about syllables. We suggest that you use this term when working with your child. If your child is learning about syllables at school, explain to her that this is different, it is all about the way we hear chunks in words.

Goal #3. To understand that we can read multisyllable words by blending sounds into chunks and then chunks into meaningful words

When reading multisyllable words, we teach children to blend sounds into chunks and chunks into words. So if we were to have before us the word 'containment,' we would first blend the sounds 'c' 'o' 'n'. Once blended, we have a neat little package that we can carry forward to the next chunk, 'con'. Then we go for the next chunk, 't' 'ai' 'n'. Now we have two neat little packages 'con' 'tain' to forge forward with 'm' 'e' 'n' 't' . . . 'con' 'tain' 'ment'. If your new reader isn't offered practice at this chunk building, she will jump in there with the same strategy we've encouraged up to this chapter. She would diligently say all ten sounds straight through the word and then try to blend them all at the end. She might, after failing at this for a few weeks, develop the right strategy on her own. She might start trying to blend as she makes her way through the word. But then again, she might not. Trying to blend ten sounds is quite an undertaking. Her auditory memory gets overloaded. This is why the hyphen in phone numbers came to be. If we can group the seven numbers into two packages 378 pause 6782, we can more easily remember them.

In addition to memory overload, multisyllable words present another problem. In our example word 'containment' for instance, the adjacent sounds 'n' and 'm' <containment>, cannot be blended. Try to think of a single-syllable word that contains these two adjacent sounds. There isn't one. There isn't one because the sounds simply do not articulate well in blended sequence. We call these "unfriendly sounds." Many multisyllable words contain sounds like this. Asking a child to read such a word without giving her an appropriate strategy to do so is a mean trick. She will try to blend all the components and will, surprise, surprise, have considerable trouble. Typically one of the unfriendly consonants gets squeezed out of the word, and sometimes, the entire syllable. The result might sound something like this: 'c' 'o' 'n' 't' 'ai' 'n' 'm' 'e' 'n' 't' . . . 'coment.' In this example, which was read to me just last week by a seventh-grade client, the child's natural desire to find meaning lead him to a real word, 'comment,' but not the right one. Having no strategy for getting all those sounds to go together, he lost a few.

Even after children learn about chunks and stop losing sounds, they can have trouble pushing the chunks together. Frequently, vowel sounds will be added between chunks so you get what we kiddingly call the "Latin effect." Our example word 'containment,' for instance, ends up sounding something like this:

'con' 'tain' 'u' 'ment'

The Latin effect tends to happen when the adjacent syllables end and begin with consonant sounds, especially unfriendly consonant sounds. It is the reader's natural tendency to bridge the two. The Latin effect can also happen because of the pause between syllables. As your child speeds up and gains fluency, the pause will shorten and the margin for error will decrease.

Goal #4. To understand that we can spell multisyllable words by building the sounds into chunks and then the chunks into words

When spelling multisyllable words, we encourage children to say the word, determine what the first chunk is, and then represent the sounds in that chunk in sequence. So if we were to spell the word 'containment,' we would first ask ourselves, "What are the chunks we hear?"

'con' 'tain' 'ment'

Then we would ask, "What are the sounds in 'con'?"

'c' 'o' 'n'

Then we would ask, "How do we show 'c', 'o', and 'n'?"

con

Then we would move on to 'tain'. "What do we hear in 'tain', and how do we show those sounds?"

con tain

And finally we would represent the last chunk, 'ment'.

con tain ment

Goal #5. To understand that multisyllable words contain a dominant chunk

We have natural highs and lows in our speech. With more than one chunk in most words, it is only logical that some chunks will be louder or more pronounced than others. This high and low is a subtle characteristic, but if read in the wrong order, can cause meaning to be lost or even changed. Let's look at this example.

bu tton

If pronounced normally, the first chunk in 'button,' 'butt,' is a bit more pronounced (louder, higher) than the next chunk, 'on'.

bu
tton

Let's imagine that you're working with your child and she reads the word with the second chunk a bit more pronounced than the first.

tton
bu

Suddenly, a fairly easy little word is sounding less and less like those things that hold your trousers up. Your child's natural desire to find meaning drives her to make sense of this word. She says it again, this time more slowly and with even more emphasis on the second chunk.

tton
bu

And suddenly she gets it, or what she thinks is it, and she proudly proclaims the word to be 'baton'! You grope for a moment, because to you the word is, always has been, and always will be 'button.' Then slowly you begin to form a mental image of a parade you took her to last Christmas. "Daddy," she asked, "what's that stick the lady's throwing up in the air?" "Why that's a 'baton,'" you explained.

Can this Saturday afternoon nightmare home reading lesson be saved? Or are you doomed to give up and tell her the word? "No, 'baton' is spelled with an 'aye' and only one 'tee.' This word is 'button' . . . 'bu' 'tton' . . . 'bee' 'you' 'double tee' 'oh' 'en' . . . 'button.' Of course you won't do that. You know better. Wouldn't it be easier to avoid this situation altogether by giving her a strategy for managing the highs and lows in words with multiple chunks? By teaching your child to try making the other chunk a bit louder, when a word isn't making sense, you will increase her odds of success significantly.

Goal #6. To understand that many multisyllable words contain a weak vowel sound

Saying more than a mouthful can cause more problems than just poor reading. It can cause imperfect pronunciation. When pronouncing multiple chunks in words, we frequently fail to correctly enunciate the vowel sound in the subdominant, or quieter chunk. In our current example word 'button,' for instance, the second chunk sounds more like 'un' or 'in' (depending upon the region of the country you live in) than 'on'. Pronounce these two words and you see that one of them sounds just fine to you.

buttun buttin

For me it's the first one. Yup, 'buttun,' that thing that holds up my trousers.

We're not advocating that you force your child to speak the Queen's English. The weak vowel sound in multisyllable words is a common and accepted part of our speech. We are suggesting that you make your child aware of it. If she isn't aware of it, she may tend to spell these words exactly as she pronounces them. The above two spellings for 'button' are typical examples of the kinds of errors that children make when they are unaware of the weak vowel sound in many multisyllable words. Here are a few more examples.

luggage = lugguge
control = cuntrol seven = sevin
forest = forust pocket = pockit
multiply = multuply mitten = mittin
hurricane = hurrucane kitchen = kitchun

To overcome these kinds of errors, we teach children to make what we call a "perfect recording" of words. To make a perfect recording we simply look at the word as we say it perfectly, as the Queen would. If your child notices that 'button' is spelled <button> and if sounded perfectly would be 'button,' she can say 'buttin' or 'buttun' all she wants as long as she knows to refer to her perfect recording when she spells the word. Experience with written language will also help your child notice such spelling errors. The more she reads and sees the word 'button,' the more likely she will be to notice that it doesn't look quite right when she writes <buttin> or <buttun>.

Goal #7. To understand that many multisyllable words have "special endings."

Many multisyllable words end in what we term "special endings." These are syllable chunks which are not phonetically decodable according to the English written code. Let's look at the word 'occupation,' for instance. The original word from which this word was derived was 'occupy.' 'Occupy' is a verb which simply means "the act of taking up space,"

The Germans 'occupied' France during World War II.

or time,

I 'occupy' myself by reading a lot.

When the special ending **<tion>** is added to the word 'occupation,' the meaning is changed to a 'thing,' a noun which refers to taking up space,

The occupation of France was a travesty.

or time,

Real estate is her occupation.

Although understanding this kind of meaning structure of words is beneficial to vocabulary development and to comprehension, it only becomes critical to reading and spelling when part of the word is not decodable given the code we have to work with. The special ending **<tion>** for instance, if sounded out according to our English sound symbol code would sound very different from the 'shun' that we say when we see it. This has occurred in our language because we have borrowed from Latin and Greek to make special endings which change the meaning of words. In Latin, **<tion>** means "to take form." In other words, to become a 'thing,' a noun. Instead of being adapted to the English written code, special endings often got adopted as they were written in Latin or in Latin-based languages such as French.

Children need to be made aware of the special endings in words. They need to know that they cannot decode them according to the code we have taught them. There are so few special endings, about eight, that your child can learn them as a unit easily enough. This kind of whole syllable memorization is exactly where the visual memory is best used. Your child cannot memorize the twenty thousand words that she needs to be able to read and spell, but she can memorize the sound symbols that you taught her in Chapters three and five, and the special endings that you'll be teaching her in this chapter.

Eleven-Year-Old Georgiana, the Worst Reader in Her Class

"I'm the worst reader in my class," Georgiana sorrowfully reported when she was presented for testing at the Altamonte Springs Read America clinic. "If my teacher asks me to read out loud, I tell her I've got a headache. Sometimes she lets me off the hook. When she makes me read, I really do get a headache!"

"We brought her to the doctor and the ophthalmologist for the headaches," Georgiana's father explained. "There's nothing wrong with her."

"Except for this reading thing," her mother added. "I just don't get it. She was an A and B student through third grade. Last year she took a turn down and this year it's the headaches."

Georgiana's testing revealed no problems with auditory processing or blending. Her segmenting was quite good. Even her code knowledge was not bad at 82 percent. But when asked to read words with more than one syllable her accuracy rate deteriorated, and her code knowledge seemed to degrade. On the standardized reading test she made the following errors:

wonderful = wonderfully, dangerous = dungarees,
allowable = allowance, prudent = purdent,
circumstance = circumcise, occasionally = occasional
tranquility = tranquality

Georgiana's therapy consisted of six sessions. The first two sessions were spent on advanced code knowledge and multisyllable management. During her first session, as her therapist explained that many words contain chunks of sounds, Georgiana proclaimed, "Oh yes, syllables. We learned about that last year" (in fourth grade). When asked to isolate the three chunks in 'deposit,' she clapped her hands three times as she said, 'de' 'pos' 'it'. She explained that last year her fourth-grade teacher, Mrs. Tobin, had taught the children to do this as an aid to determining the syllables in words. Georgiana's therapist showed her that this step was unnecessary, and that she could easily determine the syllables without clapping her hands together. Not only is syllable clapping unnecessary, but in Georgiana's case it was confusing. By clapping while saying the syllables, she was causing background noise that inhibited her ability to hear the individual sounds in the syllables. Georgiana's problems did not arise from being unable to hear syllables in words. She, like most children, could do that with ease. Her problems came from not knowing how to read words in chunks, and from not keeping track of where she was in the written word as she read. She tended to add a vowel sound between chunks or to leave out an entire chunk altogether. In addition, she was just as likely to push two or three words together as if they were syllables in a single word, as she was to read a multisyllable word as two or three separate words. Even after she began to make steady improvement, she would occasionally lapse back and make a blatant error in reading a multisyllable word. As she improved and started to catch her errors, she often found them amusing, such as the following error which she made while reading a nature book about baby animals with her therapist at her third therapy session. The passage read:

> The mother kangaroo has an area of very soft fur on her tummy. There is a pouch on this for her baby kangaroo.

She read the passage as,

> "The mother kangaroo has soft fur on her tummy. There is a pocahontas for her baby kangaroo."

I had not observed that session, but Georgiana's therapist told me of it later. She was happy to report that Georgiana immediately caught her error, found it wildly amusing, and proceeded to read the passage with perfect accuracy.

Georgiana's last four sessions were dedicated exclusively to multisyllable management. At the close of the sixth session Georgiana's standardized reading score had gone from third grade, eighth month, to seventh grade, fourth month, two years above grade level. During her last three sessions the therapist had started her reading Tolkien's *The Hobbit*. Her mother reported, in a follow-up survey the following year, that Georgiana had happily finished *The Hobbit* and gone on to read *The Lord of the Rings*.

If your child is in first grade, sixth month, or older, proceed only with the multisyllable lessons that are indicated with a graduate Sound Doggy. If your child is older than first grade, sixth month, make your way through the lessons until they start to get too difficult for her. A good rule of thumb is that second graders should be able to read and spell two-syllable words, third graders should be able to read and spell three-syllable words, and children older than that should be able to read and spell four-syllable words whose meaning they know.

READING AND MAPPING MULTISYLLABLE WORDS WITH VISUAL STOPS

Readiness

Do this lesson with any child who has successfully worked in Chapter five. With a child in first grade, sixth month, or younger, try this lesson and see how she does. If she has a lot of trouble and doesn't respond to the error correction procedures, discontinue the lesson and wait about two months.

Goals

To offer your child practice at reading words in chunks.

To cause your child to understand that there is an exact visual location of the verbal pause in multisyllable words. EX: If the word is 'Santa,' we make a verbal pause after the sound 'n'. As we read 'Santa,' our eyes should also pause, and that visual pause should match the verbal pause.

To offer your child practice in spelling words one chunk at a time.

Materials

Use the first set of multisyllable word lists (with coded text and visual cues) following this lesson plan. Start with two-syllable words. Continue on to three-syllable word lists with visual stops but not with coded text, on page 316, as your child shows that she has mastered each level.

Presentation

1. Explain to your child that the words on the list have two chunks, and that there is a marker between the chunks so that she will stop there and say what she has so far before she goes on to the next chunk.
2. Have your child read the first chunk in the first word on the two-syllable list.
3. Ask her to map the word on her paper, leaving a space between the chunks in the word.

continued

Reading and Mapping Multisyllable Words, continued

Note: At the multisyllable level, it is no longer necessary for your child to say each sound when mapping. The following procedure should be used when mapping multisyllable words.

a. Read the word Tues - day.

b. Say the first chunk slowly, 'Tues' as you write it. It is not necessary to say each sound separately, but be sure to say it slowly, trying to pace yourself so that you start and finish saying the chunk at the same time that you start and finish writing the chunk.

Tues

c. Repeat step (b) for the next chunk.

Note: If you are still working on advanced code knowledge in Chapter five, or the lesson in Chapter four, do not allow your child to map those lessons in this way. All mapping in chapters preceding this chapter (six) should be done one sound at a time, as previously explained.

Correcting Problems

She tries to sound each symbol separately. She reads the ***<ai>*** *in 'contain' as 'a' 'i'.*

Point to the **<ai>** and say the sound 'ae'.

She misreads or guesses part of the word. She reads the word 'safety' as 'safely.'

Say, "You made a mistake in the second chunk. Try again." If she is a frequent guesser say, "You guessed the second chunk. Please read the word. If she repeats her error say, "You are saying 'l' here. Try again, please."

continued

Reading and Mapping Multisyllable Words, continued

*She misreads a sound, but it is a possible option for that particular sound picture. For example, she reads **<table>** using the sound 'a' as in 'cat' instead of 'ae' as in 'table.'*

Say, "This (indicate as shown below) can be 'a', but it can also be 'ae'. Try 'ae'."

She adds a sound when reading a word. For example, she reads containment as 'containument.'

Tell her specifically what she did wrong. "You said 'u' between these two chunks."

Indicate the spot as shown below.

She attempts to say all the sounds in one chunk. She doesn't stop and blend after each chunk.

Tell her what she did and have her try again, blending after each chunk.

	b i **gg** ✋ **er**
	m o **pp** ✋ i **ng**
f u **nn** ✋ y	r u **nn** ✋ **er**
l i **tt** ✋ **le**	b a d ✋ l y
b u **tt** ✋ o n	f a s t ✋ **er**
h a **pp** ✋ y	r a **tt** ✋ **le**
g l a d ✋ l y	p u **dd** ✋ **le**
s i m p ✋ **le**	s o f t ✋ l y
s o ✋ **rr** y	r i **pp** ✋ **le**
s u **nn** ✋ y	m i **dd** ✋ **le**

fu**nn** y ________ ________

li**tt** **le** ________ ________

bu**tt** on ________ ________

ha**pp** y ________ ________

glad ly ________ ________

simp **le** ________ ________

so **rr**y ________ ________

su**nn** y ________ ________

bi**gg** **er** ________ ________

m o **pp** ✋ i **ng** ________ ________

r u **nn** ✋ **er** ________ ________

b a d ✋ l y ________ ________

f a s t ✋ **er** ________ ________

r a **tt** ✋ **le** ________ ________

p u **dd** ✋ **le** ________ ________

s o f t ✋ l y ________ ________

r i **pp** ✋ **le** ________ ________

m i **dd** ✋ **le** ________ ________

p o l i **sh**	s t r u **gg** **le**
m o n k **ey**	l **oy** **al**
sh a d **ow**	r a p i d
a **dd** r e **ss**	p **ea** n u t
p r e v e n t	r o b i n
w i **gg** **le**	s **urr** **ou** n d
r e p **ai** r	r e **qu** e s t
f e **ll** **ow**	f l **ow** **er**
l e m o n	g o **ss** i p
p i **ll** **ow**	**sh** a m p **oo**
wh e **th** **er**	t **ea** **ch** **er**
p l e n t y	t e n d **er**

a - c o r n

s a m - p **le**

c a m p - i **ng**

b **oo** k - l e t

c r **ay** - o n

c r u m - b **le**

s n i **ck** - **er**

ch i m - n **ey**

h a **pp** - e n

t r a - v **el**

p u m p - k i n

p r o - d u c t

b r **igh** - t e n

c l o s - e t

r a **bb** - i t

t a - b **le**

p a - p **er**

s i m - p **le**

a **pp** - **le**

p **ur** - p **le**

h a **pp** - y

r u **nn** - **er**

m u - s i c

l e **ss** - o n

b e - f **o** r **e**

m a g - i c

l **ou** d - l y

m o n - **ey**

m **ou** n - t **ai** n

w a t - **er**

w i n - t **er**

w **orr** - **ie** d

c a n - d y

c **er** - t **ai** n

j **ew** - **el**

h o **ll** - **ow**

Two-Syllable Words with Coded Text and Visual Stops, continued

i n - s t **ea** d	qu i **ck** - l y
f o r - e s t	s o f t - **er**
d **ur** - i **ng**	T **ue** s - d **ay**
ear - l y	**aw** - f u l
e n - j **oy**	c i n - d **er**
e x - p **er** t	l **igh** t - n i **ng**
f **ea** - **th** **er**	p r i n t - **er**
e x - c **u** s **e**	u n - d **er**
c o s - t **u** m **e**	c **ou** n - t r y
o - v **er**	s t a p - l **er**
d a n - c **er**	**w** i **th** - **er**
th u n - d **er**	c a - **rr** y

Three-Syllable Words with Visual Stops

hos - pi - tal	pre - si - dent
ha - ppi - ness	mul - ti - ply
de - po - sit	es - tab - lish
ex - am - ple	hes - i - tate

un - ea - sy	cu - cum - ber
mon - u - ment	nur - ser - y
nav - i - gate	mul - ti - ple
ob - sta - cle	mu - si - cal
o - ver - flow	ob - serv - er
prin - ci - ple	re - co - mmend
cel - e - brate	pub - lic - ly
won - der - f u l	pros - per - ous
op - er - ate	boun - ti - ful
mech - an - ic	simp - li - fy
burg - la - ry	occ - u - py
cal - cu - late	sym - bol - ic
cann - i - bal	mo - ment - ous
car - pet - ing	inn - o - cent
cen - ti - grade	de - scrip - tive
reg - i - ster	char - ac - ter
cap - i - tal	es - ca - pade

MULTISYLLABLE WORD ANALYSIS

Readiness

Do this lesson with a child older than first grade, sixth month, who has successfully done the lesson Reading Multisyllable Words with Visual Stops.

Goals

To remind your child that syllables contain sounds which are represented by sound pictures.

Materials

Use the multisyllable word lists on pages 325-329. Start with two-syllable words. Continue on to three syllables as your child shows readiness.

Use your dry erase board.

Presentation

1. Have your child read the first word on the two-syllable list.
2. Ask her what the first chunk is, and then the second chunk.
3. Ask her what the first sound in the chunk is. Have her write it down. Ask her for the next sound in the chunk and have her write it down. Proceed through the chunk. Each time a sound is represented by more than one letter, ask her to underline it as a reminder that it is just one sound.
4. Proceed to the next chunk. Repeat steps 2 and 3.

Correcting Problems

For the word 'tractor' she says the first chunk is 'trac' and the second chunk is 'tor', but she writes the word like this: t r a c t or .

Say, "You said the first chunk was 'trac'. What does the first chunk you've written say?" When she reads 'tract' say, "Please write what you said, 'trac'."

She says the first chunk is 't'.

Correct this problem by saying, "That's the first sound. There are two chunks in the word 'tractor.' What's the first chunk in 'tractor'?"

continued

Multisyllable Word Analysis, continued

She says the first chunk is 'tr'.

She is still having trouble separating adjacent consonants. She needs additional segmenting work. Mix her multisyllable lessons with some additional practice in the Auditory Processing lesson in Chapter four.

She says the first sound is 'tr', and she underlines it.

She needs additional segmenting work. Mix her multisyllable lessons with some additional practice in the Auditory Processing lesson in Chapter four.

She reads the word correctly. For instance, 'contain.' But she writes it like this:

c o n t a i n

as if the **<ai>** *were two distinct sounds, when it should look like this:*

c o n t ai n

Say, "Let's check the sounds. Please say each sound as you point to the sound picture." When she reaches the **<ai>** she should notice her error.

She misreads or guesses part of the word. She reads the word 'safety' as 'safely.'

Say, "You made a mistake in the second chunk. Try again." If she is a frequent guesser say, "You guessed the second chunk. Please *read* the word." If she repeats her error say, "You are saying 'l' here (indicating as shown below). Try again, please."

safety

She misreads a sound, but it is a possible option for that particular sound picture. For example, she reads <table> using the sound 'a' as in 'cat' instead of 'ae' as in 'table.'

Say, "This (indicating as shown below) can be 'a', but it can also be 'ae'. Try 'ae'."

table

FINDING THE LOUD SYLLABLE IN MULTISYLLABLE WORDS

Readiness

Do this lesson with a child older than first grade, sixth month, when she has completed the Multisyllable Word Analysis lesson.

Goals

To understand that the chunks in multisyllable words are not spoken in monotone. They are loud and quiet.

To establish a process for reading multisyllable words correctly by saying a different syllable loudly when the word doesn't make sense.

Materials

Starting with two syllables, use any of the word lists in this chapter which have the words separated by syllable chunks.

Have your dry erase board handy.

Presentation

1. Tell your child that words with more than one chunk have loud and quiet chunks. Explain that in this lesson you're going to find the loud chunks.
2. Have your child read the first word. Have her map it on your white board.
3. Explain that you're going to read it to her with one syllable louder than the other. Read it to her with the first syllable louder. Ask her if it sounds right to her. Then read it to her with the second syllable louder. Ask her how that sounds.
4. Now have her read the word both ways. Ask her which she thinks is the right way to say the word.
5. Proceed to the next word.

continued

Finding the Loud Syllable, continued

Correcting Problems

Your child has trouble hearing that one chunk is louder than the other.

Accentuate this even more.

Your child names the wrong answer. For instance, she says that the second chunk is louder in 'slowly.'

Say, "So the word is 'slow' 'ly'?" Then say it like that in a sentence. "I walked 'slow ly' to school."

FINDING "MR. SCHWA" IN MULTISYLLABLE WORDS

Readiness

Do this lesson with a child older than first grade, sixth month, once she has completed the lesson Finding the Loud Syllable in Multisyllable Words.

Goals

To understand that some multisyllable words contain a weak vowel sound that can be easily misspelled.

To establish a process for avoiding misspelled words by creating a perfect recording of the word as it is spelled.

Materials

Starting with two syllables, use any of the word lists in this chapter which have the words separated by syllable chunks.

Have your dry erase board handy.

Presentation

1. Tell your child that some words with more than one chunk have sounds that are weak, and that we call this sound "Mr. Schwa." Show her the picture of Mr. Schwa and tell her he's out to ruin her spelling tests.
2. Have your child read the first word, 'button.' Ask her what the first chunk is in 'button.' Then the second chunk.
3. If she says 'tin' or 'tun' for the second chunk, ask her if she hears a sound that doesn't match the sound picture that she sees. If she says 'ton', say, "That's right, 'button.' You said it perfectly, but if I say that word normally, like most people do, it sounds kind of sloppy like this, 'buttin.' When I say it like that, 'buttin' (bring your pencil along the word as you slowly say it), this sound (indicate the **<o>**) isn't quite perfect.

It sounds more like this." Print **<i>** on your white board.

continued

Finding "Mr. Schwa," continued

4. Explain that although we can speak normally most of the time, when we spell words with a sloppy sound it's good to have a perfect recording of the word, so that we spell all the sounds correctly. Have her make a perfect recording of 'button.'
5. Have your child read each of the words, find the weak vowel sound, make a perfect recording of the word, and then map the word.

READING AND MAPPING MULTISYLLABLE WORDS WITHOUT VISUAL STOPS

Readiness

Do this lesson with a child older than first grade, sixth month, who has done the lesson Finding the Weak Vowel Sound in Multisyllable Words.

Goals

To offer your child practice at perceiving the natural verbal pause in multisyllable words.

To cause your child to attend to the exact visual location of the verbal pause in multisyllable words without the aid of visual cues.

To offer your child practice spelling words one chunk at a time.

Materials

Use the multisyllable word lists on pages 325 through 329. Start with two-syllable words. Continue on to three syllables as your child shows that she is ready.

A piece of lined paper or your dry erase board.

Presentation

1. Have your child read the first word on the two-syllable list.
2. Ask her what the first chunk is, and then the second chunk.
3. Ask her to write the word leaving a space where she hears a pause between the chunks in the word.

Correcting Problems

For the word 'tractor' she says the first chunk is 'trac' and the second chunk is 'tor', but she writes the word like this: tract or .

continued

Reading and Mapping Multisyllable Words, continued

Say, "You said the first chunk was 'trac'. What does the first chunk you've written say?" When she reads 'tract' say, "Please write what you said, 'trac'."

She says the first chunk is 't'.

Correct this problem by saying, "That's the first sound. There are two chunks in the word 'tractor.' What's the first chunk in 'tractor'?"

She says the first chunk is 'tr'.

She needs additional segmenting work. Mix her multisyllable lessons with some additional practice in the Auditory Processing lesson in Chapter four.

She tries to sound each symbol separately. She reads the ***<ai>*** *in 'contain' as 'a' 'i'.*

Point to the **<ai>** and say the sound 'ae'.

She misreads or guesses part of the word. She reads the word 'safety' as 'safely.'

Say, "You made a mistake in the second chunk. Try again." If she is a frequent guesser, say, "You guessed the second chunk. Please read the word." If she repeats her error say, "You are saying 'l' here (indicating the **<t>**). Try again, please."

She misreads a sound, but it is a possible option for that particular sound picture. For example, she reads <table> using the sound 'a' as in 'cat' instead of 'ae' as in 'table.'

Say, "This (indicating **<a>**) can be 'a', but it can also be 'ae'. Try 'ae'."

She adds a sound when reading a word. For example, containment = containument.

Tell her specifically what she did wrong. "You said 'u' between (indicating the spot) these two chunks."

She attempts to say all the sounds in one chunk. She doesn't stop and blend after each chunk.

Tell her what she did wrong and have her try again, blending after each chunk.

Two-Syllable Words Without Visual Stops

gopher	parrot
hammer	orange
hanger	parade
lumber	oyster
jungle	panther
lobster	numbers
handle	mustard
infant	service
husband	rocket
insect	reptile
helmet	powder
lettuce	poison
luggage	quarrel
maple	quarter
olive	absent
muffin	vanish
office	transform
muskrat	reflect

talent	tractor
torment	simple
transport	balance
target	ginger
wrinkle	Tuesday
whisker	spider
bishop	cattle
beyond	circus
blizzard	Thursday
bitter	chimney
gather	concert
budget	control
garbage	cashier
advance	candle
active	monster
gamble	camel
garage	dinner
gadget	desert

Two-Syllable Words Without Visual Stops, continued

dentist	river
cottage	tunnel
cricket	forward
father	freezer
dirty	reckless
eagle	stickers
eclipse	trombone

Three-Syllable Words Without Visual Stops

feverish	explosive
recorder	graduate
finishing	develop
forgetful	expressway
fingerprint	exercise
fantasy	engineer
celebrate	embroider
certainly	embarrass
calculate	elephant

electric	governor
dynamite	gentlemen
detective	generous
department	satisfied
destroyer	accident
detergent	achievement
December	acrobat
customer	sensible
cucumber	gardener
crocodile	galaxy
criminal	disappear
carpenter	discover
cosmetics	deliver
telephone	consequence
Saturday	threatening
saturate	horrify
gratitude	bitterly
gravity	rectangle

recover	parakeet
transparent	parallel
vanishing	operate
absolute	multiply
umbrella	monument
trampoline	minister
tolerant	museum
reporter	microscope
pharmacy	microphone
petticoat	kangaroo
propellor	magnetic
principal	magazine
projector	lollipop
pottery	hurricane
pocketbook	happily

SPECIAL ENDINGS

Readiness

Do this lesson with a child older than first grade, sixth month, when she has completed the lesson plan Reading Multisyllable Words Without Visual Stops.

Goals

To understand that some multisyllable words contain special endings that should be remembered as a unit.

To get practice reading and spelling words with special endings.

Materials

Use the Special Endings word lists following this lesson plan. They offer a few words to practice the concept and skills needed to read special endings.

Have your dry erase board handy.

Presentation

1. Tell your child that some words with more than one chunk contain a special ending.
2. Write **<tion>** on your dry erase board. Say, "This is 'shun'. It sounds like it should be spelled like this **<shun>**." Say each sound as you write **<shun>**. Say, "'Shun' is a special ending that we can just remember like a picture."
3. Show your child the Special Endings 'shun' Word List. Have her read each word. Offer assistance as needed.
4. After reading each word, have her map the word on a piece of lined paper or your dry erase board. She should leave a space between each chunk. She should say each chunk slowly as she writes it. Do not allow her to say letter names as she writes the special ending.

Special Ending 'shun'

physician
musician
nation
mission
vacation
suspension
explanation
election
plantation
dimension

Special Ending 'zhun'

immersion
collision
television
vision

Special Ending 'shus'

precocious
delicious
fictitious
nutritious
malicious
atrocious
conscious
ferocious

Special Ending 'kshus'

anxious
obnoxious

Special Ending 'shu'

militia	inertia
Patricia	dementia
facia	Marcia

Special Ending 'zhu'

amnesia	Persia
Asia	freesia

Special Ending 'cher'

structure	gesture
furniture	posture
future	adventure
capture	pasture

Special Ending 'zhure'

treasure	pleasure
measure	leisure

MULTISYLLABLE PROCESS SPELLING

Readiness

You can do this lesson with a child older than first grade, sixth month, once she has completed the lesson Special Endings.

Goals

To offer your child practice at spelling multisyllable words using the skills she has learned so far.

Materials

Use the words on the multisyllable word lists without visual cues on pages 325-329. Start with two-syllable words. Continue on to three syllables as your child shows readiness.

Use your dry erase board or a piece of lined paper.

Presentation

1. Explain to your child that you are going to play a spelling game. Show her the first word on the list. Have her read the word.
2. Ask her what the first chunk is, and then the second chunk.
3. Ask her to say each sound as she looks at the corresponding sound pictures.
4. Ask her if there is anything in particular that she needs to remember about this word if she is going to spell it correctly. Work with her to isolate everything about the word that needs to be visually recalled, anything that is not obvious in the way the word sounds. She should do this one chunk at a time.

   For example, she should notice the following pictures, sounds, and endings.

   a. The picture of any sound that can be represented differently. For instance, the sound 'ae' is represented by the **<ai>** sound picture in <contain>, or the sound 'l' is represented by **<ll>** in the word <pillow>.

continued

Multisyllable Process Spelling, continued

b. Any weak vowel sounds that are not represented as they sound. For instance, the **<o>** in <button> sounds like 'u'. When a word contains a weak vowel sound your child should make a perfect recording of the word. In other words, she should say the word as the sound should be said: 'button,' accentuating the sound 'o' as in 'on', not 'buttun.'

c. Any special endings and the way in which they are represented.

5. Once she has completed her check of the word, you can cover the word up so that she can't see it. Ask her, "What's the first chunk?" When she tells you, say, "Good, say each sound as you write the chunk." When she has completed that chunk, go on to the next.

Correcting Problems

She misspells a sound. For example, 'contain' is shown as <contan>.

Say, "You forgot what you noticed about the sound 'ae' in this word. If she still can't recall, write down some of the 'ae' sound pictures. See if she can recall which is the correct one for this particular word.

a-e ay ai

If she still isn't sure, have her write it out each way and see if she remembers.

contane contayn contain

If all else fails, tell her what she did wrong.

She misspells a weak vowel sound in a word.

Say, "You forgot to use your perfect recording." If she can't recall the perfect recording, say it for her.

READING UNCODED TEXT CONTAINING MULTISYLLABLE WORDS

Readiness

Begin reading uncoded text containing multisyllable words when your child is working with stability on the multisyllable lesson plans. Do not begin until she has completed the lesson plan Reading and Mapping Multisyllable Words Without Visual Stops.

Materials

To start we suggest short stories that are about a year below your child's current capability. By now you are an expert at what your child can and can't do, so find something that you know will be easy for her.

For young children (younger than first grade, sixth month) large, dark print is good, with just a few words on each page. Avoid stories that contain words your child doesn't use regularly.

For older children we recommend *Aesop's Fables* and *American Tall Tales*. Move on to more challenging text as your child shows readiness.

Have your dry erase board handy.

Have a sharp pencil handy.

Presentation

1. Invite your child to come read a story with you.
2. Have her read, allowing her lots of time and patience. Offer her help as needed, using the mentoring skills you've learned so far.

Correcting Problems

Generally, you will be using all of the mentoring skills you've been using so far in your work with your child. There are a few points to be made about working with uncoded text in a book format.

Use your pencil point to indicate sound pictures and special endings as needed.

continued

Reading Uncoded Multisyllable Text, continued

If you have a need to write in order to help your child, use your white board. The problem word can be recreated on the white board so you don't have to write in your books.

If your child still needs to sound words out one sound at a time, allow her the time and patience. In addition to working in books, she should be continuing with the earlier lessons in this book. Her retest should reveal why she is still reading slowly. She may need more advanced code knowledge work, or additional practice at the earlier lessons in Chapter four.

AFTERWORD

Congratulations! Your careful mentoring has led your child to literacy. She is now able to read and spell with success. As a conscientious parent, you know that your work has just begun. Just because your child is able to read doesn't mean she will read. She is perfectly capable of brushing her teeth and cleaning her room. But does she do so without your constant reminders? If she is like most children, she will need lots and lots of encouragement to read. But read she must. It is very important that you and she understand that if she doesn't use her reading capability, it may wither. Reading, like any other complex cognitive skill, requires practice. She must read daily in order to keep her reading reflexes sharp. It would be a mistake to accomplish all your hard work, all your effort, and then suddenly stop. You have come so far. You and your child are used to working together. Why stop? Why not keep it up? Why not take the time you have been spending working on developing her reading skills, and start using that same time to practice them?

How Much and How Often

We recommend that children read aloud to an adult for at least thirty minutes each day until the age of ten, or until they have been reading well for about a year. Oral reading is advisable for two reasons. By having your child read out loud you are assured that she is actually reading. And by reading out loud, your child will be less likely to allow herself to make all those mistakes you've worked so hard to overcome or avoid. If your child's reading is not yet as good as you would like it to be, you should supervise closely when she reads aloud. We recommend reading in the same location that you have been using for your reading lessons. This will allow you to maintain the mentor relationship that you've accomplished. We also recommend that you continue to offer her lessons in the areas in which she still needs work. Your child's most recent subskill test and her actual reading will guide you.

If your child's reading is at the level you hoped for, your supervision of oral reading can be much looser. Many parents have their children read to them while they prepare dinner. Riding in the car is also a good time for reading. But be warned, some children get car sick when reading in a moving vehicle.

From Comic Books to Classics

What should your child be reading? You should split the time equally between the challenging and the easy. By allowing her to read easy and fun books, you will be giving her a chance to keep up her current reading skills. By having her attempt more difficult books you are forcing her to stretch her capabilities just a bit. Depending on her age and current reading capability, easy reading might consist of comic books, short stories, and magazine or newspaper articles. More challenging reading would be chapter books. Please encourage your child to read the classics. If a particular book is especially difficult, you can take turns reading. It could even be a family event. Everyone could have a turn to read. We also like *Aesop's Fables* and *American Tall Tales*, as well as the *Just So Stories*. These are a nice mid-length choice that is not too overwhelming. However, they are literature, not just any book. When you give her something difficult to read, tell her it's hard. Let her know that she's attempting something challenging and she should take her time and be very patient with herself. This will make her work seem more important, and lend a bit of excitement to her endeavor. It will also allow her to forgive herself when she falters.

Retest

The following copies of the tests in Chapter two are offered here so that you can retest your child and see how far you've both come. If she still needs work in certain areas, continue with the lessons that teach those issues. Refer to the goals section of the lesson plans to determine what you should be doing to continue to improve on your child's reading.

On Comprehension

Completing the Phono-Graphix activites presented in this book will improve your child's overall reading speed and accuracy—important components of comprehension. In addition to the Phono-Graphix reading method, the authors have developed a method for addressing the other important components of reading and oral comprehension—vocabulary, logical reasoning, creativity, memory, and grammar. Information about the Language Wise comprehension method can be obtained from Read America. Call us at 1-800-732-3868 or at 352-735-9292; fax us at 352-735-9294; write to us at P.O. Box 1246, Mount Dora, FL 32776; e-mail us at RAchat@aol.com, or visit our Web site at www.readamerica.net.

BLENDING TEST

Do not allow your child to see the test. Tell your child that you are going to say some sounds, and that she should tell you what word it sounds like. Sit near enough that she can hear you clearly, and see your mouth. Explain to her that you can say the sounds only once and so she should listen and watch carefully. Say each sound in the first word, with a one-second interval between each sound 'p' 'i' 'g'. Do not repeat the word. Write down her first response.

PART ONE	
p i g	________
b u g	________
h a t	________
p i n	________
r a t	________
b **ir** d	________
sh e **ll**	________
f i **ve**	________
b **oa** t	________

PART TWO	
f r o g	________
g r a **ss**	________
s t i **ck**	________
p r i n t	________
c r u n **ch**	________
p l a n t	________

Interpretation of Scores   14+ = good   -14 = low moderate   -11 = poor

Less than a perfect score on part one indicates that your child has trouble blending or pushing together the sounds in three-sound words. This will require lots of work in Chapter three.

Less than a perfect score on part two indicates that your child has trouble pushing together sounds in four- and five-sound words. This will require lots of work in Chapter four.

PHONEME SEGMENTATION TEST

Do not allow your child to see the test. Explain to your child that you want her to tell you all the sounds in the word 'dog.' If she offers a letter name say, "That's a letter. What's the *sound?*" If she persists at responding with letter names, mark those responses wrong. Put a check for each correct answer in the corresponding space. If she omits a sound, mark it wrong, EX: 'frog' = 'f' 'o' 'g'. You would mark these responses like this ✔ X ✔ ✔. If she gives the wrong sound, mark it wrong, EX: 'frog' = 'f' 'r' 'a' 'g'. You would score these responses like this ✔ ✔ X ✔. If she blends two sounds together mark both sounds wrong, EX: 'frog' = 'fr' 'o' 'g'. You would mark these responses like this X X ✔ ✔.
'f' 'ro' 'g' would be marked like this ✔ X X ✔.

PART ONE	
dog	___ ___ ___
hat	___ ___ ___
pin	___ ___ ___
pot	___ ___ ___
rat	___ ___ ___
nut	___ ___ ___

PART TWO	
frog	___ ___ ___ ___
black	___ ___ ___ ___
nest	___ ___ ___ ___
trip	___ ___ ___ ___
milk	___ ___ ___ ___
drum	___ ___ ___ ___

Interpretation of Scores   40+ = good   - 40 = low moderate   - 36 = poor

Offered a letter name more than 2 times, EX: 'dog' = 'dee' 'oe' 'gee'. Your child may not understand that letters are symbols for sounds. She may be trying to recall the sound of the letter by thinking of the letter name, an unnecessary step requiring a translation. This will require lots of work in Chapters three and four.

Omitted vowel sound or chunked it to a consonant sound 2 or more times, EX: 'dog' = 'd' 'g' or 'do' 'g' or 'd' 'og'. Your child may have a vowel sound hanging on the end of her consonants and may need retraining in the pronunciation of consonant sounds. This will require lots of work in Chapter three.

Chunked consonants together or omitted one of them more than 2 times, EX: 'frog' = 'fr' 'o' 'g' or 'f' 'o' 'g'. Your child may be having trouble isolating the separate sounds in words, causing her to leave sounds out and add sounds that aren't there. This will require lots of work in Chapter four.

Repeated the wrong sound 2 or more times, EX: 'frog' = 'f' 'r' 'a' 'g'. Your child may have a low auditory memory. This will require lots and lots of work at the basic code level (Chapters three and four).

AUDITORY PROCESSING TEST

The results of this test are not reliable for children under age six.
Do not allow your child to see the test. Ask your child to say the word 'pig.' Now ask her to say 'pig' without the sound 'p'. If she has trouble doing this, offer an example. Say, "OK, if I wanted to say 'dog' without the 'd' it would be 'og'." Continue with all the words.

PART ONE

say **pig** w/o the **'p'** ________ **(ig)**

say **pog** w/o the **'g'** ________ **(po)**

say **sip** w/o the **'s'** ________ **(ip)**

PART TWO

say **stop** w/o the **'s'** ________ **(top)**

say **nest** w/o the **'t'** ________ **(nes)**

say **flag** w/o the **'f'** ________ **(lag)**

PART THREE

say **plum** w/o the **'l'** ________ **(pum)**

say **best** w/o the **'s'** ________ **(bet)**

say **grill** w/o the **'r'** ________ **(gill)**

say **lost** w/o the **'s'** ________ **(lot)**

Interpretation of Scores +8 = good +5 = low moderate -5 = poor

Was unable to score correctly on all of the first 3 test items. Your child is experiencing difficulty segmenting and isolating single sounds in simple words. This requires lots of work in Chapter three.

Removed the adjacent consonant to the target sound in part two or three, EX: flag without the 'f' = 'ag'. Your child is experiencing difficulty segmenting adjacent consonant sounds. This requires lots of work in Chapter four.

Unable to perform (no correct responses). Your child is having difficulty understanding the nature of sounds in words. Extensive work in Chapters three and four is needed.

CODE KNOWLEDGE TEST

This page is the key for the code knowledge test on the next page. Use the next page as the cue sheet to test your child. Do not let your child see this page. Place a barrier between this page and the next. A piece of cardstock or a clip board will do. After each sound is a word or words containing that sound or sounds. This is to assist you if you are uncertain of the sound or sounds that the sound picture represents. For example, the sound picture <ie> in the last column, can represent the sound 'ie' as in the word 'die,' or 'ee' as in the word 'chief.' Indicate the first sound picture and ask, "If you saw this in a word, what sound would you say?" If she offers any of the correct sounds, mark her answer as correct. If she offers a letter name, tell her, "That's a letter. I want to know what sound it stands for." If she proceeds to offer letter names, you must mark these answers incorrect. Only the sounds are correct answers. Keep track of the number of correct and incorrect responses. The total correct times two is the percentage of code knowledge your child has at this time.

__ b	**b**oy	__ y	**y**es / happ**y** / fl**y**	__ oa	b**oa**t
__ c	**c**at / **c**ity	__ z	**z**ipper	__ ow	n**ow** / sn**ow**
__ d	**d**og	__ i	r**i**p	__ igh	n**igh**t
__ f	**f**at	__ e	n**e**t	__ eigh	**eigh**t / h**eigh**t
__ g	**g**ot / **g**entle	__ a	m**a**t	__ ay	pl**ay**
__ h	**h**op	__ o	m**o**p	__ ie	d**ie** / ch**ie**f
__ j	**j**ob	__ u	n**u**t	__ aw	s**aw**
__ k	**k**id	__ sh	**sh**ip	__ ee	s**ee**n
__ l	**l**ap	__ ch	**ch**ip	__ ey	k**ey** / th**ey**
__ m	**m**op	__ th	**th**is / **Th**ursday	__ ue	bl**ue** / c**ue**
__ n	**n**od	__ ck	du**ck**	__ ew	f**ew** / n**ew**
__ p	**p**at	__ qu	**qu**ick 'kw'	__ au	**Au**gust
__ r	**r**at	__ ce	ni**ce**	__ oo	w**oo**d / m**oo**n
__ s	**s**at	__ ai	r**ai**n	__ ui	s**ui**t
__ t	**t**op	__ ou	**ou**t / gr**ou**p /	__ oy	b**oy**
__ v	gi**v**e		t**ou**ch	__ oi	s**oi**l
__ w	**w**ith	__ ea	**ea**ch / st**ea**k /		
__ x	fo**x** 'ks' / e**x**it 'gz'		br**ea**d		

Interpretation of Scores

Raw score times 2 equals percentage of correct answers.

	good	low moderate	poor
6 years old	60-100%	50-60%	-50%
7 years old	70-100%	60-70%	-60%
8 years old	80-100%	70-80%	-70%

If your child falls in the low moderate to poor range, extensive work in Chapter five will be needed. If she scores in the good range, you should still complete the lessons in Chapter five, but your child will move through them with much greater ease.

CODE KNOWLEDGE CUE CARD

b	x	oa
c	y	ow
d	z	igh
f	i	eigh
g	e	ay
h	a	ie
j	o	aw
k	u	ee
l	sh	ey
m	ch	ue
n	th	ew
p	ck	au
r	qu	oo
s	ce	ui
t	ai	oy
v	ou	oi
w	ea	

COMPOSITE READING SCORE

Date of test________________

Total number correct from Blending Test ______ X 6.66 = _________

Total number correct from Segmenting Test ______ X 2.38 = _________

Total number correct from Auditory Processing Test ____ X 10 = _________

Total number correct from Code Knowledge Test ____ X 2= _________

Total score of the above four tests _________ divide by 4 = __________

Enter the above total score in the grade your child is currently in, or if it is summer, the grade your child is entering in the next school year.

1st grade	score X 1.10	__________
2nd grade	score X 1.05	__________
3rd grade	score X 1.	__________
4th grade	score X .95	__________
5th grade	score X .95	__________
6th grade	score X .90	__________
7th grade	score X .90	__________
8th grade or older	score X .90	__________

Interpretation of Scores

90 or above indicates a readiness for the reading material your child will encounter in her current or upcoming grade.

89 or lower indicates that your child is not ready for the reading material she will encounter in her current or upcoming grade.

GLOSSARY

Note: Boldface text represents the term or technique being defined or identifies a synonym; [r.a.] identifies a term developed or used by Read America, Inc.

auditory processing or **phonological processing** The ability to segment, blend, and manipulate sounds in words.

adjacent consonant sounds [r.a.] Two or more consonants occurring in sequence which represent two or more sounds.

accented syllable or **stressed syllable** or **dominant syllable** The one syllable in a multisyllable word that is louder than the others.

blend This is the term that phonics methods use to describe two adjacent consonant sounds. Phono-Graphix uses the term *adjacent consonants* as readers blend all sounds in a word as they read, not just the adjacent consonant sounds.

blending Pushing together sounds in words, so that they become a blended unit. This is one skill involved in auditory processing.

CCVC A word which is constructed with a sequence of consonant sound, consonant sound, vowel sound, consonant sound. This is more difficult for many readers than CVC, VCC, or CVCC.

chunk [r.a.] A single vowel sound, or a group of sounds with only one vowel sound, within a word that has at least two such chunks. A chunk is determined by linguistics rather than orthography, so two adjacent chunks in a word are determined by the spoken pause between them rather than set rules for splitting syllables. We use this term to replace the word "syllable" when we are speaking to children or adult students.

code knowledge The reader's knowledge of the sound picture to sound correspondence of the English written language.

code overlap [r.a.] This is inherent within the English written language. It refers to the fact that some sound pictures can represent more than one sound.

code variation [r.a.] This is inherent within the English written language. It refers to the fact that sounds can be represented in more than one way.

coded text [r.a.] Text that has been made explicit by bolding all of the sound pictures that contain more than one letter, and underlining all of the vowel + e sound pictures. This process was developed by Read America.

CVC A word which is constructed with a sequence of consonant sound, vowel sound, consonant sound. This is easier than VCC, CVCC, and CCVC.

CVCC A word which is constructed with a sequence of consonant sound, vowel sound, consonant sound, consonant sound. This is more difficult for many readers than CVC or VCC, but is easier than CCVC.

decoding Reading by using the sound–to–sound picture code of the language.

digraph or **sound picture** The linguistic term for two or more letters that represent one sound. Read America uses the term *sound picture* instead to describe any single letter or group of letters that represent a single sound.

directed reading [r.a.] A lesson in which a reader is asked to decode or read a word by saying each sound and then blending the sounds into a word.

directed reading, variation of [r.a.] Readers who have trouble blending sounds into words first are told the word and then are asked to map it on paper or a dry erase board. Directed reading is done to exemplify the decoding process to the learner.

dominant chunk [r.a.] The stressed or accented chunk in a multisyllable word.

encoding Spelling by representing each sound in sequence.

formal operational thought A level of logical reasoning that was described by the psychologist and theorist Jean Piaget, which is demonstrated in most children by about age eleven. At this level children can reason abstractly.

lesson The activities described at the back of each chapter of this book.

letter name interference [r.a.] A situation in which the reader is either saying letter names instead of sounds or attempting to determine the sound by using the letter name.

letter name interference, correction of [r.a.] The technique developed by Read America in which the reader has said a letter name when attempting to read a word, EX: "ef," and the mentor corrects the problem by saying, "'ef' is two sounds. What's the first sound in 'ef'?"

linguistics The study of language.

look say A method of reading instruction used from about 1920 to about 1962. Look Say taught children to memorize and recognize whole words, with no instruction in the relationship of the sounds in words and letters.

mapping [r.a.] The technique of saying each sound as you write the sound picture (letter or letters) which represents that sound.

mapping and sorting [r.a.] The technique of saying each sound as you write the sound picture (letter or letters) which represents that sound, while sorting the words according to sound pictures.

Mr. Schwa [r.a.] The character developed by Read America to represent the schwa sound.

multisyllable analysis [r.a.]The technique of determining the spoken pause in multisyllable words and finding its exact visual location in the written word.

multisyllable mapping [r.a.] The technique of saying each chunk slowly as you write the sound pictures which represent that chunk.

new reader [r.a.] A term used in this book to describe a child who is in first grade, sixth month, or younger, including children who have been retained.

nonsense words Words with no meaning that are used in the Auditory Processing with Adjacent Consonants lesson in Chapter four.

on-set rhyme Refers to the phonics technique of using rhyming words to teach reading. EX: 'ot'... 'pot,' 'dot,' 'hot,' 'lot.'

orthographic tendency [r.a.] A tendency for a sound to be represented with a particular sound picture when it occurs in particular locations in a word or after other particular sounds. We never teach rules, but do sometimes point out orthographic tendencies in our language.

orthography Refers to the written representation of a spoken language.

paired associate learning A term used by psychologists to describe the rote learning of two arbitrarily paired items.

phoneme The smallest unit of sound in a language.

phonetics The systematic study of the sound to symbol relationship and correspondence of a language.

phonics A nickname for the specific method of teaching the sound to symbol relationship and correspondence of English, as it was developed by Noah Webster.

phono-graphic logic [r.a.] Thinking about reading and spelling from a perspective that words are made up of units of sounds and that sounds are represented in writing by sound pictures.

Phono-Graphix ™ [r.a.] The trademarked name of the reading method taught in this book, as developed by Read America, Inc. Phono-Graphix means "sound-picture."

phonological awareness The awareness that words are made up of smaller units of sounds.

phonological processing or **auditory processing** The ability to segment, blend, and manipulate sounds in words.

primary strategy [r.a.] The strategy that the reader relies most heavily on when trying to read and spell.

process spelling [r.a.] The technique of spelling by slowly saying each blended chunk in a multisyllable word as you write the sound pictures of the chunk.

propositional logic The term used by philosophers and psychologists to describe reasoning which involves propositions. Phonics instruction relies heavily on the use of propositional logic. An example of propositional logic in phonics is, "If there are two vowels side by side, the first one is sounded with its 'long' sound." The Phono-Graphix method does not use this logic in its instruction, as it is considered by psychologists to be a skill of the formal operational level of logic as described by Piaget, which children do not achieve until about age eleven, well after they are expected to be able to read and spell.

Reading Reflex [r.a.] The name of this book, which refers to the automatic learned response of using the skills taught in the Phono-Graphix method.

rules As taught by phonics methods, rules are the way that phonics explains two letters representing a single sound. Rules rely heavily on propositional logic. After careful analysis, the authors of this book have determined that the average accuracy of the combined phonics rules is 40%.

schwa A weak vowel sound in an unstressed syllable of a multisyllable word. Schwa occurs naturally in speech.

scratch sheet spelling [r.a.]The technique developed by Read America of trying the code variation (various sound pictures that can represent a particular sound) when spelling.

segmenting The ability to separate sounds in words, in the correct sequence.

segmenting, technique of correcting errors in [r.a.] When the reader is asked to say the sounds in a particular word, EX: 'frog,' and he says that the first sound is 'fr', the following technique is applied: "'fr' is two sounds. What's the first sound in 'fr'?"

session A single sitting of lessons with a reader.

sloppy 'u' [r.a.] A character developed by Read America and used to describe the 'u' sound some readers have lingering at the end of consonant sounds. EX: 'tu' instead of 't'.

sloppy 'u', technique for the correction of [r.a.] The technique developed by Read America for the correction of sloppy 'u', in which the mentor says, "You said 'tu' here (indicating the sound picture **<t>**). 'Tu' is two sounds, 't', 'u', but this (indicating the sound picture **<t>**) is one sound 't'."

sound The smallest unit in spoken language. It is synonymous with the term *phoneme*.

Sound Doggy [r.a.] The Read America mascot, who guides the mentor through the lessons to be done with a new reader.

sounding out Saying each sound aloud and then blending the sounds into a word.

sound picture [r.a.] A term developed by Read America and used to describe a letter or group of letters which represent a single sound.

sound sorting [r.a.] A technique developed by Read America in which the reader reads a list of words containing a common sound picture which can represent two or more different sounds. He then sorts them into lists according to which sound they represent.

special endings [r.a.] A term developed by Read America to describe the suffixes in words which are spelled according to the Greek, Latin, or French written code, and are taught as units.

syllable A single vowel sound, or a group of sounds with only one vowel sound, within a word that has at least two such chunks. A syllable is determined by the orthographic rules of phonics, rather than linguistics, so two adjacent syllables in a word are determined by a set of rules for splitting syllables rather than the spoken pause between them.

strategy A thing or things that the reader does in order to ascertain meaning.

subskill A term used by educators and psychologists to describe one of the integral skills involved in a behavior.

VCC A word which is constructed with a sequence of vowel sound, consonant sound, consonant sound. This is more difficult for many readers than CVC, but is easier than CVCC or CCVC.

visual stops, technique of using [r.a.] A technique used to stop the reader between chunks so that he will learn to read a chunk and then blend it before going on to the next chunk.

vowel + e A sound picture which is made up of a vowel and the letter e, with a consonant sound occurring in between the vowel and the e. EX: c**a**k**e.**

whole language A method of reading instruction which has been widely used since about 1980. Whole language originators stated that "the systematic instruction of the sound to symbol correspondence of the English language is distracting and detrimental to readers." They believed that children would "emerge into literacy" if exposed regularly to literature.

word analysis [r.a.] A technique developed by Read America in which the reader is asked to look at the word and determine what the sound pictures are.

word building [r.a.] A technique developed by Read America in which the reader is asked to construct a word using sound pictures on isolated pieces of paper or boxed on a work sheet.

word families A term used by phonics methods which refers to the technique of teaching chains of words with like vowel-consonant or vowel-consonant-consonant endings, or like consonant-vowel or consonant-consonant-vowel beginnings. EX: the 'unk' family... 'hunk,' 'sunk,' 'bunk;' the 'sta' family... 'stab,' 'stack,' 'staff.'